The Command Decisions Series

• VOLUME 2 •
Pilot Proficiency

The Command Decisions Series • Volume 2

Pilot Proficiency
Skillbuilding for Every Pilot

Richard L. Taylor

Belvoir Publications, Inc.
Greenwich, Connecticut

Also by Richard L. Taylor

IFR for VFR Pilots: An Exercise in Survival
Understanding Flying
Instrument Flying
Fair-Weather Flying
Recreational Flying
Positive Flying (with William Guinther)
The First Flight
Pilot's Audio Update (Editor)

ISBN: 1-879620-03-0

Printed and bound in the United States of America by Arcata Press (Fairfield, Pennsylvania).

Contents

Preface

The ability to ride a bicycle has become a hallmark of achievement in our society. Initial success with a velocipede—when the problems of balance and coordination are overcome—seems to be hugely significant in just about everyone's life.

Most people assume that once learned, the skill is never forgotten. This must be so; you can probably think of a dozen tasks that are characterized as "just like riding a bicycle," referring to the commonly held belief that even many years downstream, anyone who ever mastered a two-wheeler can once again climb aboard and ride away as if there had been no break in his experience. Perhaps, perhaps...but when a former cyclist attempts to demonstrate his power of recall and finds his abilities wanting, the result is probably no worse than a moment of embarrassment or a skinned knee.

Is flying one of those tasks that's akin to riding a bicycle? Some would argue yes, once you learn to fly you never forget. To be sure, resuming piloting after a long layoff might not be a pretty sight as you flounder through a series of aerial maneuvers; the basics may still be there, but the smoothness, the technique and the good judgement would return only after a period of practice and reacclimation to the airborne environment.

Flying may bear some relationship to bike-riding, but when a pilot attempts to climb back on his aerial steed after a long layoff, the situation changes remarkably. "The Basics" may not be enough to cope with the circumstances that might arise on even a local flight; a simple trip around the pattern has the potential of turning into an exercise in emergency procedures—aircraft systems have been known to malfunction every now and then, with absolutely no respect for the proficiency level of the pilot.

Back in the Saddle...But Only Now and Then

The economics of non-professional aviation keep many pilots out of the air except for occasional weekend forays, and that introduces another proficiency problem...staying sharp (and safe!) when you fly at something less than frequent intervals. The infrequent flyer faces a difficult task, because proficiency maintenance requires a structured program (including the services of a CFI) that leaves little time for the sheer enjoyment of flying; no one likes to spend precious time and money on nothing but takeoffs and landings and stalls, and the temptation to go flying anyway, to forego the proficiency exercises is extremely strong.

Pilot proficiency encompasses much more than the ability to wrestle an airplane onto the ground in a crosswind or to perform a flawless Lazy Eight; it includes the ability to make good decisions on the ground and inflight, the ability to handle emergencies, the ability to communicate with efficiency and accuracy, and the exercise of good sense in all your aviation activities.

Proficiency is difficult to achieve and even more difficult to maintain. Even when a pilot has flown for years and has built up a reservoir of experience from which he can draw as needed, the FAA minimum requirements—a current medical certificate, a Flight Review, and three takeoffs and landings every 90 days—represent perhaps the most minimum of all the hoops through which aviators must jump. A pilot certificate is the legal key that opens the door, but pilots must keep in mind that they are expected to perform as if they were completely current and proficient; controllers and other aviators assume that every pilot is able to ride his bicycle, and ride it well.

Not surprisingly, proficient pilots don't often get into trouble; most of the unhappiness is visited upon pilots who for whatever reason are not up to speed on technique and procedure, who are not properly trained, or who have gotten themselves into situations they simply can't handle.

In the material that follows, you'll find examples of all these circumstances except hazardous weather encounters—those were discussed in the first volume of *Command Decisions*. We've included cases in which it appears that even a very light application of common sense would have saved the day because we believe that every pilot has the potential to act that way under certain conditions. If you pride yourself on your exercise of good judgment and common sense, please don't be miffed at this inclusion; stupidity can be committed by *any* pilot, and perhaps on that highly unlikely day when it's about to happen to you, you'll remember something you have read here.

Richard Taylor
Dublin, Ohio
February 20, 1991

The Training Process

Pilot proficiency is a very subjective matter; an operation that seems proficient to one aviator may appear downright dangerous to another. Proficiency has a lot to do with a pilot's reservoir of basic skills, how he was trained to use those skills, and how much he applied himself to advancing his competence after being certificated. Training is the keystone of proficiency, and unless a pilot continues to train—one way or another—after passing a checkride, the skills erode in a hurry.

One of aviation's hoariest cliches says that in acquiring the private ticket the pilot is just "getting a license to learn." Apparently, for some pilots, that license doesn't always get much exercise.

A detailed study of what really happens to piloting skills after the ticket is in hand reveals that when a pilot gets a license, school is usually out. For pilots who don't do a fair amount of flying during the first two years after the private pilot checkride, piloting skills drop like a plane without wings.

Graphing the percentage of correct piloting actions against time produces a fatal curve in which a steep initial drop gives way to a slower but continuing decline in skills.

And when it comes to airplane handling skills, not only are new pilots losing it, but they aren't even aware of what's happening. In the words of the study conducted for FAA under subcontract by Embry-Riddle Aeronautical University, "Pilots' ability to predict and evaluate their own skill retention levels for specific flight tasks was negligible." Not that other methods of prediction provide much help. "Written test scores," the study reports, "are not useful for predicting actual flight performance."

Use It or Lose It

While the study that reached these conclusions focused on newly minted pilots, the information gathered contains an important message for all pilots. In short, "use it or lose it." Pilots who don't fly regularly make mistakes when they do fly. Those who do fly regularly make mistakes on seldom performed maneuvers such as emergency procedures. The non-flying pilot, beginner or pro, is a hazard when he or she does get into the air. "Simply put," says the study, "no pilot is immune to the loss of flying skills if those skills are not exercised. Further, much of the loss can be expected to occur in the initial part of the time period in which the skills are not exercised."

To get a detailed look at the life and death of flying skills, the researchers started out with 42 pilots, all of whom were FAA employees. They were well trained, having earned their private pilot certificates in a carefully monitored program as part of another FAA study. Of the 42 pilots, 33 were available for testing eight months after getting their licenses; 26 were tested after 16 months; and 21 were available for the concluding evaluation at 24 months post-licensing. Nineteen people made it to all three retention checkrides, and those tested after two years had accumulated an average of 162 total hours, and had flown an average of 89 hours since passing their flight test, though there was a hiatus averaging almost five months since their most recent flight at the time of the two-year check. This is a pattern not atypical of private pilots who spend considerable time and money acquiring a license, only to see actual flight time decline as time and monetary demands of other activities assert themselves.

The checkrides were conducted in a Cessna 172 by an experienced CFI. The pilots were all familiar with the plane, since it was the same type in which all had received their primary instruction.

Super Checklist

Performance measurements were made using a highly structured, standardized list of flight tasks called the Pilot Performance Description Record (PPDR). This was, in effect, a super checklist covering an entire flight from startup to shutdown.

Each of the 29 tasks on the PPDR was made up of one or more segments, and for each segment there were specific criteria and permissible deviations within which the operation was considered satisfactory. Anything beyond that was recorded as an error.

For example, under "Climbout," there were four segments: airspeed (plus or minus 5 knots); track from extended runway (left or right error, if any); proper pattern exit (yes or no); and proper climb trim (yes or no). For those factors which weren't "yes or no" responses, the checkpilot indicated the direction and magnitude of any deviation beyond the permissible limit.

Each term used in evaluating segment performance was tightly defined. The instructions under trim read, "A measure of ability to trim for hands-off flight. Mark 'Yes' if little or no control is required to maintain level flight; otherwise, mark 'No.'" For "proper pattern exit," the instructions said, "When exiting the traffic pattern, mark 'Yes' if exit is timely, at the proper location, altitude, and correct angle. If any one of these conditions is not satisfied, mark 'no.'"

Before each set of checkrides, the researchers checked out the check pilot to make certain all criteria were being accurately and consistently applied according to the specific definitions they'd set out. Little was left to subjective interpretation, since most of the definitions called for specific, measurable limits or actions.

All the pilots had been evaluated using the PPDR on their licensing checkrides, and the idea was to use the identical measures to see how sharp their skills were eight, 16 and 24 months later.

Just to add a bit of spice, the investigators also wanted to know how well the pilots could predict and evaluate their own flying skills on each of the 29 tasks. To get at that information, each pilot was asked to fill out a prediction questionnaire just before each checkride, and an identical (except for wording of instructions) questionnaire just after the checkride (but before debriefing with the checkpilot).

Losing It

Virtually without exception, overall performance declined with time since training. About the only task to escape unscathed was the runup, which was accomplished using a checklist. "If subjects could remember to consult the checklist," the report states, "error-free performance was virtually assured." At the time of their license checkrides, the pilots' error rate on all segments of all tasks averaged 8.9 percent. By 16 months post-license, this soared to 38.1 percent, and at the end of two years the error rate climbed to a staggering 42 percent. Bad as this news is, it conceals even worse news about specific tasks.

Of the 29 tasks on the original list, two were eliminated from computation due to anomalies in the data. That left 27 tasks to be gauged, and they varied greatly in the rate at which skill in executing them declined, and in the total decline.

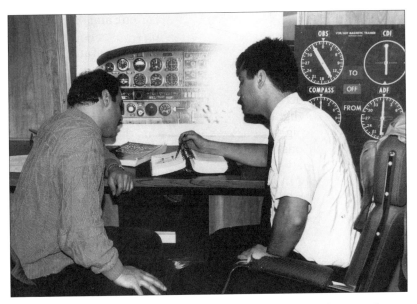

Research shows that regular recurrent training is a fundamental element of pilot proficiency.

Some skills began evaporating almost as rapidly as the ink on the new license, with most of the loss that was to take place happening within the first eight-month period. Among those skills that suffered rapid total loss were landing (uncontrolled field), unusual attitude recovery, crosswind takeoff, accelerated stall, S-turns across a road, short field landing, VOR tracking, straight and level flight, soft field takeoff, and turns about a point. Under the hood, 180-degree turns, magnetic compass turns and rate of climb all suffered most of their losses up front.

At 16 Months: A Closer Look

The 38.1 percent error rate at 16 months represented an increase of 29.2 percent from the time of licensing, and error rates increased on all tasks but runup...using a checklist.

Crosswind landing, crosswind takeoff, landing at an uncontrolled field and steep turns are the tasks that showed the greatest decline from the time of the private pilot exam.

However, there's another set of numbers that needs to be examined, and that's the absolute measure of correct performance. While accelerated stalls showed the greatest drop in proficiency from private test to 16 months (90 percent down to 52 percent correctly performed, a loss of 38 percent), some other skills started out much lower on the private exam and were a real disaster by 16 months.

Among these were magnetic compass turns under the hood (74 percent correct at licensing, 40 percent correct at 16 months), minimum controllable airspeed (37 percent correct at 16 months), VOR tracking (48 percent at 16 months), and steep turns (51 percent). For this critical set of skills, pilots are getting it right less than half the time 16 months after getting their licenses.

Things Could Be Worse: 24 Months

The final checkride was given 24 months after licensing, and it was a real eye opener...if the check pilot dared to open his eyes. The average PPDR error rate was 42.4 percent, meaning that four times out of ten, when called upon to perform some common cockpit function, the pilots got it wrong.

For the 11 tasks in which there was the greatest absolute amount of skill loss, the average loss was 44.5 percent. By 24 months, magnetic compass turns under the hood were happening correctly only one-third of the time, rate of climb under the hood stood 38 percent correct, as did steep turns, and minimum controllable airspeed had dropped to 39 percent correct.

The large number of pilots who wander around lost can be explained by the finding of a 50 percent error rate in ability to track a VOR after 24 months. And if those lost pilots blunder into bad weather, their chances of simply making the proverbial 180 seem rather poor, since only 52 percent of the efforts to execute such a turn under the hood came off correctly after 24 months.

What's Wrong?

A closer look at what went into some of the errors was revealing, and tells much about why pilots are getting into trouble. Every single person tested at 24 months failed to acknowledge at least one ATC instruction during the checkride, and 83 percent of the people failed to identify the VOR station before tracking it. Correctly estimating fuel requirements for a cross-country flight escaped 52 percent of those tested, while 83 percent incorrectly estimated time en route and 61 percent miscalculated ETA.

Almost two-thirds of the pilots failed to perform a cockpit check before entering an uncontrolled field traffic pattern, and the same percentage then proceeded to enter either at the wrong altitude or the wrong distance out. More than half didn't turn on carb heat during a simulated in-flight engine failure, 70 percent didn't enter a stall correctly and 48 percent either didn't achieve a stall or didn't recognize one when they did accomplish it.

And despite these high percentages, most people were woefully inadequate at assessing for themselves specifically what skills had deteriorated. One of the most startling findings in this study was that pilots could have their performance decline to where they performed a maneuver correctly only one-third to one-half the time, yet not know they had a problem.

Pilots demonstrated a moderate ability to predict and assess their own overall performance," wrote the researchers. "However, for specific flight tasks, their prediction and evaluation ratings failed to show any relationship to actual PPDR errors. The lack of such a relationship is of ultimate concern from the standpoint of operational safety, since it suggests that the individual pilot is not able to diagnose specifically his own training needs."

What's To Be Done?

The easy and obvious answer to the problem is more flying time for everyone, something almost every pilot would readily agree to. However, it's highly unlikely the FAA will, in the interests of safety (or for any other reason), provide a substantial subsidy so everyone can fly another 50 hours a year.

And the current requirement for a Flight Review (formerly the Biennial Flight Review, or BFR) certainly isn't the answer, as we reported in 1984. Our article analyzed data on accidents vis-a-vis pilots with Flight Reviews and found a strong suspicion that the Flight Review program may be "ineffective, superfluous and irrelevant. There is a strong chance that it has no effect on safety—neither positive or negative."

That conclusion was echoed in this skills-degradation study which concluded that "the Flight Review does not sufficiently address the cognitive/procedural types of skills that are rather rapidly lost during lapses in operations.

Data from the present study indicate that Flight Reviews are not sufficiently frequent to upgrade flight skills lost by relatively inexperienced private pilots. The same is probably true for more experienced pilots who do not operate over prolonged time periods.

In view of the above problems, effective and efficient continuation training programs are needed to maintain and upgrade safety among general aviation pilots.

The study also added a data point to the matter of instrument proficiency and its value to low-time pilots. The researchers tracked sub-groups of the pilots—those who took no IFR dual after getting their license, those who got some IFR time before their eight-month checks, and those who got IFR time later than that. Essentially, they found that the IFR training did have a beneficial effect, in postponing the loss of flight skills. But the bottom line was still the same—if the skills are left unused long enough, they degrade just as seriously.

Again, the researchers look to new ideas in "continuation training" as a way to address the problem. In order to accomplish such training, some major overhauls of training attitudes will be needed. There is a substantial bias in favor of airborne training, an attitude which is hardly discouraged by flight schools.

Yet airborne training is expensive, and when forced to choose between using limited cash on reviewing stalls with an instructor or flying somewhere with his family for the weekend, it is a rare pilot who will opt for more training.

But that's only when the choice is between two relatively expensive alternatives. The researchers pointed out that there are equally effective methods of continuation training at costs ranging from moderate to very cheap. If a few dollars would buy some "Rustoleum" for rusty skills, pilots might lay down the cash.

Pointing out that the greatest loss is in "cognitive" skills—for example, 100 percent of the pilots at the 24-month check failed to acknowledge at least one ATC instruction—the researchers called for training methods and "media" to cope mainly in the cognitive area. Among these, full-blown simulators, the familiar GAT-1 and GAT-2 simulators and even desk-top simulators or personal computers with simulation software—especially if enhanced with outside-the-cockpit visual cue devices—were lauded.

A training concept known as "full mission simulation" was mentioned as potentially effective, as was a combination of audio tapes, slides or video presentations, and written text.

Still too expensive? "A training medium that appears to be largely underused by general aviation pilots, but one which can be effective if used seriously and intelligently, consists of photographs, slides and mock-ups of aircraft cockpit instrumentation and external scenes," the researchers said.

And for the ultimate in low-cost skill refurbishers, there's "mental

For instrument pilots, regular practice, either with a safety pilot or an instructor, dramatically reduces the rate at which proficiency is lost.

rehearsal." This is a fully validated technique of "mental rehearsal of what one does, step by step, in performing a task." Although it could be further enhanced by using a cockpit mock-up, the basic equipment is free. "Effectiveness requires only a sufficient prior experience in the task to make cues and actions comprising each step meaningful and imaginable." Clearly, the study points out that innovation in the area of ground-based training methods and devices—as opposed to automatically jumping into an airplane for instruction that is four or five times as expensive—may be the key to keeping the nation's piloting skill level high, and the accident rate down.

Moving Up
Once in while we hear of a pilot whose flight training takes place in a high-performance airplane right from the start...but that's very much the exception. Economics dictate that almost all aviators learn to fly in slow, low-powered, uncomplicated trainers, then progress "through the ranks," as it were, to more sophisticated machinery when money and circumstances permit.

The regulations require at least a modicum of training and an instructor endorsement for operating a "high-performance" airplane, but like most FAA-dictated proficiency requirements, these are minimum standards; they don't consider the additional complications of very powerful engines, turbochargers, STOL conversions and the like. In most cases, the safe operation of an airplane with goodies like these on board requires some additional, type-specific training.

Graduation to a high-performance retractable single, complicated by a short, tree-lined grass strip, were among circumstances surrounding the crash of a Cessna T-210F in which all four persons aboard suffered serious injuries.

The NTSB investigator said the owner of the plane had purchased it two weeks earlier and had incorporated it to be used for business and pleasure. Another pilot of similar experience also planned to rent the aircraft, and was named on the insurance policy as an authorized pilot.

The plane owner maintained the grass strip, located behind his house. The strip, 1,200 feet long and 40 feet wide, is oriented north-south. The landing area slopes upward to the south and has trees lining that end. Consequently, it was standard policy at the strip to land south and take off north. Also, policy called for making only full-stop landings and never attempting a go-around once the wheels were down.

The two pilots had obtained high-performance checkouts a month earlier, but the 210 represented their retractable-gear experience. The owner, who occupied the right front seat at the time of the crash, had some 725 total hours. The other pilot, in the left seat during the accident episode, had about 672 total hours, investigators said. Each eventually got about eight hours in the aircraft prior to the accident.

The Centurion, which was equipped with a Robertson STOL conversion, was brought to the grass strip a few days prior to the crash. Each pilot got a chance to shoot several landings the day it arrived.

On the day of the crash, the pilots took the plane out for landing practice, with the owner in the right seat. The plane was flown for two or three landings, which witnesses described as slightly fast. At this point, the owner noticed two spectators next to his house and invited them to go flying. They occupied the rear seats.

One more landing was safely accomplished with all four aboard. On the next attempt, witnesses described the aircraft as high and fast on the approach. They said it touched down about 300 feet down the runway, bounced, and then the sound of a power increase was heard, as though the pilot intended a go-around.

The plane now veered off to the left side of the runway, dropped its left wingtip to the ground and cartwheeled. It struck an embankment traveling backwards and came to rest. The two rear-seat passengers and the pilot were able to exit by themselves, but the right-seat pilot was knocked unconscious and had to be assisted from the aircraft, investigators said.

Pilots: Teach 'Em to Think

That accident smacked of monumental bad judgement; too much airplane, too little runway...to say nothing of taking passengers along on a training flight. It's obvious that you can lead a pilot to an airplane, but can you teach him to think once he's inside it?

Actually, the question researchers have been asking for some time is whether or not it is possible to teach that intangible essential known as "judgment." Judgment, a subtype of thinking, is like pornography in being one of those "I'll know it when I see it" things which is hard to define precisely, but which we all know exists.

The U.S., Canada and Australia have all been conducting major research programs intended to develop programs to teach judgment to pilots. Some consider this like trying to teach table manners to a pig, but the effort represents a widespread recognition that judgment—or lack of it—underlies a depressingly large number of the aviation incidents which occur every year. Teach the pilots to exercise good judgment, make it okay for them to do so, and watch the accident rates drop—so goes the theory.

The Australians recently published some results of their efforts, referred to as the Australian Pilot Judgment Training (PJT) study. Judgment, the researchers write, is a function of values and beliefs, and these in turn are derived from the family, the peer group, school and the media, among other sources.

"To intervene in the formation of attitudes that will influence pilot judgments," the researchers note, "it is necessary to either control or override the influence of these agencies. Given the age at which student pilots obtain their license, the only major intervention possible is in terms of the process of flight instruction."

In the Australian study, three groups of student pilots were given either an academic approach (provided a manual which included judgment training), an experimental condition (manual plus special instruction) or were part of a control group which received conventional instruction.

A series of tests convinced researchers that the intervention group had in fact made significant progress in learning good judgment. To put that to the test, they conducted a flight test in which performance on matters of judgment was evaluated by the flight instructors.

"The intervention group," the researchers report, "consistently outperformed the control group in the actions they took to overcome hazards and interferences initiated by the flight tester. Of importance are those hazards affecting the serviceability of the aircraft, terrain and cloud clearance, and controlled airspace."

One of the important findings to emerge from the study was that students, who normally have a tendency to blindly follow their instructors' directions, were much more likely to take charge and make their own decisions because they knew that command decision-making was going to be tested from time to time during flight training. Several of the instructors made note of the value of this.

"The term 'judgment' appears to include 'decision,'" the Australian researchers conclude, "and is itself included by 'airmanship.'" They make a plea for an integrated approach to teaching people to fly in which airmanship, judgment, and cockpit resource management (CRM) are introduced as they exist in the real world: commingled.

"Introducing airmanship to the PJT scene is rather like the Crocodile Dundee task of administering suppositories to our Northern Territory crocodiles: an activity unlikely to be rewarding to either the impatient or the excessively cautious. Why should we introduce airmanship as soon as people begin to learn to fly, PJT a little later, and CRM later still?"

We need, the researchers argue, to train pilots completely, correctly (and completely correctly) from the beginning, and that includes attempting to harness the elusive butterfly called judgment.

Teaching Judgment

It's always been held that certain pilot skills were either inborn or learnable only from experience, but over the years more and more of those "experience only" items have been found to be teachable. The latest addition to the list is judgment.

Judgment is something every flight instructor agrees students should have, but it's something few of them think of as teachable in

Once a relative rarity in general aviation, flight simulators are now practically standard equipment at most flight schools. These devices improve the quality of training while reducing costs.

any specific way. Yet one study of the judgment problem found that 52 percent of the fatal general aviation accidents involved poor flying judgment, suggesting that finding a way to teach judgment would be like finding a way to teach pilots how to stay alive.

Embry-Riddle University of Daytona Beach, Florida, went to work and developed judgment training materials for instructors and their students. In an initial trial of the materials, those who had been judgment-trained made correct judgment decisions 75 percent of the time on test flights, while those not schooled specifically in judgment scored only 58 percent.

The Canadian Air Transportation Administration recently completed a study of the effectiveness of an improved version of the Embry-Riddle materials, and it offers further encouragement about the teachability of judgment.

The study rated 50 pilots' judgment on 18 aspects of flight, from planning and preflight inspection to traffic awareness and steep turns at low altitudes. The pilots, all of whom had just received their licenses, were unaware of the purpose of their rating flight, and they were asked to perform certain maneuvers such as steep turns at a low altitude for a credible purpose, such as picture taking.

Half the pilots had been given judgment training, the other half hadn't. Based on pre-defined criteria, students were rated as having either good or poor judgment for each situation, and assigned one point for each good judgment decision. The results showed that the judgement-trained group did far better than the untrained pilots. In 13 of the 18 items their performance was better by a statistically significant amount, and in four situations (stall at low altitude, flying beyond gliding distance from shore, low flying along a beach and attempting to land from an abnormally high approach) the judgment-trained group made correct decisions 100 percent of the time.

From these results it appears that judgment can be taught. What remains uncertain, though, is whether the lessons linger, whether refresher training of some kind would help, and ultimately whether this improved judgment ability translates into lower accident rates.

Training Pilots to Stay Out of the Weather

"Pilot continued VFR into IFR conditions" appears with saddening frequency as a cause of aviation accidents. And when the VFR-into-IFR bell tolls, it very frequently is a death knell for the pilot and any unfortunate passengers.

Typically a VFR-rated pilot takes off in decent-enough weather which deteriorates as he flies along. Yet for reasons which always seem a mystery, he simply keeps flying along until he's IFR and either loses control of the airplane or crashes into unseen terrain lurking behind the clouds or fog into which he's flown.

How do people get there, and in what ways do their pre-flight and in-flight actions differ from those who don't make such fatal errors? That's the question which interested two Ohio State University researchers. They've developed a methodology for exploring the question, and in the process of doing that have some preliminary results which make interesting and instructive reading.

The flight scenario presented to those being tested is an early October departure from Greensboro, North Carolina to Athens, Ohio at 5 p.m. in a Cessna 172. The "pilot" gets a WAC chart and can retrieve flight path, aircraft characteristics and weather information from a computer display.

The weather is marginal VFR, 1,500 to 2,000 scattered, chance of thunderstorms along the route. There's a stationary front centered over West Virginia, and the pilots can retrieve weather from a number of surrounding stations, and can also get forecast weather, SIGMETs, winds aloft and area forecasts. No PIREPs are available.

As of the time the preliminary report was prepared, 45 pilots had "flown" the mission, ranging from 100-hour private pilots to an ATP with more than 20,000 hours. There were 30 private pilots, 11 commercials, eight CFIs and four ATPs, though only 32 were used in the final analysis since some alterations were made to the system at the beginning.

Of the 32 pilots, 13 took one look at the situation and simply bagged the flight. Cancellation received, thank you very much, you live. Two others hung out for varying periods of time, checking later weather, then departed, while 17 launched immediately. Of the 19 who flew, 13 continued through to Athens on the simulated flight, while six diverted somewhere along the route.

In examining the pre-flight weather-seeking strategies of the pilots, eight were graded as "poor." Some failed to check destination weather, plan for an alternate, make use of all available information, or get a forecast for the route. Some selected an altitude which made things worse. And some committed several of these errors together.

In post-flight debriefing, the pilots expressed enthusiasm for what they had learned by being confronted with the situation, and felt the computer-simulated flight had provided a realistic task that encouraged them to think.

This suggests yet another avenue by which pilots might be taught to think as part of their flight training, and thus avoid having the bell toll for them later.

Currency: The Requirements

Recency of flight experience and compliance with recurrent aircraft and equipment inspection provisions are frequently the sources of FAA enforcement action as a result of information discovered on routine investigations of unrelated matters.

Since a comprehensive accident report is required of all operators involved in accidents or incidents, the data required may disclose a lack of currency on the part of the airman or a lapse of some recurrent inspection required on the aircraft or its installed equipment. Our experience with such cases has shown that virtually all non-compliance has been inadvertent. However, this mitigating factor has never been successfully used to exculpate the operator/airman involved. With a thorough understanding of the regulations, an airman or aircraft owner should have little difficulty staying compliant.

Although many airmen keep meticulously detailed logbooks relating to all aspects of their flight time, such recordkeeping is not required by the FARs. Only that experience which is required for a particular rating, or which is required to demonstrate recency of flight experience must be logged. And even this experience need not be entered into a formal logbook.

Oddly enough, the regulation that pertains to these requirements is listed under a section of the FAR's entitled "pilot logbooks." FAR 61.51 merely requires a "reliable record," which, for example could consist of an invoice for time on a rented aircraft, entries made in a personal notebook or diary, or even a computer generated printout. The only problem with presentation of records other than a meticulously kept formal pilot logbook, is that the person examining same will be less inclined to accept its authenticity. On the other hand, it would be simple to relate the number of cases that our office is familiar with concerning meticulously kept totally fraudulent pilot logs which have passed unquestioned through the hands of various FAA inspectors and employers.

The fact of the matter is that it is extremely difficult to corroborate pilot logbook entries without examining underlying documents such as aircraft logbooks, rental invoices, etc., or in the case of alleged actual instrument flight, obtaining weather reports for the date and locations indicated.

Thus we start with the proposition that the entries for proof of currency need only be shown by a reliable record, but a regularly kept formal pilot logbook will surely be given less scrutiny than some penciled notes on the back of an envelope.

The most oft-violated currency regulation is the Flight Review (formerly the Biennial Flight Review, or BFR), which is covered by FAR 61.56. Contrary to the general requirement that only a "reliable record" is required, this section specifically requires a log book endorsement by the flight instructor. To make things a little more illogical, the FAA itself supplies a calling-card size form, which some flight instructors give out in order to show compliance with the check.

The Flight Review is actually good for 25 months, since it is required within the 24 preceding months, and is not required if during that same time period the pilot has passed a pilot proficiency check given by the FAA, a check airman or the military.

The next most violated currency regulation is FAR 61.23 which requires physical examinations by an Aviation Medical Examiner (AME) within the preceding 6, 12 or 24 months, depending on whether the medical required for a particular operation is a Class I,

II or III. Again, assuming the medical examination is passed on the first day of any given month, it in effect will be good for 7, 13, or 25 months, respectively.

For single place aircraft, and solo VFR flight, that's all that's required. A Flight Review and Class III medical every 25 months and away we go!

For passenger carrying operations, however, FAR 61.57(c) requires three landings within the preceding 90 days, which landings must be to a full stop if made in tailwheel aircraft. Which reminds me of the fact that I have never seen a formal, printed, genuine pilot-store logbook that had columns that differentiated between full-stop and touch-and-go landings. Presumably stop-and-go landings would fulfill the requirements of this section in a conventional gear aircraft.

For night passenger-carrying operations, three full stop landings within the last 90 days are required, regardless of whether the aircraft is a taildragger or not, and these must be made within the period between one hour after sunset and one hour before sunrise as published in the American Air Almanac. In theory this would require a "reliable record" showing not only the date that these were accomplished, but the location and time, so that anyone attempting to verify the record would have some means to do so. Most pilots would suspect that if it were dark enough that landing lights were necessary, this requirement would be fulfilled, but this would not be technically true if the landings were made outside of the prescribed time periods.

Air Almanacs used to be standard items in the libraries of airline dispatchers and local Flight Service Stations, as not too many years ago we had day and night IFR minimums for certain approaches. Navigators also carried the Air Almanac in order to obtain the necessary data for celestial navigation. I haven't asked lately, but I suppose the FSS is still able to provide the information required to make "night" landings legal.

In the case of instrument flight, currency can be remembered by using the 6-6-6 rule. The requirements are six hours of simulated or actual instrument time, and six instrument approaches within the past six months. In addition, if currency has lapsed for more than 12 months, an IFR competency check ride with the FAA, military or CFI is required. When making the "reliable record" make sure that if the IFR is simulated, the name of the safety pilot is recorded, and if it is actual, a brief notation on the actual en route and/or terminal weather makes the record ring with authenticity.

That's it for pilot currency, except that it is easy to see how difficult it may be for infrequent fliers to keep a running record, since currency is continuously moving. For example, assuming three full stop night landings on June 1, 1988, landing currency would expire on September 1, 1988 (assuming for the sake of argument that this is a 90 day period). Two more night full stop landings on July 30 would not extend the period of currency one day, and a single night full stop on August 30 would only extend the currency period to October 30.

By the way, the FAA has a very short and simple policy with regard to logbooks that are lost: "To replace a logbook, estimate your flight time to the best of your knowledge, enter the data in a new logbook, and have the entry notarized." Unscrupulously interpreted, this policy could be used as a quick way to deal with a lack of documented currency or qualification in one's logbook.

At some point perhaps a hacker will develop a program for personal computers which will automatically compute the currency expiration date after each data entry for landings and IFR.

Impossible Rules

Learning the rules is a large part of any pilot's training, and it goes without saying that *following* those rules is expected throughout one's flying career. But then, many people dream the impossible dream, so perhaps the Federal Aviation Administration shouldn't be judged too harshly for dreaming a bit when it put together the Federal Aviation Regulations. Tucked into its pages are some rules that are virtually impossible to follow to the letter.

Some of the feats requested (no, demanded) by the rules would qualify a pilot for a guest appearance on "That's Incredible." Unfortunately, failing to perform can get him an invitation to appear before the FAA which might be considering suspension of his license. And sometimes, the belief that compliance is possible can lead to accidents—even though the crashes may be blamed on standard "probable cause" statements from the government computers.

In many cases compliance is virtually impossible because the rules ask people to do things which eyes, brains or other body parts simply can't do, according to competent medical and behavioral researchers. In other cases the regulations call for medical judgments pilots are not qualified to make, or measurements of things for which there is no available instrument that measures with the required degree of precision.

While many pilots may on occasion have felt that ATC was asking them to do the impossible, they could at least negotiate with a person. In the case of FARs which ask for the impossible, there are no negotiations. When it comes time to discuss the problem, nobody's home. The FAA is not required to prove it's possible to comply before citing a pilot for violation of the regs. It's Catch 22 in Part 91. Listed below are 10 of the specific FARs we consider impossible.

91.17— "No person may act as a crewmember of a civil aircraft while using any drug that affects his faculties in any way contrary to safety." Many physicians would be hard-put to comply with this, and for someone without medical training and access to the right publications, it's simply impossible to determine what all the side effects of most drugs are, let alone judge whether those sometimes-subtle effects are "in any way contrary to safety." It's obvious, of course, that certain types of medications are debilitating and that flying while under their influence would be clearly contrary to common sense and the desire to live a long life.

In other cases, however, the situation is a lot less clear. It was certainly not clear enough for a young first lieutenant making night approaches to the aircraft carrier *Nimitz* in an EA-6B. He'd been on a two-and-a-half-hour training flight, he'd had a long hold, then aborted two approaches. On his third try, running low on fuel, his sink rate was too fast. In response to the Landing Signal Officer's pleas he applied power, but drifted to the right of the centerline coming onto the deck. The plane, with no room to spare, tore a path through men and equipment. The final toll was 14 dead (including all three on board the aircraft); 11 planes bent, some irretrievably; and a $58 million tab for damages.

The investigation revealed the airman had removed himself from the flight schedule earlier in the day, due to a head cold, and then returned himself to duty after a few hours sleep. At autopsy, he had brompheniramine in his body fluids at a concentration six to 11 times the normal therapeutic level.

Brompheniramine is an antihistamine that shows up in over-the-counter cold remedies such as Contac, Sudafed Plus, Chlor-Trimeton and Comtrex. Even normal doses of the drug can cause drowsiness, dizziness, vision disturbances, and lack of coordination. The Navy ruled the drug a contributing factor to the accident.

What most non-medical people, and apparently the FAA, fail to realize is that every drug has side effects some of the time for some people. Any drug thus could affect a pilot's faculties in a way "contrary to safety." Asking pilots to choose which drugs will have what effect, when, is asking the impossible.

91.151— "No person may begin a flight in an airplane under VFR unless (considering wind and forecast weather conditions) there is enough fuel to fly to the first point of intended landing and, assuming normal cruising speed, during the day to fly after that for at least 30 minutes, or, at night, to fly after that for at least 45 minutes."

There is only one way to comply with this regulation, and that is to top the tanks and make the calculation based on the handbook capacity of the tanks. Even then, the handbook could be wrong.

Anything else is a sheer guess because there is no device available for the general aviation pilot which can, with any meaningful degree of accuracy, consistently say how much fuel is in the tank. That information certainly won't be provided by the wavering hands of the typical GA fuel gauge, and anyone using any sort of dipstick arrangement and then pretending to calculate fuel reserves down to the nearest 15 minutes is doing just that—pretending.

In fact, even "topping" the tanks and calculating leaves a lot of room for error. Depending on whether the plane is sitting level, what the line crew considers "topped," and whether or not they do some sloshing to eliminate air bubbles, a topped off Cessna 172 can wind up carrying 40 gallons usable or 36 gallons usable—a difference of about half-an-hour's flying time.

In other words, given the realistic and attainable precision of fuel measuring systems, the half-hour reserve is very easily left on the ground, good intentions aside.

This is not an apology for poor planning, failure to plan at all, or reluctance to make a fuel stop when a pilot knows things are getting tight. But as written, the regulation demands a level of precision in measurement which simply doesn't exist. Suggesting that it does may tempt many airmen to believe they know more about exactly what's in the tank then they really can.

Worse still, having left the half-hour's worth behind at the start of the trip, the general aviation pilot typically gets no help from his fuel gauges, which often lie about the last quarter-tank.

Virtually all accidents that arise due to these factors are blamed on the pilots (and it's true, the utterly prudent pilot adds his own fudge factor into the fuel equation), but the effects of a misleading FAR and inaccurate gauges cannot be ignored.

91.155— "...no person may operate an aircraft under VFR when the flight visibility is less, or at a distance from clouds that is less, than that prescribed for the corresponding altitude in the following table..." There then follows the table which every student pilot spends terror-filled moments trying to conjure up when asked by the examiner how close to the clouds he or she can play when within controlled airspace, more than 1,200 feet above the surface, and less than 10,000 feet MSL; or when outside controlled airspace, above 1,200 feet above the surface and above 10,000 feet MSL.

The answers are impossible. Study after study confirms that even under earth bound viewing circumstances, with plenty of familiar objects around to help in gauging distance, people cannot tell with much precision when something is 500 rather than 1,000 feet away. Imagine the accuracy to be expected when judging, without any other reference, how far away a cloud is in the sky when the visibility is as little as one mile.

Make that one statute mile. The rule also sets limits for flight visibility, and it does so in statute miles, implying the ability of most pilots to visually distinguish a statute mile from a nautical mile, by which all other things aeronautical are measured. Should anyone ask at the FAA hearing, the visibility was exactly 15,840 feet (3 statute miles). This presumably is easily distinguished from the 18,228 feet in three nautical miles.

The airport control tower determines visibility by identifying familiar local landmarks whose distance has previously been found using a map. The regulations are silent on what objects a pilot might use to determine, while idling in the sky, when he can see only 14,274 feet rather than the required 15,840 feet. Maybe that's because this is impossible.

To get some idea of just how far off distance judgment can be, particularly when it comes to clouds, gather a group of 10 or so pilots together next time there's a deck of clouds within a few thousand feet of earth. Ask everyone to write down their estimate of the ceiling and sign it. Put the estimates in a bag. Then listen to the ATIS. Don't feel bad. It takes many months of training before official weather observers can call it by eye with even a modest amount of proficiency.

91.175—"...no pilot may operate an aircraft...at any airport below the authorized MDA or continue an approach below the authorized DH unless the flight visibility is not less than the visibility prescribed in the standard instrument approach procedure being used." This one is impossible on the same grounds as the one above, except that this one is an even bigger impossibility because it asks for discrimination not in units of miles, but in quarter-miles. For example, it might be okay to land with a flight visibility of three-quarters of a mile, but not if it's only one-half mile. That's learning to see a visibility difference of 1,320 feet. While flying an airplane at 90 or more knots. With no outside references to judge size and distance by. Sure.

91.175—"No pilot operating an aircraft...may land that aircraft when the flight visibility is less than the visibility prescribed in the standard instrument approach procedure being used." See above. The FAA has become a co-conspirator in maintaining this fiction by even writing the "flight visibility" statement, which is the pilot's license to override a tower's visibility report. The tower says it's visibility one-half blowing snow, which they've measured by their ability to see fixed objects whose distance they already know. The minimum is three-quarters of a mile and the pilot sees or thinks he sees the lights. He suddenly has above-minimums flight visibility.

The irony in this particular regulation is that the plane, in order to land, must eventually get down near the ground and face exactly the same visibility circumstances being reported by the tower controller, who knows how far away three-quarters of a mile is. That's more than we can say for the pilot.

91.107—"...a person who has not reached his second birthday may be held by an adult who is occupying a seat or berth..."

This is an FAR where it is possible to comply with the letter of the law but to entirely violate the spirit. What's impossible is not the act of holding a two- year-old on an adult's lap (though that can be difficult at times), but the utter impossibility of holding onto and protecting that child in the event of impact, which is what the seat belt rule is all about.

The laws of physics are immutable, and sometimes harsh. They tell us that a 30-pound child in a sudden deceleration from 65 knots becomes more weight than even Arnold Schwarzenegger could hope to hold on to. To the extent that this rule is intended to assure safety for all passengers, it's impossible with an unbelted two-year-old. California recently recognized adult responsibility by making it illegal to carry an infant in an automobile without an approved car seat. Yet the FARs encourage not only no car seat, but no seat belt of any kind, for an infant.

91.309— "No person may operate a civil aircraft towing a glider unless the towline used has a breaking strength not less than 80 percent of the maximum certificated operating weight of the glider, and not more than twice this operating weight..."

With a brand new towline, it's possible, because whatever is written on the package about breaking strength may be some reasonable approximation of reality. However, it ceases to be reality the day the rope is put to use, and exposed to the deterioration from combined effects of sun, stretching, water, smog, fraying and such.

There is no ready means for testing breaking strength, nor any requirement for retesting. It is impossible to say if a rope that had a breaking strength 100 percent of the maximum certificated operating weight of the glider on Monday is still 80 percent on Friday, or a month later. It's impossible to tell by look, and measuring is a lab procedure pilots aren't prepared to perform.

Short of using a new rope on each flight, or starting with a high strength and replacing at an absurdly high frequency, it's impossible to know whether a pilot is complying with this rule on any given flight. The only thing that may help is that it's probably impossible for the local GADO to determine compliance, at least until after an incident, when they send the towline to the lab.

91.119— "Except when necessary for takeoff or landing, no person may operate an aircraft below the following altitudes: over any congested area of a city, town or settlement, or over any open air assembly of persons, an altitude of 1,000 feet above the highest obstacle within a horizontal radius of 2,000 feet of the aircraft."

Once again the pilot is asked to make utterly impossible judgments of distance. This time there's the added interest of distance judgments in two dimensions. Since the pilot is asked to judge horizontal and vertical range simultaneously, it's impossible.

91.117— "Unless otherwise authorized or required by ATC, no person may operate an aircraft within an airport traffic area at an indicated airspeed of more than 200 knots.

They don't bother saying whether that's true or indicated, but it doesn't matter. This is typical of many regulations which imply an absolutely absurd degree of accuracy when the measurement process is at best approximate.

Saying 200 knots implies there's a significant, measurable, knowable difference between that speed and some number rounded to the nearest 10 knots.

What makes this rule laughable is the knowledge any pilot (and any FAA rule writer) should have about the variations and vagaries of the airspeed indicator. When planes are test flown for certification, special, sophisticated instrumentation is installed in order to get precise numbers for the flight manual. Yet the general aviation pilot is left to fly the airplane with an airspeed indicator which is just one step above a piece of yarn tied to the cowling in accuracy.

Furthermore, given the normal diameter of a general aviation airspeed indicator, it is sheer folly to pretend the possibility of reading the numbers to one knot accuracy, even if parallax weren't given distorting the view. So even if your airspeed indicator reads in mph, you may not be able to keep it exactly on 200.

91.113—"When weather conditions permit, regardless of whether an operation is conducted under Instrument Flight Rules or Visual Flight Rules, vigilance shall be maintained by each person operating an aircraft so as to see and avoid other aircraft..."

The "see and avoid" rule. What a fitting end to a tour of impossible FARs. This is one of the FAA "gotcha" rules. If one airplane hits another airplane, somebody obviously didn't see and avoid. That's always the conclusion when there's no evidence of other transgressions. Somebody must have done something wrong or they wouldn't have run into each other. Gotcha.

It is, of course, both possible and necessary to be vigilant for other traffic. But when it comes to application of the rule, the human eye has great difficulty perceiving a light-colored object against a light-colored background. Place a white airplane against a background of haze or snow and "see and avoid" may well be a physiological impossibility unless there is enough time for repeated scans.

A not-infrequent traffic pattern accident is one plane descending on top of another. It's really a collision of blind spots, yet somebody will get blamed for failing to see and avoid.

If it seems like a sick joke to fault a pilot in this type of situation, on balance, the probable cause report usually "forgives" one pilot where the facts clearly show he could not have seen the collision coming. But when there are no such clear facts, the report typically blames both pilots.

The doctrine is so ingrained that during the investigation of the San Diego collision of 1978, in which a Boeing 727 ran down from behind a Cessna 172 in VFR conditions, killing all aboard both aircraft, the Safety Board in all seriousness used special binoptic cameras and analysis to study what the instrument student and his instructor could have seen out the back window of the Skyhawk!

These 10 are just a sampler of FARs whose intent is entirely good and honorable, but whose design is truly dreadful. They ask the impossible, and in some cases suggest strongly to the pilot that the impossible is possible.

The regulations are due for an overhaul, this time with an eye to human factors as well as regulatory goals. Areas that need careful consideration include:

Degree of Precision. Find out with what accuracy a pilot can actually expect to estimate distance, and cast the regulations with that number in mind. The military expects its ground-based observers to average a 750-foot error in spotting targets, and several experiments have placed that error at close to 1,000 feet. This makes the distinction between 500 feet below and 1,000 feet above a cloud meaningless.

Units of Measurement. Inconsistencies such as statute vs. nautical miles should be eliminated. Of greater importance is finding meaningful units of measurement that can be applied by the flying pilot. Experiments might well develop the fact that most pilots can gauge a distance more accurately by how long it takes to get there in their plane than by how far away it is in feet.

Ability to Discriminate. It is both foolish and dangerous for the regulations to codify an imperceptible difference such as one-half vs. three-quarters of a mile visibility, or 30 vs. 45 minutes fuel reserve, because doing so implies it's possible to do, and that can only lead to dangerous attempts on the part of pilots to do the impossible.

Perhaps someday in the not-too- distant future (say, three-quarters of a mile away, rather than one-half), the FARs will no longer be a Mission Impossible.

So Much for You—How About the Aircraft?

Aircraft currency is the responsibility of the owner or operator. However, since the pilot in command is precluded from operating an aircraft which fails to meet the maintenance requirements, some means should be available, such as an abbreviated logbook, to advise crewmembers of the status of those mandatory recurrent maintenance requirements.

Although each particular aircraft may have recurrent AD requirements, except for those aircraft on some type of approved continuous airworthiness program, no aircraft may be operated unless within the past 12 months it has undergone and passed an annual inspection. Thus, an inspection "signed off" on the first of any given month is good through the last day of that same month the following year, under FAR 91.409.

FAR 91.411 prohibits flight unless the altimeter/encoder has been inspected and calibrated within the past 24 months, which again means that for an inspection "signed off" on the first day of any month, the inspection period is good through the end of that same month two years later.

The only other aircraft requirement is for IFR flight, which requires a VOR ground, airborne or comparison check within the past 30 days. This is a pilot-conducted check and requires the VOR to be within four degrees of error for ground and dual VOR receiver comparison checks, and six degrees for airborne checks.

The regulations may be spread out all over the lot, but these currency requirements will most assuredly be looked at by the FAA on a random ramp inspection or when something as innocuous as a ground loop occurs. Pilots should make a list, log it, and stay current.

Flight Instructors Have Training Problems, Too

One of the most difficult things for a budding CFI to learn is the advanced technique of sweating only on the right side of the face; after all, if the instructor can't stay "cool" during training, what can be expected of the student? But sooner or later, all students must be kicked out of the nest, and on occasion, the solo experience brings to life some of a CFI's worst dreams, nay, even nightmares at times.

Flight instructors may suffer from a variety of nightmares—one of them is watching a solo student crash in the pattern. But perhaps even more fearsome is the student who insists on "doing his own thing," despite instructions to the contrary.

The crash of a Cessna 150 was a nightmare come true for one instructor. His solo student walked away with minor injuries when the Cessna snagged powerlines over Interstate 10 at Banning, California. The airplane, however, may well have been a write-off.

The flight had started as some solo touch-and-go practice at Banning Airport. The student pilot, with some 37 total hours—all in the C-150—had been told by his instructor to remain in the pattern and practice takeoffs and landings. The session started at 11:40 a.m.

The instructor stood by, watching the student make his rounds in the pattern. The instructor later characterized these first few landings as "satisfactorily performed." But there were hints of what was to come.

In his report to investigators, the instructor noted, "The

student remained in the pattern and the immediate vicinity of the airport for approximately 1.5 hours, and left the immediate area for two periods of approximately fifteen and twenty minutes." Despite this, the instructor felt "the flight appeared to proceed normally, and after the first half-hour no communication between instructor and student was deemed necessary."

At about 1:30 p.m., the Cessna left the pattern and flew out of sight. It was next spotted by an air traffic controller who was driving east on Interstate 10 about ten miles east of the airport. The controller noticed the C-150 go over his car at about 30 feet, heading in the opposite direction.

Minutes later, the Cessna buzzed over him again, this time going eastbound at 30 or 50 feet. The controller kept an eye on the airplane until it got about a quarter-mile ahead. The controller watched as the Cessna snagged a high tension wire 50 feet above the highway. The airplane pitched over and slammed into the ground on the median. The controller drove by the wreckage and kept on going. He never stopped.

Minutes later the phone was ringing back at Banning Airport. The instructor now learned where his errant student was—on the highway in a heap.

A nightmare for instructors? In the space on the accident report where pilots are invited to comment on ways the accident could have been prevented, the instructor seemed at a loss for words. His response: "None, at this point."

Flight Instruction—How Dangerous Is It?

Some CFIs consider flight training to be a form of hazardous duty. In sort of a peace-time version of the Dawn Patrol, instructors get up nearly every day to face whatever their students can dish out. Flying airplanes that get more use during a year than some get in a lifetime, coping with students who run the gamut from exceptionally gifted to exceptionally slow, performing daily some of the most dangerous maneuvers known to private pilots, flight instructors might not be expected to have very long life expectancies.

Yet for all the hazards of instructing, there are surprisingly few accidents during training flights. For a given three-year period we studied (1982 through 1984), there were some 393 accidents during dual training flights, or about 131 per year.

In perspective, how does instructional flying compare with the rest of general aviation? NTSB publishes data on several categories including personal/business flying, corporate/executive, aerial application, and instructional flying. On the basis of accidents per 100,000 hours flown, instructional flying is the second safest category (corporate/executive is the safest).

In a typical year, instructional flying accumulated a total accident rate of 8.32 accidents per 100,000 hours. This is less than the total accident rates for personal and business flying (13.23) or aerial application flights (13.22). The fatal accident rate for instructional flights of 0.45 crashes per 100,000 hours is again better than that for personal and business flying (2.84) or aerial application (0.83).

Aviation Safety not only scanned the NTSB data, looking at ways instructors wind up in trouble during training flights. We also called on instructors around the country for answers to the critical question: How does a flight instructor avoid the hazards of dual flying?

Way Ahead

One of the most common answers instructors gave with regard to the question of keeping out of trouble was that they were ahead of both the student and the airplane. Some instructors categorized it as almost a sixth sense.

Henry Sollman, Chief Instructor and an FAA designated examiner at Panorama Flight Service of White Plains, New York, shared some of his views with *Aviation Safety*. Sollman has some 50 years of instructing experience. How has he stayed safe? "I know just what the student is going to do before he does it. I've been at this so long, I know what's coming. I know what to look for," he told us.

He offered as an example a pilot he had recently checked out. The pilot had gotten a private certificate only a month before she came to his FBO. She wanted to rent a Cessna 172 for the weekends for some local flying. "I could see from the start of the flight that she wasn't really on the ball," said Sollman. It all came to a head when he asked her to demonstrate some stalls.

"I asked her to show me a departure stall. Well, she just pushed the power in and hauled back on the yoke and we ended up pointing straight up. I knew what was coming from there. I could see she didn't have the ball centered, and she just wasn't really concentrating on what she was doing. Sure enough, the stall broke, a wing dropped, and we started over and down. I knew this was coming, so I was already on the rudder as it started over. We went back to the airport right after that, and she never did rent any of our airplanes."

Sollman's "sixth sense" about what to expect was echoed by many other instructors. Many felt very confident that they could spot trouble before it developed, and keep the student out of it.

When Least Expected

But instructors shouldn't put too much faith in their "sixth sense." Students can, and do, surprise their instructors. One instructor found that sometimes the student can do things no one would be able to anticipate.

He had been out practicing touch-and-goes with his student. The instructor later told investigators the student was having trouble aligning the Cessna 152 with the runway during landing. As they came down short final, he told the student to "get the nose up." According to the accident report, "At an altitude of approximately three feet, the student pushed the controls full forward. The instructor was not able to react fast enough to prevent the aircraft from colliding with the runway"—nose first.

Over Their Heads

Some instructors put a lot of faith in their own abilities as pilots. They feel it's best to let the student "get in over his head" and then pull him out. This is particularly true with students seeking advanced instruction, like an upgrade to a complex aircraft or an instrument rating.

One instructor we spoke with explained, "I let them get in the airplane and let them get in over their head. That humbles them. You gotta get them in over their head so they realize their limits." He went on to qualify his method, adding, "I never let them get into it so far that recovery may be questionable."

But this philosophy hinges on the instructor's flying ability—something which may not increase in proportion to experience. A rather inexperienced instructor from North Carolina, who also believed in the "over the head" principle, coupled this approach with a healthy respect for the dangers. "I haven't had much experience. I've only been instructing for about 100 hours, but I don't let the student get too close to the edge. I base the student's limits on my own," he told us.

"For example, if I'm teaching stalls, I'll let it progress to just before a wing drops. If I see or feel that it's not going right, I'll take it." He's also putting stock into his future experience. "Later, when I get more comfortable with instructing, I may let them go farther," he explained. But for now he's holding the reins tight.

And with good reason. One instructor learned this the hard way while giving multi-engine instruction in a Piper Turbo Seminole. The instructor "failed" one engine and let the student fly it out. The CFI later told investigators the student treated the simulated emergency like he would a loss of power in a single-engine aircraft. He turned to the nearest runway, which would entail landing downwind. Also, the student forgot to extend the gear.

The report continued, "The CFI was aware of the situation, but elected to wait until the later part of the approach to see if the student would realize his mistakes. The CFI had found this technique of teaching to be successful in the past. However, he became distracted and allowed the student to forget to lower the landing gear. Subsequently, the student landed with the gear retracted."

Another instructor was training a pilot in a Beech 300 Super King Air. As they came down final, the King Air was a little high, so the pilot under instruction pulled off the power and ran the props up to max RPM. Despite the best efforts of the instructor to get the engines/props spooled up again, the increased drag caused by the props caused the aircraft to sink to the pavement and hit hard—hard enough to damage the wing spar.

Surprise, Surprise

"Good communications with the student, both before and during the flight, is the bottom line," said an instructor from Minneapolis. "Most problems can be prevented by a good preflight briefing. That's where the key is. You discuss every aspect and maneuver with the student on the ground so you both know what to expect."

Yet, some instructors still feel the element of surprise can be a good teaching tool. It's a sort of variation on the "over the head" theory of instructing. Unfortunately, both student and instructor can end up surprised. For example, there was the case of a pilot receiving multi-engine training in a Piper Aztec. During the first takeoff, the instructor failed the right engine by turning the right fuel selector off. The student responded properly by landing back on the runway and stopping. They taxied back for another takeoff. Again, the instructor turned the fuel off to the right engine. The Aztec roared down the runway and lifted off. As it became airborne, the right engine failed. Again, the student landed back on the runway. Unfortunately he had retracted the gear as they broke ground, leading to a gear-up slide down the pavement.

Another, sadder case involved a commercial pilot getting multi-engine instruction in a Beech 76 Duchess. The commercial pilot reported, after the accident, that he noticed the airspeed was low as they came down final. Nonetheless, the instructor reached up and failed the right engine using the mixture control, and the Duchess promptly stalled. It crashed in a residential area, killing the instructor and seriously injuring the student.

Equally Shocking

Of course, it's often not the instructor who's packing a surprise for the student. Sometimes it's the other way around, and both pilots can end up worse for the experience.

One instructor from New York related a classic tale of a student surprising him. He was checking out a private pilot in one of his flight school's airplanes. The flight had gone well, and they returned to the airport. As they entered downwind, the private pilot reached down and switched tanks. He explained that this was what he'd been taught to do where he learned to fly.

The instructor didn't think much of this habit, and he thought even less of it when the engine failed on a one-mile final. The private pilot had switched to an empty tank. They both escaped injury in the ensuing forced landing short of the runway.

An instructor in Albertville, Alabama, told us of the surprise a new student had for him. They had taken off and climbed to 2,000 feet when the instructor smelled booze. He asked the student if he'd been drinking, and the student said yes, he'd had "three or four belts before the flight to loosen up."

"So I took his hands off the controls, went back to the airport, and told him to never come out to fly again. I run him off, just like that," said the instructor.

Sometimes the surprises from the student just come too fast to be dealt with. An instructor was giving a private pilot transition training in a Great Lakes biplane. On the third touch-and-go landing of the day, the private pilot started to lose control. The instructor took over and got the airplane back under control. He gave the controls back to the private pilot, who promptly stomped on the brakes and flipped the plane over.

Too Much, Too Fast

Another variation on the "over the head" theory of instructing is to string emergencies together and have the student deal with them one after the other. But, things can get carried too far.

An instructor from Oregon bragged to us of his prowess in drilling his students. "I have this one guy who owns a Cessna Skymaster. He came in a few months ago for some recurrency training and IFR proficiency. It was a miserable night. Rain, clouds, winds up to 40 knots, but we went anyway.

"Well, the airwork went pretty well, so we came back to the airport for some approaches. We went for the ILS first. That's when I started to work on him. From the initial approach fix outbound, I started covering up his vacuum instruments, giving him partial panel. Then I pulled the glideslope on him so we were on a localizer-only approach. Once we got inside the marker, I pulled the front engine. I also pulled the gear motor circuit breaker.

"We broke out at circling minimums, and he'd powered back so that the gear warning horn was on. He worked us around to final and hit the gear selector. Now the gear horn had been on for a while at this point, so it had stopped being a warning and was just part of the background noise. I let him get into the flare before I pushed the power up and went around. He'd forgotten to check that the gear had actually gone down. He was really surprised to be caught like that."

Wasn't that just a little dangerous? "We had another instructor who went through the same thing," he explained, "But he ended up landing with the gear retracted." Evidently this didn't faze our instructor in the least.

But things don't have to get that severe for problems to overtake the crew. An instructor giving multi-engine training in a Piper Seminole found this out the hard way. He failed the left engine as the Seminole was on approach for a touch-and-go. The student handled it well, and when they got on the runway the instructor pushed both throttles up for the takeoff.

The Seminole had accelerated to 85 miles per hour when the instructor failed the right engine. The student again handled it well, pulling off the power to land straight ahead on the runway. Again the instructor pushed both throttles up and the Seminole climbed for a bit at 100 mph.

People on the ground saw the Seminole climbing with the right wing high. Suddenly, the wings rolled level and the nose pitched down. The CFI had taken control. After leveling the wings, he pulled off the power and landed off the runway. Unfortunately, the gear was on its way up as the Seminole was on its way down, making for a wheel-less arrival. Although the CFI would later claim the left engine wasn't responding, the NTSB saw it differently, laying the cause of the accident squarely on him.

I've Got It!

One of the first things taught to a student pilot is that when the instructor says "I've got it!" the student should let go of the controls immediately. Presumably, this allows the instructor to extricate the airplane from whatever mess the student has gotten it into. Failure to clearly release the controls can lead to confusion over who's actually flying the airplane.

> Just such a lack of crew coordination apparently caused a mishap that left a 29,475-hour, 73-year-old CFI and his 165-hour, 47-year-old student uninjured, but which damaged the Cessna 182 they were flying.
>
> The Cessna was on approach to runway 22 at Smith Ranch airport in Napa, California, at about 3 p.m. Winds were calm, and as the student began his approach, it became apparent that he was not lined up properly with the runway.
>
> The instructor took control on short final. He later stated that he thought the student was applying right rudder; but the student later stated that he was not doing so. The instructor applied left rudder, but the aircraft did not respond. On touchdown, the 182 swerved to the right, running off the runway and colliding with a wire fence. Damage to the Cessna was relatively light, including a bent propeller blade and a damaged horizontal stabilizer.
>
> FAA officials were on the airport at the time of the accident, and inspected the airplane's rudder cables and pedals. The cables were found intact and properly rigged, and the pedals operated normally.
>
> Both the student and instructor noted in their written statements that the autopilot was on at the time of landing. Neither could account for it being activated, and it is not known how it was switched on.
>
> The autopilot was a Cessna 300 series Nav-o-matic, a single-axis system that is connected to the ailerons, but not the rudder.

Who's Got It?

There is one irrefutable rule of the sea: When aboard a boat or ship, the captain is The Boss, and when it comes to operating the vessel he is in absolute control. It works the same way in aviation, at least in theory. The pilot-in-command is supposed to be running the show unless he very clearly delegates the task to another crewmember. In practice, things don't always work out that way.

Lack of clarity on just who was making the decisions led to a mishap in Lexington, North Carolina. A Cessna 172 with two pilots aboard ran off the end of the runway after landing long and fast. Neither pilot was injured, though the airplane suffered substantial damage when it slowly flipped inverted in a ditch.

The pilot-in-command, a 36-year-old, 285-hour instrument-rated commercial pilot, was in the left seat. The right seat was occupied by the PIC's former flight instructor, who had logged 860 hours.

On the day before the accident, the PIC called a fixed base operator in Lexington, North Carolina, to reserve the C-172 for two hours the following morning. At the same time, he asked if his former flight instructor would like to go along; the pilot wanted to get in some simulated instrument time to maintain currency. The flight instructor, who was scheduled to take his checkride for the instrument instructor's rating that afternoon, also wanted to get in some practice and readily agreed.

The flight departed Lexington shortly after 9 in the morning. The PIC was acting as safety pilot for the instructor, who was flying the airplane and wearing foggles to restrict his vision. The two flew to Rowan County Airport in Salisbury, where the instructor flew two NDB approaches, then handed the foggles to the PIC and acted as safety pilot. The PIC flew the NDB and VOR approaches, then proceeded back to Lexington, North Carolina.

While approaching Lexington, the instructor acted as controller, giving vectors for a simulated radar approach. According to the PIC's written statement, he did not provide distance-from-touchdown information.

Just short of the end of the runway the PIC took off the foggles, and here the stories given by the two pilots begin to diverge somewhat. The instructor's said, "About 500 MSL from the runway [sic] I told him to remove the hood and land. We touched down halfway down the runway and at three-quarters of the way down he said 'I think we need to go around.' I said, 'We can make it.' I didn't feel there was room for a go-around because of obstacles at the end of the runway.

He was still in control at this point." Both pilots were applying brakes and had the wheels locked up. The Cessna ran slowly off the end of the 3300-foot-long runway, down an embankment, and nosed over in a ditch.

The PIC's statement is somewhat more revealing. "When I took the foggles off, I thought we were too high to commit to a landing (we were still losing altitude and approximately 100 feet high almost on the approach end of runway 26) and suggested that we go around. The instructor then stated that we had 'plenty of room.' I continued to lose altitude, although I was prepared to execute a go-around at any moment. In fact I still had full intentions of going around. About 25 feet AGL he stated, 'Flaps coming down.' Although I had been prepared to go around, after he started extending the flaps, I assumed he really could get it down. Upon touching down full brakes were applied. However, there was not enough room to come to a stop and we ran off the end of the runway. We had slowed down considerably, and with perhaps another 15 to 20 feet we could have stopped."

It's apparent from the PIC's statement that at some point he felt he had given actual command of the airplane over to the instructor, though he never actually told the instructor this. He wrote that he "assumed the instructor could get it down," indicating that he believed the instructor was in control. He also said that he was specifically intending to go around, yet he never took action, choosing instead to follow the instructor's suggestions. The instructor, on the other hand, specifically states that the PIC was in command of the airplane right up to the end.

The Ice Man Cometh

A final variation of the "I've got it" game is the student who freezes at the controls. Many instructors told us this is their biggest fear. Many also had their own horror stories to relate.

An instructor from Florida told us of checking out a student in a Mooney. They were doing accelerated stalls when the student got them into a cross-control condition and they snapped over into a spin. "He just froze there on the controls. He was a big old farm-boy type, real strong, and I couldn't overpower him and he was just hanging on for dear life. I finally had to slap him in the face to snap him out of it so I could take it and recover."

Other instructors had similar stories. One, however, pointed out that for male instructors it was usually not too much of a problem. His concern was for "little female instructors who aren't strong enough to either overpower the student or hit him hard enough to wake him up." (We've never seen any accident or other data to show any distinctions between male and female instructors.)

Yet, chauvinism notwithstanding, a frozen student can be a hazard for any instructor. There was, for example, the 40-year-old male CFI giving a student his first lesson in a Cessna 140. From the accident brief: "This was to be the student's first flight and the CFI had him follow through on the controls. As the tail came off the runway, the student began overpowering the CFI at the controls. The CFI was unable to maintain directional control and the aircraft ran off the runway into a drainage ditch."

Or the case of pilot trying to add a helicopter rating to his ticket. He and his instructor had just completed a successful practice autorotation to a landing in a Bell 47 when the student abruptly pulled the collective all the way up. The chopper shot into the air, and the student then pulled the cyclic "full aft and to the right and froze," according to the instructor. The CFI was trying to overpower the student and had moved the cyclic back to level the chopper when they hit the ground. Both pilots escaped injury.

The Most Dangerous Game

Perhaps one of the most dangerous maneuvers in the pilot curriculum is the simulated engine failure. For every rating from solo student to ATP, instructors are killing engines. The student, of course, must then either handle a "simulated" forced landing or single-engine event in the case of a twin. But the test seems most severe for pilots of single-engine airplanes.

One instructor told us he'd pull an engine at any time, with no fear. "I get a lot of guys who fly a B-52 pattern—high, wide, and far from the field. If I get them on a Flight Review and I see them on a wide pattern, I'll yank the engine on them and challenge them to get to the airport," he said.

But sometimes the challenge is too much and the simulation becomes real.

A typical case involved a private pilot getting ready for a commercial certificate. He and his instructor were flying in a Piper Lance. They had completed a spiral descent from 4,000 to 2,000 feet when the instructor called for a simulated forced landing. They picked a field and headed for it, clearing the engine at 1,000 feet and again at 500 feet. They continued the approach down to 100 feet, but when they tried to power up and climb, the engine would not respond. The simulation was now real.

Despite their best efforts, the engine would not power up. The CFI took over. Since the gear was down, the CFI decided to skid the Lance sideways into the plowed field to collapse the gear. As the Lance settled into the furrows, the engine started to come back to life. Unfortunately, it stopped again when the prop hit the ground.

A variation on this is the "simulated" engine failure on takeoff. A private pilot getting checked out in a Grumman AA-1 got a little more than he bargained for when the instructor pulled the throttle at 50 feet on takeoff. The CFI later explained that he expected the pilot to make a low speed, low-altitude 120-degree turn to land on another runway. The private pilot didn't bank steeply enough, so the CFI took control and collided with trees in an attempted resumption of the takeoff climb.

Sometimes the simulation can get carried too far in other ways. A student and instructor in a Grumman AA-5B Tiger were out practicing one morning. The instructor failed the engine and let the student go through the restart procedures. Having declared the restart unsuccessful, the instructor let the student proceed to the forced landing portion of the exercise.

To make the problem more realistic, the instructor had a policy of letting the student actually move each control as if the emergency were real. He would be following the student's hand, repositioning each control after the student had moved it.

The student played along, turning off the mags (the instructor then turned them back on), pulling the mixture (the instructor then pushed it back in), and turning the fuel selector off (the instructor missed this one).

The simulation continued down to about 550 feet, when the instructor took over and applied power to climb out. The engine, however, was dead from lack of fuel. The instructor then noticed the selector in the "off" position and reset it to the left tank. It was too late, though, so he was forced into a landing. The Grumman hit hard and swerved, wracking up substantial damages, but leaving the two occupants unharmed.

A truly extreme case, illustrating the hazards of both the simulated engine failure and the "over the head" theory, involved the crash of a Beech Baron. The student and instructor were practicing Vmc maneuvers, and the instructor had shut down the right engine by turning off the fuel. Things unfortunately went too far and the Baron entered a flat spin from which it did not recover. The student survived with serious injuries; the instructor died.

The Real Deal

As mentioned previously, most instructors feel the key to their safety is to be ready for anything. This goes beyond being ready for the student to pull something. The airplane itself can malfunction, thus providing the student with a chance to either handle a real-life emergency, or more likely, to observe the instructor handling a real-life emergency.

An example is the case of a multi-engine student and instructor in a Piper Apache. They had been practicing touch-and-goes when the left engine failed at 200 feet during takeoff. The CFI took over, feathering the left prop.

The student released the controls and looked out at the left engine to see oil coming out of the cowl. The Apache was vibrating and shaking, indicating 100 knots as the instructor lowered the nose to maintain best single-engine rate of climb. But the Apache was not climbing; instead it started going down. The ground below was rough and the CFI held on, trying to gain airspeed and get the ship to climb.

But the Apache wouldn't fly. There were powerlines ahead, so the instructor turned toward what seemed to be the most suitable terrain and crash landed. Both student and instructor escaped with minor injuries. The engine was later found to have a broken oil cooler line, as well as some carburetor problems which could have made the engine run rough or flood.

Multi-engine training work, which includes a fair number of simulated engine failures, should have both pilots alert, practiced, and ready for a real one. But sometimes the real thing is just overwhelming.

A case in point was the crash of a Piper Aztec. From the accident brief: "The aircraft made a forced landing in an open field near the airport when the right engine stopped at 50 to 100 feet AGL during a touch-and-go landing. During the emergency the landing gear was not retracted, a right engine restart was not attempted, the right engine was not feathered, and a turn of 145 degrees was made into the dead engine. A runway aligned with the takeoff runway was less than three miles ahead. The aircraft landed gear-down and flaps up. Both main gear separated on landing." Post-accident investigation found the right engine had failed because the fuel selector had inadvertently been turned off.

Unsafety Pilot

Instrument instruction holds hazards all its own. Under actual IFR conditions, there is always the chance the student may get the airplane into some predicament the instructor can't recover from. Fortunately, this occurrence is quite rare.

But when the weather is VFR, the danger increases. While the student is under the hood, the instructor is supposed to be looking outside, watching for traffic. But sometimes he must divert his attention inside to point something out to the student, or at least monitor the student's performance. That's when the door opens to disaster—with one pilot who can't see and one who isn't looking.

A well-known case was the Wings West midair collision near San Luis Obispo, California in 1984. The commuter airliner was hit by a Rockwell 112TC on an instrument training flight as the airliner climbed outbound on the localizer and the Rockwell was shooting the localizer approach. The student was under the hood, unable to see. The instructor, his attention perhaps diverted to the instruments or the student, didn't spot the Beech C-99 airliner. The commuter crew, preoccupied with contacting controllers and cleaning up the aircraft in the climb, failed to see the Rockwell. They collided nearly head-on.

Another, lesser known incident was the collision of a Piper Seminole and a Beech Bonanza near Stockholm, New Jersey. The Seminole was on a multi-engine instrument training flight, while the Bonanza was on a local flight.

The student, the sole survivor of the incident, told investigators he was flying, under the hood, straight and level on a heading of 240 degrees. He did not remember the instructor giving any sign of the impending collision.

The two aircraft collided nearly head-on, sending the Bonanza out of control. The instructor took control of the Seminole and crash landed it in a wooded area. He died, however, from his injuries—he was not wearing a shoulder harness.

But instructors on instrument training flights are not only responsible for traffic watching. They must also keep ahead of the student, the airplane, and the flight. Getting behind any of these can hold serious consequences.

A case involving an instructor and student on an instrument training mission in a Cessna 172 over Arizona exemplifies the point.

The night flight had gone well until they started their descent for the destination. The student was under the hood as they started down out of 10,500 feet, heading for the airport some 30 miles away.

As they descended through 7,000 feet, the instructor obtained the local altimeter setting and dialed it in. That's when he realized they were far too low for their position. He called for the student to climb, but it was too late. The instructor caught sight of the trees in the landing light just before they hit a mountain. Fortunately, all aboard escaped serious injury.

Staying Ahead

Many of the instructors we spoke with said staying ahead of the student, the airplane, and the flight were the most important parts of preventing accidents. They owed their continued survival to anticipating the actions of student and airplane.

Other instructors pointed out communications and pre-planning with the student. Still other instructors based their safety on knowing the limits of both the airplane and themselves.

But the pilot who will live to retire is the one who adheres to all of these principles. Staying ahead of the airplane and the flight, planning ahead for both, and knowing the limits are perhaps the best forms of accident prevention available.

Good Training Means *Current* Training

The advantage that a twin offers over a single is a two-edged sword: The pilot must be able to handle the complex and difficult task of flying a twin with an engine out in order to realize any safety gain at all. Experience has shown that the only way to give a pilot this capability is through rigorous training, and, more importantly, continuing practice.

> Just such a lack of current experience in multi-engine aircraft precipitated an accident in which the owner/pilot of a Cessna 310D and his three passengers escaped injury, but the aircraft was extensively damaged. The 53-year-old private pilot was intending to make a local flight from a private dirt airstrip near Yermo, California at about 4:45 p.m.
>
> Just after liftoff, at about five feet AGL, the left engine lost all power. The aircraft yawed, uncontrolled, to the left, and drifted off the edge of the runway. The pilot aborted the takeoff, and the airplane hit some rough ground off of the

airstrip. The gear collapsed due to side loading, and the airplane slid to a stop 165 feet from the point of impact. Damage areas included both props, the nose section and both wings in addition to the gear.

The engine-out had caught the pilot by surprise, in more ways than one. The 1,517-hour pilot had logged a total of 17.7 hours in multi-engine aircraft, none of which had been accrued in the preceding 90 days (though he was current in single-engine aircraft). No indication was made of the cause of the engine failure, though it was noted that the last annual inspection had been performed two and a half years before the accident.

Emergency Training

There are times when it might be argued that training for an emergency poses as great a threat as the emergency itself. Every year, dozens of aircraft are damaged or destroyed as pilots simulate emergencies that become all too real.

A case in point is the February 22, 1986 crash of a Cessna 402B at Plainview, Texas. The 4,302-hour, ATP-rated pilot, age 27, and his safety pilot escaped injury, but the Cessna was substantially damaged.

The flight departed Lubbock International on an instrument proficiency flight to Plainview. The pilot was using a hood to simulate instrument flight. During the flight, the pilot shut down the right engine for training purposes and left it caged. The Cessna proceeded on course to Plainview.

When they got within three miles of the field, the pilot removed his hood. Everything went well until the Cessna was on the approach to Plainveiw. As they swung down final, the pilot realized that the aircraft could not land from the position it was in. He initiated a single-engine go-around.

But the Cessna wasn't performing as expected. Obstructions loomed ahead, and the pilot didn't think he could clear them. Rather than plow into them, he elected to land gear-up on the airport instead. The Cessna slid to a halt with substantial damages.

NTSB laid the blame for the accident squarely on the pilot. In a rather long listing of probable causes, the Board faulted the pilot for improper procedures, inadequate inflight planning, his failure to restart the caged right engine, and his attempted go-around on one engine, among other things.

The safety pilot provided an interesting footnote to the accident. Recounting the details of the flight, the safety pilot recalled, "I was unaware of any difficulty with the approach until the pilot tried to go around."

The Fatal Fallacies of Training

Given the importance of the training process in aviation safety, it is remarkable how little research has been done on how to train civilian pilots. Many of the methods and materials in use are similar or identical to what was employed 30 years ago. For aviation education, as practiced at the average FBO, filmstrips seem to be the cutting edge of technology.

Now a learning expert suggests that several fallacies, rather than any facts, may be guiding the way many high-performance skills (including flying) are taught. His data comes from studying air traffic control training methods.

No. 1 on the fallacy list, according to University of Pittsburgh researcher Walter Schneider, is the concept that "practice makes perfect." It's the notion which underlies the bump and grind approach to teaching pilots to land an airplane. The novice flier is made to circle the pattern endlessly, in the vague hope that repeating mistakes will make them go away.

"In air traffic control training," says Schneider, "a large portion of the training time is occupied with the student simply practicing the task. However, many students show only very slow acquisition rates by practicing the task and do not obtain acceptable performance levels by the end of the training program.

"The statement that practice makes perfect is an overgeneralization. Not only does practice often fail to make perfect, it sometimes produces no improvement in performance at all."

Fallacy No. 2 is that it's best to train a skill in the form in which it will finally appear. Turning again to the example of an air traffic controller trainee, Schneider points out that it's very difficult to teach controllers to perceive where an aircraft should be started on a turn because the skill is taught by waiting for such turns to occur on radar, where it's difficult to really see the turn radius, and where "the trainee may experience only eight 90-degree turns in an hour."

The answer, he argues, would be a training regimen that teaches the task in a different form. "A training module designed to teach this component could expose the trainee to hundreds of accelerated observations of a turn radius in an hour." That's not the way it would ever happen on a real scope with real airplanes, but it is the best way to get the point across. Reality is not always a good teacher.

The third fallacy cited by Schneider is that "skill training is intrinsically motivating and thus, adding extrinsic motivators is inappropriate." The beginning pilot is there because he wants to learn to fly, so why should the instructor have to worry about interesting him in the flying task at hand? Perhaps because he'll learn better. When Schneider added bells and whistles (in the form of interesting sounds and visual displays) to training air traffic controllers, failure rates in certain experiments dropped from 30 percent to 5 percent.

And of course, aviators always train for high accuracy. Everyone should want to be good, holding those headings and altitudes to within a whisker. That's another training fallacy, says the expert. The problem with such standards, argues Schneider, is that it produces a person who isn't very skilled at the larger and more important task of dividing his attention between the many things which do have to be maintained in the real-world cockpit.

"Training programs following this fallacy," he notes, "tend to produce operators who can perform individual component skills well but who cannot operate well in high workload situations.

"In air traffic control, an operator who can maintain optimal separation of only two aircraft would not be an acceptable controller. What is desired is an operator who can maintain safe separation among 10 aircraft."

The fifth fallacy is that initial performance predicts eventual outcome. This is actually a fallacy combined with a self-fulfilling prophecy. When it comes to complex skills, initial performance is often quite variable, and research shows that the more complex the skill, the lower the correlation between initial performance and final skill level. Slow learners do become excellent final performers sometimes—if their teachers' expectations don't ground them.

That's the self-fulfilling prophecy part. Initial performance often labels a student in the mind of the instructor, and instructors' expectations have a way of being fulfilled. Once a klutz, always a klutz, at least in the eyes of the person in the right seat.

And the final fallacy is the notion that understanding something intellectually will result in the capability to be proficient at doing it. This is the split between book learning and performance.

Sometimes the split results because there's no real relationship between the skill being discussed and the skill as executed. For example, controllers are taught the performance characteristics of various airplanes— essentially a long list of numbers. But the meaning of those numbers on a radar scope is an entirely different matter. The person who has the numbers memorized may or may not be any good at visualizing that information and doing something with it on radar.

Training techniques, like engines, need periodic overhauls. In the case of general aviation, training is far beyond TBO. Most of the fallacies cited by Schneider are a well-established part of the average training program, which is a barely-modified version of the way people were taught to fly decades ago. Perhaps that's one of the reasons the accident rate continues to be depressingly consistent, and unacceptably high, from one year to the next.

"With appropriate perspective, research, and guidelines," says Schneider, "the current computer revolutions can flower into a training revolution." It could start, perhaps, with general aviation, where the success of training is often measured in lives.

The Student View of Pilot Training

Although we have sought to avoid first-person articles and expressions of opinion on these pages, the following article, submitted by a 25-year-old private pilot, expresses some concerns that we believe many newly licensed pilots share. The author's honest self-assessment—which may be the first step toward safety any airman can make—is something we feel will benefit all our readers, from a student to a 20,000-hour airline pilot.

CONFESSIONS OF A ROOKIE AIRMAN

For many of us, the dream of learning to pilot an airplane requires several years and many hundreds of dollars to become reality. When I was a young boy, my father had introduced me to aviation in the form of models, primarily World War II military aircraft. Eventually, I realized that the fighting machines whose pilots I idolized were the same machines to which wives, sweethearts and children lost the men and boys they loved. While still fascinated with the technical aspects of military hardware, my interest turned to civilian aviation and how it could become part of my life. By the end of high school, I was determined to earn my private pilot license and, eventually, to buy my own airplane.

After completing my training as an avionics technician, I could wait no longer to pursue my aviation goals. I was constantly around aircraft I could not yet fly. I asked a local A&P instructor to recommend a flight school. Two weeks later, I took my introductory lesson. I was hooked. Flying was for me.

There are, however, several aspects of the pilot training I received which have caused me to ask some serious questions. I hope these concerns are shared by other members of the pilot group in which I place myself: The Licensed Rookie.

INTENSIVE TRAINING

I suspect that my training experience is typical of that of many of today's new pilots. I was able to meet the requirements of Part 141 in 37 flight hours, accumulated between June and October, 1984. I spent as much time at the airport as my work and family schedule would allow. I continued my habit of reading anything related to aviation, focusing on piloting technique, regulations and my textbook lessons. At times the weather would prevent my flying, and I would return to the books and charts. I felt that I was making the best possible effort I could to learn to be a safe and competent pilot, yet I still made some poor decisions and bounced a few more landings than I care to remember. All things considered, by checkride time, I was confident of my ability to handle the airplane in any situation the examiner could throw at me.

When that fateful day arrived, I was a well-prepared bundle of nerves. Having the FAA-designated examiner arrive an hour and a half late didn't help. We had the usual chat about paperwork, sectionals, FARs, preflight planning, etc. I felt that our discussion was a good review of my textbook work, with two areas of exception. The application of weather theory was not covered at all. At the time I was glad, because this was a weak area for me. All those fronts and pressure differentials and going from high pressure to low pressure didn't seem relevant. I wanted to fly for fun! If the weather was bad, I simply would not fly. (This attitude has changed a great deal since then.)

When I obtained current weather information for the checkride, I found good to acceptable VFR conditions forecast throughout the afternoon. I chose to activate my flight plan after takeoff—the verbal exam was not over, and I did not yet want to commit to a specific takeoff time.

WEIGHT A MINUTE!

After I hung up with Flight Service, the verbal exam continued with the weight and balance calculation for the checkride. Having taken off many times in a Cessna 152 with full (long-range) tanks and my instructor aboard during my flight lessons, I was mildly shocked to find that in the same situation with an FAA examiner who was 10 pounds lighter than my instructor, I would be 20 pounds over gross weight.

The examiner confirmed my findings and, looking across the Chicago sectional, said to me, "That's okay. We'll burn that off after a few minutes anyhow. Let's go fly the airplane."

There I sat, facing the man with the power to grant me the privilege of private flight. This man expected me to act wisely, in a law-abiding manner, conscious at all times of my responsibility to myself, my passengers, and all over whom I flew. This same man was telling me it was okay for me to fly my checkride over gross!

I thought it was a trick question, and I said so. He assured me that he was serious, putting the ball back in my court. I wanted my license. We walked out to the airplane.

BEFORE STARTING

Normally, I would perform my preflight alone, signaling to my instructor, who remained in the FBO office, when I was finished and ready to go. In retrospect, I was consistently guilty of the "cursory preflight inspection" which most pilots carry out, giving the aircraft the walk-around once-over while noticing only what was right, not things that were wrong. I was always lucky, and never had mechanical difficulty or failure.

For the checkride, preflight inspection was as brisk as that cold October day. With the FAA's examiner watching every move, I felt a bit nervous, even though I felt I knew what I was doing. I checked the aircraft as I always had, using the procedure outlined in the flight manual. But I spent the five minutes it took to perform my preflight more aware of the examiner than of the airplane. I had done what I had been taught was a correct and adequate preflight. Everything "looked" good. I climbed in and watched as my first passenger belted himself into the airplane.

Well, there I sat. The moment of truth had arrived. It had taken 25 years to happen. I expected to be flying for 25 years more, and another 25 after that. I knew I could pass.

But wait a minute—what about this guy sitting next to me? He had checked my paperwork up and down, inside and out. I had adequate flight time and good test scores. I knew the rules and the charts. But, apart from my instructor's word and the manner in which the examiner conducted himself (which I was beginning to question after the weight and balance affair), I had no evidence that he could fly any better than I could. Still, my license depended on *his* appraisal of my piloting ability. I picked up the checklist and turned to "Before Starting Engine."

The checkride was to be a round-trip cross-country flight to an airport 176 miles away. Twenty minutes into the flight, this plan was abandoned in favor of doing some airwork locally. I had activated my flight plan shortly after takeoff. I asked if I should cancel it. The examiner said, "It can wait till we get down." This was not the answer I expected. I should have reported the change in plan to Flight Service, but even from the left seat I didn't feel I was the pilot in command. At the examiner's instruction, I turned for the practice area.

En route to the practice area I was asked to perform two turns about a point; with only a slight wind present, these went well. Next we did some stalls. First was the simulated approach to landing stall, which also went well. Then came the stall after takeoff. I applied full throttle and pulled back the yoke. I neglected to add enough right rudder and aileron to counteract the left-turning tendency. We began to roll left, and almost spun. The airplane stalled just as I levelled the wings, and I recovered comfortably. The examiner, visibly alarmed, said, "You've got to control that bank!"

I was sure that my ride was over, and I was going to turn back to the airport, when the engine quit. I quickly found the mixture pulled to full lean, complements of the FAA's examiner. "Where are you going to land?" he asked. At only 2,200 feet AGL, I knew I had to get set up quickly, there being no going around from a bad approach. Sure, I had been expecting a forced landing, but I still could not decide where to land.

Several fields looked good and two large ones were staggered, allowing diversion to the farther if the closer looked too rough as I got near it. I talked about my options, which naturally began with trying to restart the engine. I was told my efforts had failed, and we were committed to a landing. As we lost altitude, the approach looked good, and the examiner gave me back the engine. We climbed out to 3,000 feet and headed for the airport.

Unusual Events

Now came simulated IFR. Under the hood, I could see only the instrument panel. The examiner took the controls, (the only time I saw him fly, but didn't really "see") and put the plane in an unusual attitude. "Now return to level flight on your original heading," came the command.

Airspeed was climbing through the yellow arc, RPMs were over 2500, left wing low, altitude decreasing rapidly from 2,200 feet AGL. I pulled power, leveled the wings, carb heat on, and began to pull out. I felt very close to the ground for this sort of thing, but I expected that the FAA man realized that whatever happened to me in the airplane would happen to him, too. After what seemed like a rather long time, we were climbing out from 500 feet AGL. I'm sure that if I had stalled on pull-up, it would have been all over. We then returned to the airport for crosswind landings, and some short-field work. This went reasonably well, and I was again confident that I would pass. We landed and taxied in.

Although this may seem like a full schedule, my checkride lasted only 42 minutes. We went into the FBO building and I was signed off. Having completed the "ride" part of the checkride, there remained only the signing of the check.

I had been prepared for a lot more to be asked of me during my checkride. Minimum control airspeed, slips, S-turns, figure eights, and a series of stalls (including secondary stalls) were all things I expected to be covered. What about radio procedures, filing a pilot report, obtaining weather information en route, coordination with other aircraft through ATC? The test had been too easy to be an accurate measure of my ability as a pilot. I didn't recognize the feeling right away, but I was disappointed.

To make matters worse, the examiner had made the only

false entry that will ever appear in my logbook: "Private flight check satisfactory. Tested on all pilot operations in the flight test guide." He then signed his name to this lie.

MY TURN TO ASK

But, beyond the questions nobody asked me, I am concerned about the questions I did not ask others.

I had developed a certain degree of skepticism as my training progressed. Even so, there were many questions I should have asked that I did not. How well was my training aircraft being maintained? I know what I did to it—what about the cumulative effects of the four years of student strut-benders before me? Where were the engine and airframe maintenance logs? I had heard some brief comments on prior aircraft damage, but don't remember seeing logbooks or other documents to verify this. I had been told that all mandatory Airworthiness Directives had been complied with. I had been told verbally that the aircraft was legally operated and inspected, and I have no reason to doubt this. Still, I should have made more direct inquiries to really know about the aircraft I was flying.

Why had I never done an actual weight and balance calculation for the airplane, instructor and fuel quantity that I flew with, in addition to the sample weight and balance problems that I practiced on? When would I learn spin recovery technique?

Why hadn't engine operation technique been more thoroughly explained? I would often "cruise" at almost full throttle before I learned of terms like 75 percent power, or 65 percent power. Also, my understanding of mixture control consisted of "full rich below 3000 feet MSL, with leaning for maximum rpm at higher altitudes." EGT? What's that? Why hadn't I actually landed without power during training? How much can one learn from a simulated emergency landing at 3,000 feet?

What frequency should I use if I'm landing after the tower is closed? What about hull insurance on the airplane? I had heard something about "One thousand deductible hull insurance." What about personal injuries?

Why wasn't more emphasis put on weather theory? With the answers in the back of the book, anyone with a study guide should be able to pass the written exam. It's too easy to memorize the answers to the more difficult questions. It's also too easy for an instructor to accept successful completion of the private pilot written as an indication of understanding and knowledge gained. If an instructor doesn't ask questions, he won't really know how much you have learned.

As the list grew, I realized that all I had to do was ask. I had expected that these and other important areas of my pilot training would be addressed in detail before my checkride, yet they were not. Too late did I realize that the training I had paid for was a bare minimum, learn-how-to-fly course (yet perfectly legal in accordance with the FARs).

POSITIVE ATTITUDE

My instructor had showed great confidence in my ability, and reassured me of a successful checkride. Looking back, everyone connected with my flight training was confident right from the start. Perhaps this was nothing more than presenting a positive environment for the student. (However, after learning that this same check pilot flew with all of the FBO's students, and considering the FBO's claim of being the "area's most successful flying school," the phrase "license factory" keeps popping into my head.)

At the time, however, I studied the books, flew my lessons, and passed the solo, written exam and checkride hurdles. I had tested my way into possession of that most sought-after of prizes, my private pilot certificate.

I wonder how many pilots remember that feeling of exhilaration at that moment in their flying careers. (The freedom of skies and all that.) For me, just as it had been at the time of my first solo, this feeling was silently absent. Instead, I found myself asking, "Is that it? Is that all there is to it?" I felt that something very important was missing.

I suspect now that there are many similarities between my experiences and those of you other Licensed Rookies out there. Lacking in time and money, I find my flight hours are few and far between. I do my share of hangar flying and reading, but my actual experience is not accumulating as fast as it did that summer, and now I find myself wondering, "Am I a safe pilot?"

When I was training, I averaged one and a half hours of

flight time a week. Frequent contact with the airplane in the airport environment made it easy to stay in touch with all that I was learning. I felt confident in my ability, and trusted my airplane. It always worked; I believed it always would. But since that October day of realization, I have logged less than 10 hours. When I checked out with another FBO to rent from, they required an hour of dual with their check pilot. I was gently but unmistakably reminded that I had been away from the airplane too long.

Stalls? No problem. Carb heat on, throttle back, pull the yoke, wings level, right rudder, buffet, break, recover, right? Sure, if you plan it that way with enough altitude to recover. No, I really don't know stalls very well at all. (But I'm a *licensed pilot*. Of course I know stalls!) Spins? Sure, I've ridden along for one or two with the instructor at the controls.

Am I a safe pilot? I don't think I am as safe a pilot as I want to be. Not the safe pilot my fellow airmen deserve that I be. And certainly not the safe pilot I want to have sitting in the left seat when my own family is aboard.

Perhaps I seem paranoid to other pilots. I don't think I am. I have a secure existence and a healthy family. Why should I jeopardize them through ignorance and mental laziness?

I encourage each of you to re-examine your abilities and knowledge. Right now, before you take your family or friends up again. They take it for granted that you know it all. Don't let them down by believing that you do.

Gap After Gap

Each issue of *Aviation Safety* makes me more aware of the flaws and gaps in my training. Until the July 1, 1985 issue, with a lead article on extra-effort preflights, I believed I could properly preflight a simple Cessna 152. No more. My pre-flight routine has expanded considerably.

It prompted me to think about the whole airplane and try to imagine what could be wrong yet go undetected by the casual once-over. I now check for proper trim tab operation, securely attached flaps and control surfaces, and absence of differential elevator movement. I look at the nosegear and steering mechanism closely to see whether there's any dam-age from improper towing. I check for cracks in the Plexiglas windshield. I confirm that the tanks were topped off with the fuel valve in the "off" position (which prevents cross-feeding of the tanks, decreasing the actual amount of fuel taken on). I make sure the proper type of fuel is used, being alert for potential misfueling.

The more I learn about possible problems, the more I wish the engine compartment were more easily accessible. Many potential gremlins are hidden by screwed-down cowlings. But FBOs might object to a pilot pulling out a screwdriver as he approaches the airplane. And anyway, I suspect that the time involved discourages pilots from uncowling the airplanes they rent.

In my employment, I have learned to look closely at an often-ignored item—the antenna that may sprout from almost any surface of the airplane. A large percentage of the avionics squawks that get reported originate from dirty or damaged antennas, not problems with the radios. A little oil or grease buildup goes a long way to reduce signal strength, both in the transmit and the receive mode. This is also true of an antenna that has been painted (antennas should not be painted). Suppose you had an emergency where you needed maximum range from your radios, but a dirty or damaged antenna wasn't caught on preflight. You might still have a 50-mile range of transmission—but the nearest receiver might be 51 miles away and *no one will hear you.*

As an avionics installation technician, I have worked with a small FBO, a helicopter service center, and a corporate jet service center. I see a lot of sick birds.

Many of these machines have problems that are commonplace and easily solved by competent mechanics. But some of these aircraft I have serious doubts about. Mechanics can only do what the owner will pay for. Beyond that, a mechanic's report and recommendations alone will not prevent accidents, if the owner doesn't act.

For example, I was involved in an avionics retrofit on a V-35 Bonanza. As the job progressed, we saw a good example of an owner's unwillingness to do the job right. The passenger area floorboards were removed in order to mount antennas on the belly, I was greeted by a layer of gummy, black sludge one-quarter inch thick (I measured it). This was the result of a leaking landing gear transmission box. I am at a loss to explain why the leak was allowed to continue long enough to cause such an accumulation of gunk (the airplane is older than I am). It's not just that the gearbox leak could be pointing toward gear system failure, but the dirty, oily connections could lead to failure of the new transponder, marker and DME antennas. After cleaning the area to allow the antenna installation, I reported this to my supervisor and the aircraft owner. Log entries of my findings notwithstanding, the aircraft left with the gearbox unchanged.

Beech King Airs are notorious for having harnesses chafed by the control chains which link the pilot's and copilot's control columns. Although most avionics installers will confirm that adequate clearance exists between the harnesses and moving parts, the pilot-owner who swaps out his own disabled RMI or HSI might not be as careful.

Most of the potential safety hazards I find in customers' airplanes deal with avionics or electrical wiring. There are thousands of sharp edges waiting to cut wires, and often I find repairs in these areas. I have seen 16-gauge wires spliced to 10-gauge buss feeders to provide power to owner-added circuit breakers. I often encounter avionics harnesses haphazardly crammed between the instrument panel and firewall or pressure bulkhead. Several times I have seen the flexible harness to the panel instruments so tightly crammed into the small space available that the instruments were pushed partially out of the panel when the mounting screws were removed.

Too many airplane owners don't understand that a good-quality, electrically functional, properly installed wiring harness takes time to build, install and check out. Often, owners are amazed at how much of the airplane we have to take apart to lay in the wire bundles. They just don't want to pay for labor that seems unnecessary and doesn't appear to contribute directly to the installation procedure. As a result, they cut us short on time or go to someone who will cut corners for them. Regardless of what we think or say, when they take the airplane it's out of our hands.

My point is that we have a federal agency to establish safety standards and to make some effort to see that they are maintained. We have federally licensed mechanics to inspect and service aircraft. The next link in the safety chain is the owner-operator. How well is he equipped to inspect, detect and correct? How financially willing is he? The bottom line is that I no longer blindly trust the airplanes I rent. I'm going to ask them many questions before we fly together again.

IN-DEPTH TRAINING

I hope that all I'm saying will not be taken lightly. Flying an aircraft is not a complex act, yet it requires a great deal of mental preparation and responsibility on the part of all who touch the aircraft. For the pilot, this means training and current experience, but this should include much more than the "skim the surface" instruction that many FBOs charge a good dollar for. I strongly recommend that the requirements for private pilots be expanded to make spin training mandatory. Not only recovery, mind you. By then it's often too late. Avoidance is the goal.

Stalls are generally covered more than spins, yet there is room for still more reinforcement of how to *avoid* this situation before airspeed and altitude are gone. Students spend real dollars for expensive lessons. The cost should not include injury or death as a result of incomplete training.

I haven't given up. All things considered, I have arrived at an attitude that will not let my uncertainties and distrust prevent me from flying. Instead, I choose to make every effort to better myself as a pilot. I need more dual time, with several different instructors, to get a more objective view of what I think I know how to do. I encourage my fellow Licensed Rookies to do the same.

I need a better understanding of the mechanical functions of airframes and powerplants. If I had a better knowledge of engine operation and assembly, control rigging, general airframe assembly and annual inspection requirements and procedures, it would help me ask the questions an airplane should answer to each pilot before the engine is started. Who can effectively inspect an aircraft when he wouldn't recognize anything out of the ordinary, even if it was about to bite him?

There were many times when, as a student pilot, I expected to be taught things and I wasn't—because I didn't ask. No one told me I would have to ask, and I didn't. Now I'm telling you: Ask questions. You're paying for the answers. I believe pilot safety depends on continuous training, study and awareness. Don't blindly trust someone else to keep you from doing something stupid.

As with many other Licensed Rookies, I will always remember the words of my examiner on that October day. As he handed me my certificate, he said, "This is a license to learn." The responsibility now lies with me.

Landings, Takeoffs, And Go-Arounds

A truly proficient pilot is one who can make every takeoff so smooth that his passengers don't know when the airplane has left the ground, whose every landing is a "grease job," and one who always knows when a go-around is required.

That also describes a pilot who lives in La-La Land. The longer you fly, the more you become aware of the infinite number of conditions that work to frustrate the admirable objective of super-smooth runway operations; but there's no good reason for not constantly trying to improve.

In this section of Pilot Proficiency, we will present two sides of the takeoff/landing/go-around issue, some tips on how to accomplish these operations more proficiently, and the results of some less-than-proficient attempts at coming and going.

What You See Is Not Always What You Get

There's a lot of emphasis on "how it looks" during the landing-training phase of a pilot's education. We depend heavily on outside visual cues for altitude, glide slope, runway alignment, and so forth; with flight simulators for tools, researchers are discovering that reality doesn't always match perception in this situation.

Training students to land is often traumatic for the student, the instructor, and the airplane, and an increasing amount of training is being carried out in simulators. As costs drop, more and more GA students will have access to simulators with realistic visual displays, which has added impetus to the drive to make the displays simulate reality better.

Just as many of the real-world cues that inform the landing decision remain obscure, the components that make up a simulator pilot's perception of reality are just starting to be revealed. Researchers are beginning to find out what it is about the simulator scene that makes land-bound pilots perceive what they're seeing correctly.

Or, in some cases, not correctly. Researchers have long known that simulator pilots have a tendency to land short and hot while "flying" in the unreal world. There's no evidence that this has any adverse affect on their real-world performance, but it's still a distressing glitch in the system.

In their search for the reason why simulators tend to make people come up short, investigators decided to look at runway texture and see if that was a factor.

As a pilot lands, he sees more and more detail as the ground approaches. What look like a few big chunks of pattern at pattern altitude (maybe that's why it's called pattern altitude?) reveal themselves as a variety of textures at 500 feet, and resolve into discernible objects lower down. Boxes within boxes within boxes, if you will.

And therein lies the clue. Or rather, the cue. To define how this visual cue is affecting landing decisions, nine pilots and nine non-pilots were put through the hoops in a simulator where they made approaches starting from either 110 or 230 feet above the runway. At 50 feet AGL the display was frozen and the pilots were asked to point with a cursor to where the plane would land.

The simu-jocks faced four types of runway displays: a plain runway outline, an outline with some dots providing a bit of texture, a grid, and a runway with a grid and additional texture provided by a large X in each grid block with some small Xs around it. The big X became visible at 100 feet and the smaller Xs at around 75 feet.

Toting up the results, investigators found that the less texture the more the error. The outline model produced a landing that was, on average, about 60 feet short. Add some dots and the error dropped to around 20 feet. The bare grid brought the error down to a few feet short, while the X pattern actually had the pilots landing long by about 10 feet. Another way of stating it is that the more texture there was, the farther down the runway a pilot tended to land.

What the research did not show was any significant affect of the trait called nested texture—the emergence of more pattern information as a pilot gets closer to the ground.

There was one other bit of surprising information to emerge from this study. The tests were run using a variety of approach angles, and pilots performed best on the steepest glideslope, which in this case was a rather breathtaking 15 degrees (a normal glideslope is three degrees). They're still trying to figure out what that means.

Flying the Straight and Narrow

The essence of a good final approach is a ground track that lies right on the extended centerline of the runway (we assume proper airspeed and rate of descent). Pilots encounter tracking difficulties due to seat position, width of the cockpit, and inability to visualize the centerline; but no doubt the most troublesome problem arises from crosswinds.

The corrective technique is simple in theory—bank the airplane to provide just enough horizontal lift component to offset the cross-wind, and keep the nose pointed down the runway with rudder pressure—but often difficult to apply. Sometimes, it's necessary to be very conscious of crosswinds even after the airplane is on the ground, as this pilot discovered.

> For the 35-year-old, 310-hour pilot of a Cessna 182RG, an attempted landing on a dirt strip at Arizona's Marble Canyon Airport ended in a flip-over off the side of the runway. The pilot and his passenger were uninjured, but the airplane was badly damaged.
>
> The flight began in the early morning at the Marble Canyon airport. The pilot and passenger had departed there at 5:35 a.m. for a few hours of local flying. By 7:30, they had returned to Marble Canyon and prepared for a landing attempt. The pilot overflew the strip once and found a fairly strong crosswind at 1,000 feet above the ground. He looked for the windsock, but it was too tattered to be readable. He brought the C-182 around the pattern for the landing attempt on runway 3.
>
> Descending through 500 feet, he found the wind seemed to be decreasing. By the time the aircraft reached to threshold, the winds had died entirely. The 182 touched down and started rolling on the dirt strip.
>
> The pilot pulled up the flaps and the Cessna slowed to about 40 knots. Suddenly, a strong gust from the left lifted the wing, driving the Cessna towards the right side of the runway. The pilot, for some reason, did not react, and the 182 left the packed dirt of the runway.

The nosegear dug, slowing the airplane dramatically. The tail started to come up, and the Cessna flipped over. The pilot and his passenger climbed out unhurt.

The subsequent investigation disclosed rather windy conditions in the area. Page, Arizona, 12 miles northeast of Marble Canyon, reported winds at 11 knots from the northwest with gusts to 18 knots. The pilot himself estimated the winds at Marble Canyon as gusting to 18 knots from about 300 degrees.

In his report to the NTSB after the accident, the pilot offered his own perceptions of the reasons behind the accident. "I feel the airplane could have been kept on the runway with quicker reaction to the wind," he wrote. "More experience would have made a difference." How much more experience would have made the difference, he did not say.

When the Wind Bloweth from Behind

Airplanes land into the wind for good reason...the groundspeed at touchdown is reduced by the velocity of the wind, making for a shorter landing roll. When, for whatever reason, a pilot manages to land with the wind, the results can be unhappy—as this student pilot discovered the hard way.

The 35-year-old student pilot suffered minor injuries when his plane bounced and went out of control during a downwind landing at the completion of a solo cross-country flight. He had 22.5 total hours, including 6.3 as pilot in command.

Upon arrival, he made a full-flap landing on runway 17, but the plane bounced and departed the runway to the left. The pilot added full power in an attempt to go around, but he left the wing flaps in the full-down position. The aircraft did not accelerate to flying speed and struck a fence and a tree off the runway.

The pilot said although he thought the wind had been from the south, he later discovered that it was from 010 degrees at 15 knots, gusting to 20. (Unicom was available, but he didn't use it to get wind information.)

The pilot also told investigators that he found no wind sock, and although he observed the traffic direction indicator. Was there some deficiency in this pilot's training?

Beware the Decelerating Approach

Bill Kelly is one of *Aviation Safety*'s contributing editors. As a naval aviator and engineering test pilot with many years experience, he's seen his share of accidents caused by lack of proficiency. Kelly believes that many landing accidents are a result of sloppy technique and a poor understanding of airspeed, power and pitch. Here's what he has to say about the subject:

The other day, I watched an older Cessna P210 make an unusual approach to the local airport. It came in fast and close on downwind, but then orbited way out there on a looping base leg. The airplane lost an awful lot of altitude during the curved base leg and barely cleared the trees a half mile from the runway.

The flaps appeared to be fully extended and the engine sounded as if it was throttled back to just a hair above idle. But the pitch attitude indicated that its airspeed was very high. The Cessna dipped down after clearing the trees, leveled out with about 5 feet of clearance between the tires and the turf, and proceeded to "glide" level for the length of the grass overrun off the approach end of the 5,000-foot runway.

It was a classic shallow-approach deceleration. The nose came up slowly as the airspeed bled off. Fortunately, the pilot played it just right. He ran out of speed and lift just as he crossed the threshold of the concrete; the airplane plunked onto the runway within the first 100 feet of concrete, leaving behind a 2,000-foot strip of tall grass still waving from the down wash.

Now that *is not* the way to make a short-field approach and landing. That 210 scared the heck out of me. I thought for sure it was going to roll through the grass before reaching the runway. And I wondered whether the nose strut on that big single would survive the two-inch lip where the grass meets the concrete.

A low, shallow approach might be the only alternative if, for some crazy reason, you just *have* to land on a 500-foot strip with no obstacles or a short sandbar in the middle of a river. But even then, you would not want a *decelerating* approach. If you have to be low and shallow, you want to be stabilized at that minimum approach speed with the power necessary to maintain altitude, as well as the low airspeed.

Decelerating approaches are bad news. They're dangerous. And it's not just general aviation pilots who get into trouble with them.

In the past few years, two highly experienced professional flight crews have run afoul of decelerating approaches. The mishaps were highly publicized. They happened to involve the same type of wide-body jetliner, the Airbus A320, which is perched on the zenith of high technology (fly-by-wire automation with auto-throttles and side-stick flight controls). Both of the winged marvels decelerated and settled into the boonies, loaded with passengers.

KILLER DEMO

One of the crashes followed a low-altitude fly-by at an air show at the Mulhouse Habsheim airfield near Paris on June 26, 1988. The crew was two highly experienced Air France pilots, who had been involved in the development of the A320. They had planned to perform two fly-bys over the relatively short (approximately 2,640-foot) grass general aviation airstrip—the first slow, with gear and flaps extended; the second in a clean configuration and fast.

The low-and-slow demonstration was a killer. The fly-by was supposed to have been made with a minimum of 100 feet of ground clearance. The A320 flew the pass at idle power, decelerating all the way, and slowly descending to 30 feet of the ground. The power didn't come on in time to clear the trees off the end of the runway. The airplane was in an incredible nose-high attitude, not climbing, when its rear fuselage and horizontal tail hit the treetops. Three passengers died, 36 of the occupants were injured and 97 people more or less walked away from the wreckage.

The airplane had descended from 1,000 feet AGL with its landing gear and flaps down, and the two engines throttled back to flight idle. The automatic throttle system had been disengaged for the fly-by. The data recorder showed a rate of descent of 600 fpm. Although the altitude-alert system broadcast a warning at 200 feet, the plane continued descending at 600 fpm, still at flight idle.

Another altitude alert was sounded in the cockpit at 100 feet (the planned minimum). Though the descent rate decreased, the airplane dipped down to 30 feet off the ground. And, still, the throttles remained at idle.

ATTITUDE CONTROL

No, the A320 didn't stall. In this airplane, angle of attack is limited by an automated system to prevent a stall from occurring, even if a pilot pulls a side-stick controller all the way back. The automatic throttle system would have prevented the disastrous loss of airspeed and, probably, helped the pilot hold his 100-foot target height. However, the auto-throttle system wasn't engaged.

Even so, normal scanning of airspeed and manual positioning of the power controls could have prevented this accident. The young trees in the impact area were only about 40 feet tall—high enough to choke the powerful engines with leaves as the airplane cut a swath through them in its nose-high attitude.

What a way to go in! I watched the film of the ill-fated low pass several times on television news programs. The way that pitch attitude kept increasing with no gain in altitude—you could just sense that there was little power applied and that airspeed was falling rapidly. The same type of dangerous deceleration was apparent when I later watched the Cessna P210 make its low, shallow approach.

WRONG MODE

The other crash occurred on Feb. 14, 1990, and involved an Air India A320 approaching to land at Bangalore. In the left seat was a trainee captain, who was being evaluated by a check pilot in the right seat.

The pilots had mistakenly selected a flight control mode called "idle open descent," in which the auto-throttles hold the power at idle. This mode is normally used only for descent from high altitude; it is not intended to be used during landing approaches. They could have selected among two other auto-throttle modes, which would adjust power to maintain the desired approach airspeed. Or they could have controlled the power levers manually.

In the last 30 seconds of the descent (in good VFR weather), still at idle, the big jet slowed to a speed 25 knots below the desired approach speed. A so-called "floor mode" automatically increased power to accelerate the A320's engines to go-around thrust, but the aircraft continued to descend until it crashed on a golf course a half mile from the approach end of the runway.

Both side-stick controllers reached their full-back positions about one second before impact; but, again, no stall. The wreckage bounced and slid almost to the airport boundary wall, and was destroyed by fire. Ninety-four of the 146 people aboard the airplane perished. Interestingly, fire crews didn't arrive until about 20 minutes after the crash.

The check pilot was playing "instructor" almost the whole way to impact, when he really should have been acting as a member of a coordinated crew, since there were passengers aboard. Instruction has its place—but not close to the ground with other people aboard.

More Questions

The A320 accidents have heightened the controversy over automated systems and, undoubtedly, have raised more questions about crew coordination. But let's not knock automatic throttles just yet.

For the U.S. Navy, getting high-wing-loaded jets onto carrier decks is a precision operation. Auto-throttles are the best thing to come along since sliced bread, the angled deck and a visual glide slope. But there is still an LSO (landing signal officer) standing alongside the landing area. Nowadays, the LSO does most of his work over the radio, and one of his most frequent, and most needed calls, is: "Power... power...power!" Just the call that the pilot of the P210 and those in the Air France and Air India airplanes needed.

Rapid Slowdown

To explore the deceleration phenomenon, I conducted some simple tests in a Cessna 152. First, I tried leveling-out from an idle descent, then holding constant altitude while slowing to just a hair above stall.

It was amazing how fast that little putt-putt bled off speed with power at idle, especially with 30 degrees of flaps extended. I also found holding a constant altitude (my target was 2,500 feet) to be a problem. I just couldn't rotate rapidly enough and consistently lost about 100 feet during the idle slowdown maneuvers.

There are a couple of lessons to be learned from the rough data I recorded in the 152. First, if you insist on gliding real

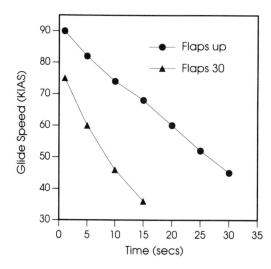

Rapid deceleration resulted when the aircraft was held at a constant altitude after idle-power descent.

fast (I used 90 knots) with no flaps and then level out just above the surface for landing, you are going to float a long way before touchdown. My data showed about 30 seconds worth of float—maybe a little longer in ground effect. That's about half of a 6,000-foot runway. And, then, when you run out of speed, you're likely to land really hard. Of course, some pilots tend to become impatient during the float and *plant* the airplane on the runway, nosewheel-first.

Second lesson: The flaps-down deceleration data shows you'd have only 15 seconds between round-out from a too-fast glide of 75 knots and stall. You would have even less time if you held altitude better than I did during the test. And there would be still less time if your glide speed was normal with power at idle. Better not round out too far before the runway, or too high. A short or hard landing would surely result.

Energy Deficit

Another test I made in the 152 was a check of descent rate versus indicated airspeed in an idle glide. Airspeed was stabilized in each case to allow a steady reading on the vertical speed indicator (VSI). Then the data was corrected to derive the descent angles.

Descent rates were high, and descent angles were steep for the airspeeds above the best-glide speed. At the speeds

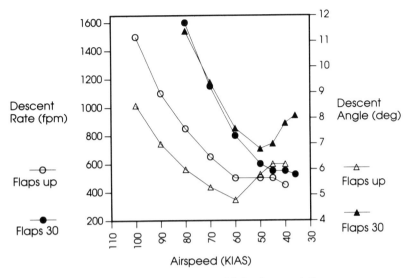

With flaps out, deceleration is very rapid during an idle-power descent. Descent rate varies with airspeed.

below best-glide, the descent *rates* don't look too bad, but the descent *angles* were uncomfortably high.

Again, there's something to be learned from the numbers. First, you sure don't want to touch down with the airplane in an idle-power glide without flaring. You have to have some excess speed and energy remaining to round out, so that you can get both the descent rate and angle to near zero for arrival. That's part of the reason why the FAA specifies approach speeds in the vicinity of 1.3 times the stall speed in landing configuration (Vso).

Therefore, if you were flying a light-weight C-152 much below 60 knots with flaps up (or 50 knots with flaps down), you'd better be ready to add some power when you're ready to flare. If you don't, you could mush in hard or, maybe, stall and land even harder. In my tests, flying just five knots above minimum speed, the descent angle was over six degrees with no flaps and about eight degrees with the "barn doors" hanging down. That's pretty close to airplane structural limits, probably. Even if something doesn't break on the airplane, you would probably have to pull up your socks or panty hose after such an arrival.

Fourth Control

The bottom line to all of this is that there are *four* flight controls. We all know about the aerodynamic surfaces—the elevator (or stabilator), rudder and ailerons. But the *throttle* is a flight control, too, and you should be ready to use it in proper coordination with elevator position, especially on final approach.

And don't forget to peek at the airspeed indicator on final approach. Pilots should stabilize *every* approach at the proper airspeed with the power necessary to hold the desired approach angle. By all means, don't decelerate your way down that crucial last leg of a flight.

High-Performance Operations Require High-Performance Proficiency

Test pilots earn their money by taking airplanes to the "edge of the envelope"—in other words, making the machine perform to the utmost of its capability. Such operations are always conducted under carefully controlled conditions and in accordance with pre-determined schedules...the pilots know rather well what to expect.

Here's a good example of what can happen when a non-proficient pilot (non-proficient in terms of maximum-performance maneuvers) pushes himself and his aircraft too far.

An Italian-built twin-engine Partenavia P68C/TC suffered very substantial damage in a hard-landing accident at the Mackay Bar Airstrip, 12 miles south of Dixie, Idaho.

The airplane was on a sales demonstration flight and had departed Boise at approximately 7:30 a.m. with two pilots and three passengers aboard.

In the left front seat was the chief pilot at Mackay Bar, who was an experienced commercial pilot and intimately familiar with the difficult airstrip approach, but who held no multi-engine rating. In the right front seat was a well-experienced commercial and multi-engine rated pilot representing the aircraft sales organization, who had never landed at Mackay Bar before.

NTSB's investigator said the high mountain airstrip, situated in a gorge, is often approached by single-engine pilots using a turning, slow, high-sink-rate ultra-short field approach, with power being chopped in the flare to allow the shortest possible ground roll. However, this technique, which the left seat pilot employed, is not usually suitable in twins, which sink sharply when the power is reduced.

The impact caused the Partenavia to veer to the left, shearing the left main gear, which caused an abrupt swerve. Although the right-seat pilot now applied full right rudder and full power to the left engine, the plane departed into a fence. Fence poles tore into the nose and fuselage, and investigators said both wings were buckled by the crash. One passenger reported a minor injury; all other occupants reported no injuries.

Landing at Night...the Hard Way

Sorting out all the visual cues for a good night landing is a difficult task at best, in consideration of all the illusions that can be present. But when major cues—such as runway lights—are non-existent, the chances of completing a safe landing shrink remarkably.

A private pilot and his three passengers got away with no injuries when their rented Cessna ran off the end of the runway during an attempted night landing.

The 89-hour pilot explained to investigators after the accident that he and his passengers had originally departed West Memphis and flew to Memphis International Airport in Tennessee. Before departing West Memphis, he had helped another pilot land when the runway lights malfunctioned. According to his statement, the lights on the single runway at West Memphis were only partially illuminated, with some of the lights on the left side working and none of the lights on the right side working.

After telling the pilot of the airborne aircraft which lights were working, that aircraft was able to land safely. The Cessna pilot and his passengers then departed for Memphis International. On their return to West Memphis, the pilot found the runway lights were now completely out.

He decided to try landing anyway; he said he was able to visually acquire the runway, but landed long and fast and ran off the end.

According to the airport manager, a NOTAM was in effect stating that the runway lights were unusable because the airport was installing new pilot-controlled runway lights at the time; a notice to that effect was posted on the door of the FBO. According to the airport manager, if the Cessna pilot had keyed his mike on the appropriate frequency, he would have gotten at least the remaining lights on the left side of the runway to work, as well as the VASI.

Formerly, the pilot-controlled lighting system at West Memphis Airport activated only the VASI. The runway lights would be on from sunset to sunrise, requiring no activation from the pilot. The new system would allow pilots to turn on both the runway lights and the VASI by keying the microphone on the appropriate frequency.

Lack of Currency and Low Experience— A Dangerous Combination

When the examiner handed you that private pilot's license and said, "This is only a license to learn," he wasn't kidding at all. Perhaps the most critical period in a pilot's career occurs between the date of the license and the 300th hour. One pilot in this category who apparently forgot several lessons crashed his Beech Sundowner in a landing attempt at California's Oakdale Airport.

The 52-year-old airman had obtained his license 18 months earlier and had logged a total of some 109 hours when he rented a Sundowner (he had 23 hours in make and model) for a trip to Merced, California. Magneto problems forced the substitution of another Sundowner, but the pilot departed Merced and stopped off at Modesto on his way back to home base, all without incident.

In the past three months, the pilot had logged just nine-tenths of an hour of dual instruction and the 2.9 hours he flew on the trip in question.

The condition of Oakdale Airport is of some interest. Investigators said for many weeks the field had been undergoing major construction. The 2,100-foot Runway 28-10 was being extended by 800 feet, with new taxiways to match. The work had been well publicized, and local pilots were requested not to use the new portion of the runway. The extension was finished on the day of the accident, but the blacktop had not yet cured. During the weeks of construction, the airport was NOTAMed closed between 8 a.m. and 4 p.m., except for a half-hour after noon.

The field was uncontrolled, but had a Unicom operator who stated he did not hear from the Sundowner pilot, although he talked with other pilots before and after the accident. Witnesses said the plane arrived at the field shortly after 3 p.m. and made a first pass down Runway 10 that appeared to one observer to be a "flat hat" or "buzz" job.

The Sundowner then made a landing attempt on Runway 10, although the wind tee indicated use of Runway 28 and the sock showed a wind out of the west at more than 10 knots.

Various witnesses described the event. They said the Sundowner touched down and puffs of smoke rose from the wheels. It appeared to skip or hop on the mains, then skidded on all three gears and slewed to the right. It then became airborne for 75 feet and finally, dropped into a drainage ditch (straight into the ditch, with no forward motion, investigators said). The pilot survived, but with serious injuries.

Investigators talked with one of the pilot's instructors, who described him as "a 70-percenter on a good day after taking instruction." The CFI said the airman "was not a natural pilot and had to work hard to maintain proficiency." In the weeks following the accident, investigators were not allowed to interview the pilot in the hospital, and were told "when he is ready to talk about the accident, he will do so only in the presence of his attorney." However, they did obtain a statement taken from the pilot by a policeman just after the crash.

The pilot told the officer, "I was coming in on what I thought was a normal landing and the plane went to the right. I corrected the plane and then before I knew it, I was going over the embankment." The officer asked, "How fast do you think you were going?" The pilot replied, "Sixty to 70 miles per hour. Just a normal landing. I thought everything was lined up just right."

More Night Landing Proficiency Problems

Proficiency (and training) includes knowing and respecting one's own limitations—no matter whether they are operations-oriented or physiological in nature; or in this case, both.

A Piper Arrow pilot got off with no injuries when his airplane struck a fence during an attempted night landing at Tulare, California. He was completing a short flight from Madera,

California at about 6:20 p.m. when the mishap occurred. The pilot told investigators he observed the airport's lighted wind sock, segmented circle, and what he believed were the taxiway and runway lights as he prepared to land. He flared out and touched down on what he thought was Runway 31, only to realize that it was a road adjacent to the airport.

The pilot told investigators he had never had occasion to use the procedures described in the FAA Airport Facility Directory to activate runway lights by radio. A witness at the airport told investigators immediately after the accident he went to a parked aircraft and had no difficulty turning on the runway and VASI lights using the microphone.

The pilot's records showed 108 hours logged in the Arrow, and a total of 3.0 hours of night flying, including half an hour in the past 90 days. The pilot presented investigators with copies of medical certificates showing he had obtained a medical on August 11, 1986, which had been amended by the FAA on October 30, 1986 to include the limitations that he have glasses for near vision and that the certificate was "not valid for night flying or by color signal control."

Good Landings Take Lots of Practice

All those hours a student accumulates on his way to a private license can have a way of fading into the ozone if a pilot doesn't keep flying after he passes his test. One of the hardest tasks for some pilots to hone is the landing flare, a judgment-intensive maneuver that takes constant practice. Such logic was reinforced for a 42-year-old private pilot whose 91 total hours (five in the last 90 days) had been spent in the same make of airplane, a Cessna 172, in which he had his latest "lesson." The accident at Hayward, California left the pilot and his passenger uninjured.

VFR conditions prevailed as the Cessna took off from Hayward for a cruise above the San Francisco Bay Area. Returning from the sight-seeing flight, the pilot called Hayward Tower to announce his intention to perform a full-stop landing. He was at first instructed to enter a base for Runway 28R, but was then told to enter an extended downwind for the same runway and informed that he would be advised when to turn base. This he did, and before long, he was on final.

In his report of the accident, the pilot gave no account of his descent to the runway, stating only that he flared but that the plane seemed to land "flat and hard." Just how hard would soon become evident. The Cessna began to porpoise down the runway and the pilot executed a go-around. Upon becoming airborne, he discovered he had little aileron control and almost no elevator control. Nonetheless, he continued the go-around.

The tower instructed him to fly by for a visual inspection but controllers could detect nothing untoward with the airplane or its gear. The pilot was then told to attempt to land the airplane on Runway 28L, 1,600 feet longer than 28R. The landing was successful and the pilot and his passenger exited the Cessna without injury.

Damage to the airplane, however, was almost shocking. Investigators discovered the firewall had buckled, caving the floor in so that the vertical instrument panel support was pulled down on the push-pull rod for the aileron and elevator. The nosewheel strut was canted and the fuselage wrinkled.

In pronouncing probable cause on the accident, NTSB issued a veritable "laundry list" of piloting mistakes. It said the pilot's first error was an improper flare, followed by an "improper recovery from a bounced landing." This was compounded by the pilot's delay in going around, and was a product of "inadequate transition/upgrade training," the NTSB report concluded.

Great Landing! But No Wheels

Perhaps the most benign of all common types of accidents is the gear-up landing. It usually comes at the destination airport—usually after an otherwise fine flight and uneventful arrival at the runway—and usually causes no injuries.

It usually is a fine landing, at least in the flare prior to touchdown. (Passengers who experience it often comment on how smooth the landing was—until that nasty sound of screeching metal started.) It usually does not start a fire. It usually leaves an eminently rebuildable airplane, one that usually can be jacked up and towed away on its own wheels.

Indeed, what is perhaps most striking about gear-up landings is how usual they are. They happen all the time, hardly anyone ever gets hurt, and the debris is quickly swept off the runway (and under the rug). Gear-up landings are so usual that every pilot transitioning to a retractable is subjected, at least half a dozen times, to intonations of the old saw about gear-upping: "There are those who have, and those who will." This is supposed to keep young pilots humble, but we suspect it actually seems to hint that the gear-up landing, being almost inevitable, represents perhaps an end of virginity—a rite of passage. The reportable gear-up landing accidents (those with damage types and degrees that qualify under NTSB rules) amount to about 110 each year. The number continues year after year, without appreciable change.

Added to that are perhaps an equal number of incidents—wherein the damage did not qualify under NTSB rules to be considered an accident. Summarily dropping an aircraft onto the trailing edges of its flaps, twisting up the propeller(s) and suddenly stopping the engine(s)—none of this yet meets the NTSB qualifications for an "accident." It is almost as though the Safety Board wrote the rules in order not to have to keep filling out paperwork on the unending stream of gear-up landings.

Beyond even this is an inestimable number of gear-ups that don't appear in official records at all. The owner, eager to keep a wheel-less landing from blemishing his own or the plane's logbooks, spirits it away to a dark hangar for a "change of landing gear doors" operation. (Gear doors, belly skins, antennas and the like, if mentioned in the logbook as being repaired, are hints of a damage history that can cut a plane's resale value sharply.) By any reasonable estimate, gear-up landings are costing the nation's plane owners (and insurers) about $2 million a year—and perhaps double or triple that amount.

The gear-up thus is often viewed as an embarrassing event, one that hurts economically, but not a grave danger and not something which can be easily changed. Throughout all the gear-up accidents runs a thread or two of conventional wisdom; it's always a dumb mistake by the pilot, and wherever there are retractables, there will be gear-up landings.

A three-year study of gear-folding arrivals on runways conducted by *Aviation Safety* has yielded results that challenge—if not totally refute—both points. It is debatable whether the lion's share of gear-ups are to be nailed to the pilot's hide, to the mechanic's, or the airplane maker's. And not all retractable aircraft must be plagued with a poor record of slides down the runway. Some have much better records than others.

Among 337 gear-up accidents studied, some 147 (or 43.6 percent) could be ascribed to pure pilot blunders. Another 137 (or 40.7 percent) were clearly mechanical problems unrelated to pilot action. The remaining 53 accidents (15.7 percent) fell into a gray area, where the pilot could be faulted for failure to assure the gear was correctly placed, but where mechanical failures complicated his task. For instance, there may have been an engine or electrical failure, a partial gear system failure, etc. Reasonable people might differ on whether these should be put in the "pilot" or "mechanical" category—thus, the scales can be tipped either way.

Among the past and present products of the currently extant "Big Four" aircraft makers, the data appear to show Cessna Aircraft trailing the pack with the worst over-all rate of gear-ups as well as rate of hardware-related gear-ups. Mooney Aircraft is the leader in both categories.

What danger there is in a gear-up accident may come from mistakes unrelated to the gear position. In the accident group under study, most people walked away unharmed. Only a tiny portion involved fatalities (five, or 1.4 percent of the accidents) and three of these were compounded by a pilot action, such as attempting to take off after the props had struck. Only four of the 337 accidents involved a fire after landing; not one of these caused any injuries.

Whatever else may be said, a gear-up landing cannot be simply laid to pilot inexperience. Of the 337 pilots, the average total time was 3,842 hours, and the average time in make and model was 571 hours. Some 209 (62 percent) held commercial, CFI or ATP licenses—a much higher proportion than the flying population at large.

Study Limits

Were one to query the NTSB computer for all accidents involving "landing gear" in a given year, the number would be inflated and misleading. Hundreds of accidents involve some damage to the landing gear, and the "hard landing" accident—often involving a student pilot in a fixed-gear trainer—would overshadow the cases of gear mis-operation. Also, a fair number of crash landings and off-airport emergency landings occur with the wheels up—often intentionally.

In our study of accidents during the years 1979-81, we screened out such things. We searched for only those landing gear accidents which involved retractable gear aircraft operating at an intended place of takeoff or landing. This did include some subgroups of accidents that are not runway/landing mishaps, but are closely akin and deserved to be part of the group, we felt.

One is a group of 16 pilots and aircraft that crashed after the wheels retracted on takeoff, not landing. This was of interest because 14 of them occurred due to pilot action, usually by retracting the gear before sufficient ground clearance was available. This we consider a form of pilot mis-operation of the landing gear of the same genre as failing to extend the gear before landing.

Likewise, there were 19 cases of amphibious floatplanes and seaplanes which had gear-related accidents. These belong in the study, we feel, because the most common accident—failure to make sure the gear is retracted when landing on water—is the exact counterpart of the landplane pilot's *bete noire*.

Further, there is a sub-group of accidents of the kind where the gear is probably down and locked when the airplane lands, but seconds later it retracts—because the pilot hit the wrong switch when he meant to retract the flaps, in most cases. There were 29 such cases, and one aircraft manufacturer's products are the unchallenged "stars" of this kind of accident: Beech Bonanzas and Barons. (More on this later.)

General Lessons

The search yielded a total of 337 accidents, or about 3.1 percent of the general aviation accidents during the period. An immediately apparent aspect is the lack of injury in most cases. All told, there were 799 people aboard these aircraft, and 787 of them walked away without serious injury.

In all of general aviation, fatal accidents occur about 17 percent of the time. In gear-up accidents, the figure is about 1.5 percent (five accidents, seven fatalities in the study group). This low mortality rate helps to explain why the unending procession of gear-up accidents is tolerated; it's not killing many people.

It can be developed even further than that, however. Two of the fatal accidents occurred when pilots tried to continue takeoffs after the gear had been retracted prematurely and the props had struck. Two others involved gear-down landings in water by seaplanes (a special danger, discussed later). And the remaining fatal accident occurred when a Cessna 310 pilot, having recognized that his nosegear was caught in the well, shut down both engines on final in an apparent attempt to save the props (they were both horizontal at impact). The airplane failed to make it to the runway and crashed, resulting in the pilot's death.

It could be asserted, then, that the "classic" gear-up accident killed no one in general aviation in a three-year period. But to go even further, it could be asserted as well that many of the elaborate preparations for intentional gear-up landings may be unnecessary. This speaks to certain questions that airmen have debated for years:

Is it better to gear-up on grass than on pavement? Is the fire hazard greater? Should the runway be foamed? Should fire equipment chase the plane down the runway? Should one land with full flaps, partial flaps, or no flaps? Well, the 337 accidents produced only five fires, and no serious injuries among them. We believe the fear of fire should be put to the back of an airman's mind. It is not necessary to land in grass, especially if you can't guarantee the smoothness of the surface. The great majority of the land accidents (319 of 321) occurred on paved runways, with no particular consequence.

The question of foam has been answered by military studies which show there is little difference between gear-ups on a foamed or unfoamed runway. It develops that if a pilot aims for a foamed area, he often misses it entirely. Even when he does hit it, the plane slides out of it. But on this and the other questions, more convincing evidence comes from both military experience and the present study: In what we'll call our "Aw, shucks" group are a collection of airmen who simply forgot to put the landing gear switch in the correct position. They thought they were going to make a normal landing, and they more or less did.

Since these airmen did nothing to anticipate a gear-up landing, it can be presumed that they set down on a paved runway in a normal landing attitude at a normal landing speed, with normal landing flaps (full, in most cases). Among 87 such cases, there were no deaths, no serious injuries and only one fire after landing (in a Beech 55 Baron). It would appear that extraordinary measures in a wheel-less landing simply aren't necessary in most cases.

A slight chance of fire still exists, so it is well to exit the airplane quickly after a gear-up, however—if only to block the firemen from unnecessarily pumping gallons of suds onto the aircraft.

Pilot Types

The population of pilots who exit at street level is not less qualified than the population of pilots at large, and in fact seems more qualified, if anything. There is a higher share of commercial, CFI and ATP certificates, and the amount of flying experience is generally higher, as might be anticipated among a group flying high-performance retractables.

Also, the group of accidents in which only pilot action was involved is about as large as the group in which mechanical failures alone were the cause (i.e., the malfunction was outside the pilot's control and beyond his ability to correct). A middle group, wherein some contributory failures of the airplane helped set the stage, could be assigned to either side, depending on one's opinion.

Our cases of "landing gear malfunction" are actually that—an example being a hydraulic rupture that defies use of the back-up pump, so that the pilot cannot lower the gear even though he tries.

Some may side with the pilot in the "gray area" cases. This group includes 13 in which a warning horn or light was inoperative—which is not much of an excuse for a prudent pilot. But it also includes 23 where there was an electrical failure, which seems a slightly better excuse, although strictly speaking, a perfectly prepared pilot should be able to get his gear down in the dark, by feel alone.

A lesson to be learned here, though, is that a pilot hasn't totally completed his job in meeting an electrical emergency unless he has the gear confirmed down on final.

The Real Boobs

Within the pilot-only group is a sub-group of 100 pilots who were landing and should have put the gear down, but just plain forgot—period, no excuse offered. We call this the "Aw, shucks" group. They included 87 ground landings and 13 water landings.

This group was of interest because, it might be supposed, they represent the boobs who have been giving retractables a bad name with insurance underwriters.

Well, there's nothing about the "Aw, shucks" group which would trigger any alarms on an incompetence meter. They averaged 3,072 hours total time, and 577 hours in make and model. They are only slightly different in these numbers than our total group of pilots here, and are well above the norm in general aviation.

Averages can mislead, so we can break it down demographically. Insurers like to believe they can screen out the higher-risk pilots on the basis of total time, or time in the make and model intended. If we could assemble the 100 pilots for inspection and let insurance agents have the floor, it might go like this:

Insurer A declares that no one with less than 500 total hours and 10 in type can remain standing. Only 22 pilots sit down.

Insurer B says he believes time in type is the more important number. He lets everyone stand up and tries again, declaring the minimums to be only 200 total hours, but 25 in type. Only 17 pilots sit down.

Insurer C decides to make it much tougher and get down to the small minority who are really prime insurables (he'll also collect fewer premiums, of course). He tells the pilots that anyone without 1,000 total hours and 50 in type will have to go home. (Imagine paying for 50 hours of dual in a retractable.) Insurer C is not rewarded by the sight of a nearly empty room—56 pilots remain.

Lesson for insurers: Make total time and in-type time lower in priority than pilot currency, the kind of airplane, its horsepower, age and complexity. For a simple upgrade from single-engine fixed-gear to single-engine retractable, 10 hours is probably enough.

"Simply forgetting" to put the wheels down before landing is a hollow excuse; there is almost always some mitigating circumstance, something that distracted the pilot to the point where the "U" in "GUMP" took a back seat to other procedures. Here's an accident which proves the point.

> While it may be a bit pessimistic to assume that every pilot of a retractable will someday forget to drop the wheels, leaving out that one vital step can be all too easy.
>
> A classic case of gear forgetfulness resulted in an embarrassing situation and aircraft damage, but no injuries to either the 1,450-hour commercial pilot or the single passenger of a Cessna 182 Skylane RG. The Cessna belonged to the pilot's company, and he was on a VFR business flight from Titusville, Florida, to Jacksonville.
>
> The pilot reported downwind for Runway 22 at Jacksonville and began his landing checklist. In his written statement, the pilot detailed the sequence of the list: fuel, mixture, prop, and carb heat. On application of carburetor heat, the engine began to run rough. The roughness was so pronounced that the pilot commented to his passenger on it. Immediately after this the tower called, putting the Cessna in sequence as "number two to land" following an aircraft on final. The pilot did not see the other aircraft, and spent several seconds looking for it. By the time he located and confirmed the traffic, he was on base leg near final. He turned onto the final approach, still preoccupied with the engine roughness. The pilot decided to turn off the carburetor heat, after which the engine ran more smoothly. The Cessna was now on short final, and the pilot proceeded on down to the flare, never realizing that he had forgotten the gear until the fuselage scraped the runway. Damage to the airplane consisted of a demolished propeller and hub, destroyed radio antennas and damaged fuselage skin.

The pilot had logged 180 hours in this make and model of aircraft. There is no indication of how much time he had logged in other complex aircraft, but he did mention that most of his experience was in fixed-gear airplanes. He suggested stronger reinforcement of the "GUMP" (Gas-Undercarriage-Mixture-Prop) pre-landing checklist in primary training, even though virtually all trainers have fixed gear, as a way to avoid similar accidents in the future.

On the Waterfront

The situation with seaplanes is not quite so sanguine with respect to risk of injury. Landing gear accidents with watercraft amounted to 19 accidents in the three-year period. Four involved mechanical failure of a landing gear—two on land, two on water.

The other 15 were pilot-action accidents—in every single case, an "Aw, Shucks" with no ameliorating excuse. It is remarkable that 13 of the 15 were landings in water with the gear down, while only two were on land with the gear up. Ten of these accidents involved a Cessna 185 on amphibious floats—all gear-down on water.

Gear-downs in water can be more dangerous than gear-ups on land because the airplane may nose over from the powerful pitching moment and introduce the added hazard of drowning. Of the 15 water accidents, two were fatal, causing a fatality each.

In view of the propensity for the pilot to make a mistake on an aqueous landing, perhaps someone can come up with a gear warning system that can smell water.

Airplane Models

We also looked at gear-up accidents from the aspect of the airplane model, and found much to praise and much to blame. But we learned to beware of pat answers. For instance, we had hoped to answer one question: Is an electrical-mechanical gear system inherently more reliable than an electrical-hydraulic one? We guessed the mechanical system would prove itself the better without debate. Most hydraulic systems can be disabled if just one hose leaks. But the answer has eluded us. When we put all the "solid linkage" gear systems on one side and the hydraulic systems on the other, there seemed to be little difference. Rather, we found the brand name and individual airplane model seemed to matter more.

In our opinion, the figures show Piper as building a far more reliable hydraulic gear system than Cessna. (Comparable airplanes

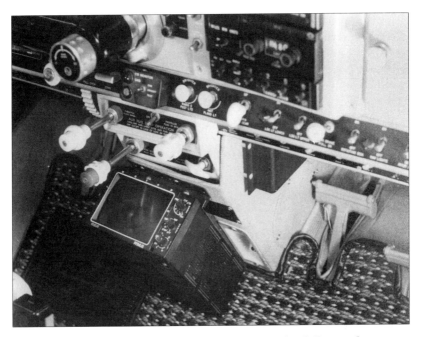

Many Beechcraft airplanes, with their non-standard flap and gear switch locations, have suffered gear up incidents after an otherwise uneventful landing.

are the single-engine Cessnas versus the Piper Arrow and Lance.) Among a fleet of 5,963 Piper hydraulic singles, we found only one accident due to a leak; among 9,504 Cessna singles (all are hydraulic), there were eight. Adjusted for fleet size, this is a five-to-one ratio.

As for the "solid" systems, Mooneys and Beech Barons and Bonanzas, some Cessna twins (310, 340)) and Pipers (Comanche, Twin Comanche) might be compared, but with no conclusion other than that some manufacturers do it better than others, in certain models.

Sheer mechanical reliability isn't the only factor, either, since ergonomics can sometimes be shown to play a part in the errors of the pilot. It's undeniable that a share of the "pilot" accidents can be laid to design-induced errors, but the exact influence probably cannot ever be measured.

Special Case

One design item is all too abundantly evident in a certain kind of accident—the "Wrong Switch Club" initiation rite in which the pilot lands and reaches for the flap lever but flips the gear lever instead.

After lots of hints at the problem over the years, an exhaustive NTSB study in 1980 showed that although other models were not immune, the Beech Bonanza and Baron are subject to this kind of accident head and shoulders above all others in their classes.

For reasons that go back more than 30 years, many Bonanzas and Barons have landing gear switches toward the right side of panel center, flap switches to the left. Some models built by other manufacturers were similar. But as many of those designs petered out, to be replaced by the arrangement favored under modern standards (gear switch to the left, flaps right), the Beech airplanes continued in production essentially unchanged.

Thus, nowadays pilots trained in non-Beech airplanes habitually reach to the right for the flaps—and join the Wrong Switch Club.

We have heard that the reason Beech would not change the location of the switches—a relatively trivial expense—is that it did not want to confuse its loyal Beech pilots. But as time has gone on, most Beech designs have been modified to the "modern" configuration, including not only the Sierra and Duchess, but even the Baron 58P and 58TC.

Among the accidents studied was one in which an 8,900-hour ATP pilot, well acquainted with the pressurized model's being "backwards" according to Beech practice, stepped out of a Baron 58P into a Baron 58. He retracted the gear on the next landing.

We found the trend NTSB identified continues to haunt Beech pilots. Of 29 cases during the study period involving inadvertent gear retraction after landing, 18 were Barons and Bonanzas (62 percent).

The Wrong Switch Club is almost certain to acquire new members as time goes on. It continues to be possible to buy either configuration Baron 58, and all Bonanzas continue to fight the grain of cockpit standardization.

We believe the total fix would involve at least conforming current models to current standards, and possibly modifying some of the older models to trade switch positions. Beech hasn't done anything resembling this.

But to its credit, after years of ostrich-like inattention, Beech finally took a small step toward dealing with the problem. It issued service instruction No. 1215, allowing owners to buy a guard that can be installed over the landing gear switch in nearly all Barons and most Bonanzas from the P35 model onward. The pilot would have to lift the guard to make the big mistake. The guard takes only an hour to install, costs very little, and might prevent thousands of dollars in damage. Beech has not offered any warranty help, and the modification is not mandatory.

Best and Brightest

Rather than dwell on the bad, we'd like to spend some time in praise of the good. Certain designs are superior, in our opinion, and could lead to a betterment of the gear-up landing statistics.

Although the fleet size was small, Rockwell singles had no gear-up accidents during the period studied—a perfect record. Another small—but much newer—fleet was the Cessna 172RG Cutlass, with zero mechanical gear-ups and only one pilot-action accident. It may be too soon to tell, but the Cutlass could signal an improvement in Cessna single-engine landing gear systems.

It has been a rocky road. Suffice it to mention that the Cessna 210 once had a special handbook procedure to cover the case of the nosewheel alone failing to lock down, and at the height of problems with the hydraulic power pack located under the center pedestal, a Centurion Society official was advised by Cessna that a kick might be the final remedy; he joked that among standard equipment on a Cessna 210 ought to be a hobnail boot.

Two relatively large fleets exhibit very good records with regard to gear-up accidents: the current single-engine Pipers (Arrow and Saratoga SP, nee Lance) and the entire Mooney fleet.

The Pipers are known for their automatic extension systems. If the pilot slows the aircraft below a certain speed, the automatic system lowers the gear for him. While we are not thrilled with the system (especially if it lowers the gear when an engine falters just after takeoff), it certainly seems to be doing a stellar job of preventing gear-ups. Of the total of nine pilot-action cases between the Arrow and Lance, two were definitely a result of the pilot using the auto system's override feature, and four others may be presumed to be, since NTSB found no malfunction of the gear system after the accident. Some insurers give a discount, or allow a lower-time pilot to transition without penalty, when the airplane to be insured is an Arrow or Lance. In our opinion, this is well deserved.

Mooneys as a fleet have a very good record on gear-up accidents, with design a likely reason. Many early Mooneys have a big "Johnson bar" system where the pilot provides all the input energy and the indicator basically is whether the handle is up or down. Others have the luxury of optional electric systems. Either way, the fleet has proven to be a reliable one, thanks (we think) to solid-linkage design.

None of the gear malfunction or mis-operation accidents involved a single Mooney 201 or 231, even though the fleet size (1,359) and time in service was double that of the Cutlass, with its fine record.

Mooney in the latter two models put the big, round gear handle in prominent view at the top of the panel (left of center, of course) and the flap lever down and to the right. The landing gear "down" and warning lights are situated just below the glareshield, well within the pilot's side vision. And there is a positive emergency extension system, including a direct-linkage set of down- indicators (flags seen through a floorboard window).

It comes as no surprise that this system compiled a "perfect" record in the time period studied. We can heartily recommend it to airplane buyers, and to others who seek to improve cockpit design.

Landings and Go-Arounds

As part of his test pilot duties, Bill Kelly has done go-arounds in just about every conceivable aircraft configuration and circumstance. Here's what he has to say about the subject:

> You can't talk about landings without first covering the go-around. Every arrival should be approached as either a landing or a go-around. Land if everything is just right, go around if anything looks wrong.
>
> But, nobody practices the go-around part. Lots of CFIs don't teach proper go-around technique, and many examiners don't look for it on check rides. Lots of students graduate into the licensed pilot ranks without knowing how to go from the approach glide into a climb without stalling and with minimal altitude loss.
>
> How about the young student pilot who switched instructors one day when his regular CFI was busy elsewhere. This student had already soloed, but needed more pattern work. His fill-in instructor called for a sudden go-around when they were about 10 feet above the runway on one of the approaches; things weren't going quite right. The student hadn't tried a last-minute wave-off during his earlier dual sessions, but he remembered from the Cessna 152 manual that flaps have to be retracted. And that's just what he did—he retracted the flaps before adding power or increasing the pitch attitude. Down came the little trainer, and only extremely rapid reaction by the right-seat pilot prevented a hard, nosewheel-first touchdown.

That is not the way to do it. Every certificated airplane has to demonstrate a balked-landing climb capability in the full landing configuration, which is with the gear down and flaps full down (or, if the flaps can be retracted in two seconds or less, they can be retracted for this climb test). Depending on the regulations under which the airplane was produced (CAR 3 or FAR 23), it will have to climb in the vicinity of 200 to 300 feet per minute to meet the 1-in-30 climb angle requirement, or the five-times-Vso (in miles per hour) climb rate. The flaps don't have to come up until the pilot has added full power, and rotated to at least the normal touchdown pitch attitude.

And don't be in a hurry to raise the gear if you have a retractable. Nobody ever dictated that a go-around couldn't touch down. A very late, last-minute decision to abort the landing may very well touch the surface. Leave the gear alone, just like the flaps, until the descent is positively arrested. As a case in point, a Learjet started a missed approach at decision height in what must have been zero-zero conditions. The surprised pilots had already reached full throttle when they impacted, gently, right on the runway centerline, then decided to continue it as a landing. They were successful in coming to a stop. But the point is, don't over-rotate just to keep from touching down. And don't raise the gear until you are sure you won't touch down.

Also consider that a go-around might commence after landing. This happened to me a few years ago flying a Piper Navajo into a 3,000-foot, icy strip in central Pennsylvania. It was an uncontrolled field, and nobody answered on Unicom. There was no windsock, but the tetrahedron showed that Runway 9 was in use. The snow was starting to come down and visibility wasn't all that good.

I put that Navajo down right on the numbers before I realized that I was going much too fast to stop. This time, "instinct" did me right—full throttle and go! We were plenty fast to do a bounce and go, but had way too much groundspeed to stop. And we went, even with 40 degrees of flap and the gear still down. Unicom came on the air at about that time and apologized. "Sorry about that," said the voice on the radio. "The wind just shifted. Use Runway 27." It was actually 20 knots worth of wind.

What made the difference on this landing abort wasn't

Kelly's "superior reactions," or anything like that. It was recent training. We had just finished a lengthy series of landing distance tests in this Navajo, and I had do to many last-minute go-arounds. Any time I made a poor approach— an approach that would just waste theodolite camera film— the engineer on the ground would radio, "Go around, Kelly. Another crummy approach." So I got lots of practice.

We all need that kind of practice. And maybe some dual training with a well-qualified instructor. That go-around procedure should be every bit as polished as the normal, short-field, and soft-field landing needed to pass the next flight check or Flight Review. And the practice doesn't have to start near ground level. Try it up high first. Set up a normal approach, gear and flaps down, and use normal approach airspeed (usually about 1.3 Vso). Go to full takeoff power while simultaneously rotating the nose up from approach angle to normal takeoff or landing attitude. Leave the flaps and gear alone. The idea is to find the nose-up pitch rate you can use without getting close to an accelerated stall, and then to accurately locate a pitch attitude (visually, over the nose, and on the artificial horizon) that will arrest the descent rate and maybe allow a slight climb in the "dirty" condition.

Then will come practice in how best to get rid of the landing flaps. Some aircraft flight manuals call for "milking" the flaps up, others just say "retract." Be careful of a sudden, full retraction—there may be a big pitch attitude change associated with it, and a big out-of-trim condition to hang on to. And there will almost always be a big sinking sensation going from 30 or 40 degrees of flaps to zero in just a second or two.

There will be some necessary difference of technique between a go-around at approach airspeed and one at over-the-fence speed. You really should be able to accomplish a go-around from just above stall speed—maybe not without continuing to settle and maybe not without touching down. Such a maneuver is really just a very-low-altitude recovery from an imminent stall. But it takes some practice.

Be careful when flying something with a high, pod-mounted engine, like a Lake Amphibian, for example. The high thrust line, way above the c.g., may tend to push the nose down when applying full power. Test pilots call it "bassackwards pitch with power." Other, more conventional planes, especially some of the high-powered turboprop twins, have too much positive pitch-up with power addition. This could lead to an excessively nose-high attitude if not handled properly, especially if retracting flaps adds to the pitch-up. It's better to do all this investigation up high first. Then try a few go-arounds from short final approach.

And, if you are instrument rated, put a little more polish into that missed approach at decision height. What I often see on instrument refresher rides is full power at DH, but a lazy, sloppy rotation to a climb attitude. Much altitude is lost before we arrest the descent rate. Too much attention is paid to getting the gear and flaps moving up, and getting into the first turn—but there's no concentration on holding climb attitude or airspeed. Dangerous!

The go-around decision gets even more critical when flying real "heavy iron." I recently got to fly right seat while the pilot of a single-pilot Cessna Citation shot a visual approach into a good 5,000-foot airstrip. It was a bad approach, with way too shallow a descent and way too much airspeed. And no plan to go around. We just plain old landed long and hot. We got stopped okay, thanks to good brakes (they were hot brakes afterwards). You have got to plan to go around if the approach is bad.

The accident summaries show an amazing number of "landed-long-and-rolled-off-the-far-end" crunches. Or landing hot and going through the fence and into the ditch. Come on now. That's no way to land. We all may make bad approaches or landings on occasion. That's no reason to crunch. Just be ready, every approach, to go around. From any point in the approach, even after touchdown.

Another problem with the last minute decision to get out of there: What if you are flying one of those machines with a fixed-wastegate turbocharger? Or a turbocharged machine where the wastegate is linked to throttle travel, but with no limiting manifold pressure? Like most of the "heavy-iron" turboprops, the only power limiting system is in the pilot's throttle hand. You can't just jam on full throttle. No fire-walled throttles or pedal-to-the-metal action is allowed. This makes it a little harder to achieve maximum allowable power in a hurry. I like to put a piece of masking tape, or a pencil mark on the throttle quadrant, approximating the maximum forward travel of the throttle for takeoff power. Sure, this won't work for all density altitudes, but at least it's a starting place for the go-around power addition.

Now, that's a lot of talk on go-arounds. All we really intended to do was land. Well then, set up a decent landing approach. Do it the same every time. Get used to what a good final approach looks like, and get out of there early when things don't look right.

Every approach won't be a landing. Especially at strange fields, or in strong crosswinds. Or when the wind is blowing hard and real gusty. Or when trying to get into a marginal-length strip, especially if the approach is down a hill or over high obstacles. You don't have to land every time. But when you do land, it had better be good.

How come the major airlines rarely go around? Because every final approach is the same—down an ILS glideslope, in the same type airplane every time, at familiar airports every landing. One airline even lets the copilot take over if he catches the PIC in two errors on one approach. How would you like somebody alongside who could take over your job after only two call-outs of off altitude/glideslope or minimal deviation from prescribed airspeed? It sure would make you work for precision. So, let's talk landing approaches.

Most of us operate from good, hard-surface strips of over 3,000-foot length. Only once in 1,000 landings do we have to go into a short strip. So, when near the end of a Flight Review, I call for a short-field landing. I see some real strange, real dangerous final approach paths. Typically, when I call for a touchdown within 200 feet of the numbers (on a long runway), I see a half-degree final approach angle, or maybe even a nose-high, dragged-in, level final approach about 20 feet above the weeds—then a sudden throttle chop just before reaching the desired touchdown spot.

That's a good way to set up a settle into those weeds. Or maybe a full stall and the beginning of a spin on short final. Or maybe flying into the ditch just short of the runway because you can't see over the nose enough to know that the shallow final approach is aimed short of the runway.

That's how the navy used to land the Hellcats and TBMs on their little carriers on the "Victory at Sea" series on TV, right? Yes, but that naval aviator had an LSO (landing signal officer) standing at the stern of the carrier, waving his paddles and watching like a hawk. And the navy still had quite a few airplanes settle in short (into the "spud locker") or land long, bounce, and go over the last-ditch barrier into a pack of parked planes on the bow.

The navy doesn't do it that way anymore, and neither should you unless maybe you're flying an old J-3 Cub, an Airknocker, or crop duster. A Cherokee, Cessna 152, or Bonanza is more akin to an F-14, and final approach should be similar to the jet. Fly a steep final approach angle. You may need it to clear the trees or power lines. Fly it at an airspeed that will permit adequate control, and sufficient energy to complete a flare to a landing attitude, but without excessive float after finishing the flare. Approaches at about 20 to 30 percent above stall speed work well for most airplanes, and are typically used for flight manual landing distance charts.

Now, setting up for a reasonably steep final approach (say 2-1/2 or 3 degrees, like on an ILS or VASI) takes care of the longitudinal touchdown problem, along with reasonable care to maintain the correct indicated airspeed.

Let's talk about the lateral problem—crosswind. My usual briefing on crosswind landings is, "Don't plan on landing." Instead, plan a final approach, then flare and add a little power to be sure it doesn't touch down before you're ready. Then fly, fly, fly until you're going down the runway, and until the nose pointing is down the runway. If you get one landing out of three approaches at your airplane's limit crosswind component, you're doing good. Don't ease off on the power and let it touch down unless the crosswind correction is perfect. Have a go-around point planned so that you don't land too long after finally achieving that proper crosswind correction. And don't land on the downwind side of the centerline in a bad crosswind. Set up final approach with an aim at the middle of the upwind side of the runway. All mistakes you might make will offset you toward the downwind side, so why not make some allowance for the errors? If the wind is from the downwind-leg side, make that downwind a little wider than normal. You don't need a steep turn to final to further complicate a landing problem. But also watch that crosswind that blows from the other side—it tends to make you turn from base to final too early and you end up angling to the approach end of the runway. It's hard to set up a crosswind correction when you don't line up until passing over the overrun.

That reminds me of the first-solo student I had back at that same short Pennsylvania field. She was a good pilot, but a little lacking in self-confidence. Also, she really listened to me, her CFI. I told her, loud and clear, before her first solo, "No landing unless it's going to be a good landing. Go around if it's no good. I can wait here all afternoon." She took me at my word, making three landings out of nine approaches. The airport manager was ready to shoot her down, especially when she touched the macadam momentarily on the second wave-off (he didn't allow touch and goes at his field). But guess what? Every full-stop landing was a good one. And every go-around was a good one, including the one that touched momentarily. She even called after the third landing and asked if she could make one more, having finally got the hang of it. And that last one was perfect.

The result: A ticked-off airport manager, a proud but hesitant student, and a very happy and proud CFI. Boy, if only they would all learn to get out of there when things don't look good.

Go-Around Gone Awry

The flaps on the Cessna Skyhawk are jokingly referred to as "barn doors" partly because of the way they look when they're fully extended but mostly because of their aerodynamic effect. They create a considerable amount of drag, which is useful for making slow, steep approaches into short fields. But they can also become a hindrance should the need arise to accelerate and climb. Therefore, retracting the flaps is one of the highest priorities while initiating a go-around. But it has to be done carefully and by the book.

The procedure for most airplanes is to retract the flaps in increments, rather than all at once, while allowing the airplane to accelerate. In the case of late-model Skyhawks, Cessna Aircraft recommends the flaps be raised initially no further than to 20 degrees extension when initiating a go-around. Dumping the flaps too quickly at low airspeeds can rob the wings of needed lift and cause an airplane to stall or mush.

That is just what happened to a Cessna 172M on a short VFR flight to a private airstrip near Norman, Oklahoma. At the

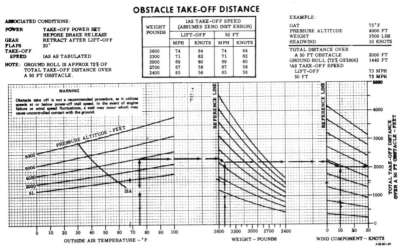

OBSTACLE TAKE-OFF DISTANCE

ASSOCIATED CONDITIONS:		
POWER	TAKE-OFF POWER SET BEFORE BRAKE RELEASE	
GEAR	RETRACT AFTER LIFT-OFF	
FLAPS	20°	
TAKE-OFF SPEED	IAS AS TABULATED	
NOTE:	GROUND ROLL IS APPROX 72% OF TOTAL TAKE-OFF DISTANCE OVER A 50 FT OBSTACLE.	

WEIGHT POUNDS	IAS TAKE-OFF SPEED (ASSUMES ZERO INST ERROR)			
	LIFT-OFF		50 FT	
	MPH	KNOTS	MPH	KNOTS
3600	74	64	74	64
3300	71	62	71	62
3000	69	60	69	60
2700	67	58	67	58
2400	65	56	65	56

EXAMPLE:	
OAT	75°F
PRESSURE ALTITUDE	4000 FT
WEIGHT	3500 LBS
HEADWIND	10 KNOTS
TOTAL DISTANCE OVER A 50 FT OBSTACLE	2000 FT
GROUND ROLL (72% OF2000)	1440 FT
IAS TAKE-OFF SPEED	
LIFT-OFF	73 MPH
50 FT	73 MPH

WARNING

Obstacle take off is not a recommended procedure, as it utilizes speeds at or below power-off stall speed. In the event of engine failure or wind speed fluctuations, a stall may occur which may cause uncontrolled contact with the ground.

PRESSURE ALTITUDE ~ FEET

OUTSIDE AIR TEMPERATURE ~ °F   WEIGHT ~ POUNDS   WIND COMPONENT ~ KNOTS

REFERENCE LINE

TOTAL TAKE-OFF DISTANCE OVER A 50 FT OBSTACLE ~ FEET

Very few aircraft manuals have very much to say about go-around performance, but the takeoff performance charts give an inkling of what to expect.

controls was a 63-year-old private pilot with 300 hours of flight time, and there were two passengers aboard.

Nearing Norman, the pilot checked in with the tower at the University of Oklahoma/Westheimer Airpark to inform the controller that he would be passing over the airport en route to the nearby private field. The pilot also requested information on surface winds. He was told the wind at Westheimer was from 260 degrees at 7 to 10 knots.

The private strip was 1,800 feet of turf, 75 feet wide, with approaches to the southeast and northwest. Had the pilot chosen to land to the northwest, he would have had a left, quartering crosswind. However, he chose to land to the southeast, which put the wind behind the airplane.

The Skyhawk's flaps were fully extended for the approach, and at some point the pilot decided to go around. A passenger in the right front seat told investigators that the airplane was climbing above trees off the end of the runway when the pilot retracted the flaps.

When the flaps were dumped, the Skyhawk settled into the trees and was destroyed. The fuselage was twisted and buckled during impact, but the cabin remained intact, and neither passenger was hurt. However, the pilot sustained a serious head injury when he was thrown into the windshield and panel by secondary impact forces. The NTSB noted that although the pilot's seat was equipped with a shoulder harness, he wasn't wearing it when the accident occurred. The safety board determined that selection of the wrong runway for landing and premature retraction of the flaps during the attempted go-around were the probable causes of the crash.

It's in the Book—Or Is It?

The no-injury crash of a Piper Tomahawk has caused investigators to point out to Piper that the plane's manual contains no discussion or procedure describing how to properly execute a go-around. The accident occurred at Miller Airfield, a private grass strip near Keyser, West Virginia.

The Tomahawk had been rented by a student pilot at Cumberland, Maryland. He flew solo for an hour and then returned to Cumberland and picked up a friend, who held a private license. With the friend in the right seat and flying the airplane, the Tomahawk completed a circuit and landing at Cumberland, then headed for Miller.

Upon arrival, the private pilot made one pass at the field and found himself to be very high. He discontinued the approach well above the airport. On the second attempt, he flew down to about 30 feet above the runway, but decided to go around.

The pilot told investigators he applied full power, pushed off carburetor heat and established a best-angle climb speed of 60 KIAS. At the end of the field, he retracted the flaps from the full-down to the one-third position. The Tomahawk was unable to outclimb the rising terrain to the northwest of the runway, and it struck trees and crashed.

Investigators noted the occupants weighed a total of about 360 pounds and there were 10-15 gallons of fuel aboard at the time of the crash. The temperature was 85 degrees and the field elevation was 975 MSL. These figures would indicate that the plane probably was well under maximum gross weight, and should have achieved a passable rate of climb.

However, investigators noted that the Tomahawk manual does not contain a go-around procedure or discussion (the

Cessna 152 and Beech Skipper manuals do contain a "balked landing" procedure) and Piper representatives stated that the Tomahawk's published best-angle speed is predicated on a flaps-retracted condition.

Speaking of Procedure...

Pilot proficiency involves good training, a lot of practice, and staying current in the kind of airplane you're flying. With these qualities, safe flight can be accomplished by applying good judgement to that pilot proficiency. Here's a situation in which perhaps none of the above qualities applied:

> Extension of the landing gear during a single-engine go-around immediately preceded a roll-over into the ground by a Cessna 310; the two persons aboard died in the crash and subsequent fire.
>
> The NTSB investigator said the plane was arriving from Tulsa, Oklahoma, and had been cleared to land while on a right downwind to Runway 8L, when the pilot reported he had lost his right engine. He immediately made a right turn, as if to angle toward Runway 8R, but an airline Boeing 727 was in position on 8R, waiting for takeoff clearance. The tower controller pointed out the conflict, and also noted that the 310's landing gear was not extended.
>
> The pilot began a go-around. Meanwhile, the 727 cleared the runway, and controllers now cleared the Cessna to make a right turn for another approach to either 8R or 8L, at the pilot's discretion. The controller advised, "Just continue around and lower the landing gear."
>
> According to evidence pieced together, the twin was about halfway through its turn (roughly on the downwind again) when, just after the controller's instruction, the landing gear came down. Immediately thereafter, the twin rolled to the right and descended into the ground.
>
> Investigators found evidence that the right propeller had been feathered prior to impact. The landing gear was in the down and locked position, and flaps were at 15 degrees.
>
> Investigators also found that almost every system in the right engine had been capable of operation prior to impact, but that the engine-driven fuel pump was out of limits (on the high side) and erratic when put on a test bench.

The pilot had a commercial license and about 900 total hours. However, he had obtained his multi-engine rating only about 11 months previously, and had logged about 67 hours of twin time, mostly in the 310. Prior to that, and for most of his total flying hours, he had flown a Mooney M20G.

During interviews with the two controllers on duty in the tower, the NTSB investigator determined that neither had a pilot's license, and neither was aware of the special concerns of multi-engine pilots about Vmc and the hazard of lowering the landing gear at slow airspeeds.

Good Decision, Bad Procedure

A 175-hour private pilot and one of his passengers were seriously injured, while two other passengers escaped with minor injuries when their Mooney crashed during an attempted go-around. The accident came as the Mooney was landing to the east after a flight from Key West, Florida.

The pilot, who had accumulated 80 hours in the Mooney, allowed it to bounce as it touched down; it bounced a second time and the pilot decided to go around. He applied full power, started climbing and retracted the landing gear.

When the Mooney had climbed to about 100 feet, it began what witnesses described as a steep left turn in a nose-high attitude. The passenger in the right front seat later said the stall warning horn came on during the turn and the Mooney started to descend. As the Mooney sank towards the ground, the pilot tried to level the wings, and had almost accomplished that when the airplane crashed onto Runway 33 and slid to a halt off the side. The horn remained on until impact.

Witnesses stated the engine sounded normal and appeared to be producing full power during the initial climb, but that the engine sounds were reduced during the steep left turn. Investigators examined propeller slash marks on the runway and determined the engine was running at about 2,700 rpm at the time of impact, which equates to full power.

Investigators also said it was likely the pilot was landing with a tailwind. Weather observations taken at nearby Palm Beach International Airport minutes before the accident showed the winds as 270 degrees at nine knots.

Flight Instructor Proficiency Counts, Too

The ability to recognize a bad situation and take over before it develops into something really unpleasant is one of the most difficult for a flight instructor to develop. This problem is made all the worse during the landing phase of a training flight, when everything comes together at once close to the ground. Indecision and changes of mind in this critical period are near-certain precursors of problems, evidenced by this Mooney episode from which the two pilots escaped without injury.

The 8,022-hour flight instructor was giving the 278-hour private pilot a checkout in the Mooney. The instructor had logged some 300 hours in the Mooney at the time of the accident, but the "checkee" had only flown the airplane for a little over one hour.

After about 45 minutes of ground instruction, the pair departed Santa Clara County Airport in San Jose. They flew first to Hollister Airport for a series of full-stop landings, then went to South County Airport in Santa Clara for more landing practice.

At this point, the statements by the instructor and the private pilot begin to diverge. In his statement to investigators, the private pilot said that on the first landing at South County Airport, the aircraft bounced twice. He recalled that the instructor had told him during ground instruction, "If you bounce two times in a Mooney, you should do a go-around or you will buy a new prop."

In his written statement to investigators, the private pilot said, "I bounced for the second time. I told him I was going to do a go-around. When I gave the plane power, he said, 'No, you're okay.' I said, 'No, I want to go around.'

"At this time, he took the control wheel, then he reduced power, then he gave power to the plane and told me to get the gear up. We started up, then he told me to get the flaps up. Then we veered to the left and the plane got rocky and slow. Then we landed with gear up in some gravel off the runway."

The instructor's statement is essentially the same as that of the private pilot's until the moment of go-around. In his written statement, he said the landing at South County Airport was made, "with the nose of the aircraft a little high. I told him to pull the throttle back, that it was a good landing.

He added power. I told him again to pull the throttle back. He did, but then added power again. I told him to pull the throttle back again, which he did, and then again added power. He said he was going to do a go-around. The nose came up and a turn to the left started due to the nose-high attitude and full throttle. The stall horn was at full noise level.

"I told him to get the gear and flaps up to reduce drag. I pushed the yoke full forward, hoping to lower the nose and get some ground effect and speed, in order, hopefully, to finish the attempted go-around. I could not get the nose down—I was pushing with both hands. We scraped the left wing, then scraped the right wing and made ground contact in level flight."

The instructor went on to state, "The go-around was not necessary and should not have been attempted as a good landing was made with the nose of the aircraft just a little high, but nothing to worry about. The private pilot panicked on the need for a go-around, in my opinion."

And from the checkee's standpoint, we would add, "But Sir Flight Instructor, you said that 'If you bounce two times in a Mooney, you should do a go-around or you will buy a new prop.'" A proficient CFI not only knows when to take over, he also knows when to abide by his own admonitions.

Don't Get Your Nose Bent

The airplane in question is a big, single-engine, six-place with 300 horses and retracting gear. The pilot has a private license, instrument rating, 500 total hours, including more than 100 hours in smaller "complex" singles. He has rented this plane after two checkout flights which included a bunch of touch-and-goes, a few full-stop landings, stalls, systems emergencies, etc.

But his checkout flights were both from home base, which has three runways, the shortest of which is 6,000 feet long. And home base is near sea level. As is usual, his checkouts were in a lightly loaded aircraft, with only our pilot—"Jake"—and his instructor aboard. The FBO staffers know Jake well, and he has never had any trouble in their Cessna 172s, or C-182s or Piper Arrows. So he gets a quick going-over before being allowed to schedule this big six-place for the next weekend.

Jake even takes a solo "refresher" in the local area on Thursday afternoon, and does a quick weight and balance calculation for his intended load of six people and light baggage. His solo practice includes some "short-field" approaches, since he plans on going up into the hills to a one-runway field with only a 3,500-foot strip. Not much effort is spent on takeoffs—the plane has such tremendous acceleration and initial climb rate that it seems there will be no trouble getting out of the intended strip, which has no obstacles.

Come Saturday morning, Jake carefully loads his five passengers into their proper seats (already calculated to put the lightest in the rear for c.g. reasons), and the small bags fit nicely behind the rear seats. Weight and c.g. are within limits.

Takeoff from Metropolis Airport goes well. There's 7,000 feet of macadam ahead, so Jake doesn't feel in a hurry to get the nose up to get into the air. Directional control during takeoff run does seem a little weak, but with the 200-foot runway width, it's no real problem.

Landing up at Hilltop Municipal, elevation 2,500 feet, comes only an hour later and 20 gallons lighter. Jake flies the flight manual airspeeds, and gets it on in good shape at 9 a.m. Before everyone scatters to the hiking trails, Jake warns them to be back aboard by 3 p.m. for the return to Metropolis.

By 3 p.m., Hilltop is hot. (Metropolis never gets this warm—it always has a cool afternoon sea breeze.) Hilltop, for all its 2,500-foot elevation, seems warm enough that Jake does a quick Takeoff Performance Chart calculation—no sweat, says the book.

Jake even holds the brakes to full throttle, at the very end of the runway. "Ole Bronco" does not exactly leap ahead at brake release, but does seem to be accelerating. But the short, narrow runway is disappearing under the nose too quickly. Jake isn't trying to hurry the takeoff, but he is having a little trouble staying on the narrow runway. Just a little back pressure on the yoke has lightened the nosewheel enough that it's no longer helping with the steering, and Jake has not gone to full rudder or a touch of brake to straighten out the left drift.

In fact, panic and incorrect instinct have taken over. As he angles gently off the left edge, Jake is holding only two-thirds right rudder, full right aileron, and full-back yoke. "Ole Bronco" drags the tailskid in the grass between runway and parallel taxiway, lifts a few feet into the air to clear the taxiway, then sits down again on main gear and tailskid in time to plow through two parked small planes. And it comes to a skidding halt because the propeller was reduced to a stump while chewing through a Cessna 152 wing.

Miraculously, nobody is hurt. But they are running like crazy to get away from the big fuel spill. Jake's ego is bruised, however. He did not even know he had hit other planes until exiting the wreck and looking back at the carnage on the ramp.

Why didn't he know? Because his plane's nose was so high during the takeoff run that he could not see ahead. He had pulled the nose up to an impossible takeoff attitude, putting the airplane into a stalled attitude while still on the ground. For all his low total hours, Jake is a good instrument pilot. After a takeoff into a low ceiling, he would never pull the nose above a reasonable climb pitch attitude. But he did just that in good visual conditions. And, in so doing, he assumed a "no-fly" attitude that also cost him his forward visibility.

Could Jake have made a safe takeoff from Hilltop? Sure. There was plenty of runway, and no obstructions on the far end. So what did he do wrong?

Well, first and foremost, he did not have a good visual yaw attitude reference. He didn't notice immediately that he was slowly swerving leftward because he had not established a "heading bug" on his engine cowling. During his checkout flights, he should have determined a point on the cowling directly ahead of his nose that would indicate alignment with the runway. In fact, he could have established this point during his first taxi-out on the first checkout flight. After a few flights in any airplane, this checkpoint on the nose comes naturally—but on any new airplane checkout, a pilot should establish "straight ahead" with a definite nose checkpoint (it makes for better crosswind landings, also).

Second mistake? Even without a good "straight-ahead" nose reference, when the runway centerline starts departing to the right, it's time to use right rudder—lots of it (and maybe a little brake, too, on some airplanes). Jake never got to full rudder, yet he continued the takeoff run, even after it became obvious that he was going to depart the left edge of the runway.

Next error? Why not be ready to abort any takeoff (or landing also) when things aren't going just right? On takeoff, things only get worse as speed builds if you are not under full control. That 10-degree angle to the left of the runway centerline is not too hairy at 20 knots groundspeed, but at 60 knots, that's a rapid runway departure. And if you want 70 knots before takeoff rotation, why try to get the last 10 knots as you are plowing through the runway lights?

And there's another serious error: Jake had never established a visual, over-the-nose pitch attitude reference for liftoff. On most nosewheel-type airplanes, this is a line-of-sight reference achieved by setting the top of the cowling on, or just below, or just above, the far end of the runway. But it will vary with the type of airplane, and with the individual pilot's sitting height in the airplane. It can be established early in the checkout, starting with the first long, straight taxi. The pitch attitude for liftoff is bound to be a little higher than the three-point taxi attitude.

Then, during the takeoff and landing practice portion of the checkout ride, a standard nose-up pitch can be established that permits liftoff shortly after commencing rotation at the prescribed speed, but which also permits acceleration to V_y after liftoff while in a shallow climb. Jake did not have such a reference established, so in the midst of a crisis, he pulled his nose way too high. It's probably just as well he never got really airborne, or he might have made it to 20 or 30 feet before stalling.

Is this accident all Jake's fault? No, not entirely. None of his instructors ever insisted on prescribed pitch attitudes for visual flying. They gave just a little commentary occasionally, like "get your nose up," or "stay on centerline" (in reference to *what?*). They never insisted on establishing prescribed pitch attitudes *without reference to the instrument panel* for various visual maneuvers. Nobody demanded that he stay on the runway centerline for takeoff, or for landing—especially on those big, wide runways.

And nobody gave Jake any real preparation for his first real heavyweight takeoff in "Ole Bronco." Those additional bodies made his takeoff weight at Hilltop about 600 pounds—or 20 percent—heavier than he had ever experienced before (except for his first takeoff earlier in the day on the long, wide runway at Metropolis). Short of loading ballast or spare bodies (not totally out of the question), his instructor could have done low-power takeoffs to simulate heavy loads or high density altitudes.

Well, Jake and his friends lived through the crash. Of course, his friends are not quite as chummy as they used to be, and now they head for the hills in a four-wheel-drive Bronco. Jake is a little more cautious, but still flies. But now he just flies, flies, flies in an airplane until he really knows it well. Sure, it costs a lot of rental money, but eventually he learns the airplane and the pitch, bank and yaw attitudes seem to come naturally.

That may be Jake's solution. But why not check, visualize and remember these attitudes right from the start, during the checkout ride? It's much safer, and it saves rental fees.

Of course, the same knowledge of attitudes, especially pitch attitude, applies not only to takeoff, but to climb, cruise, approach and landing. It is possible to fly an airplane without an airspeed indicator if you match pitch attitude with throttle position. (It's not a good idea to cover up the airspeed indicator, however, especially with a big, heavy bird with high wing loading and monstrous draggy flaps. But even for these biggies, a pilot ought to know the safe liftoff and touchdown attitudes.)

Look at the case of "Jill" and her one particularly bad landing, for instance. She has recently finished her private course, all in the Cessna 152. She is about 5'4" tall and the short distance from tailbone to eyeballs was no problem in the 152—it fits almost everyone.

But she does not fit too well into Dad's old Cessna 172. Everything has a different perspective. Even with the seat cranked all the way up, she isn't seeing much of an over-the-nose reference until established in cruise. Since she already has her private license from real CFIs, Dad is giving her a family checkout in the 172.

Takeoffs are no real problem—the 172 will lift off from a three-point attitude without really trying to wheelbarrow. But landings with Dad are a little flat and a little fast—even with Dad coaching, "Get the nose up a little higher" just before touchdown. Dear old Dad has never demonstrated "touchdown" attitude, even though he could have done it during a fast taxi. Jill doesn't really know what is a safe pitch attitude for runway arrival.

So when Dad gets out on the taxiway and says (just like a real instructor), "Take it around for three landings," Jill stretches her neck and taxis out onto the runway. Now lightened without heavy old Dad, the Skyhawk leaps into the air from a three-point attitude.

The first touchdown—really an "arrival"—is also in a three-point attitude, but Jill recovers from the ricochet with a good go-around. Without Dad there to coach, "a little more nose-up," the second touchdown is just as flat, but with a little more sink rate.

Instinct takes over, and the "let's get this thing on the ground" reaction brings on a nose-drop that really pegs the nosegear into the runway. Dad gets across the runway in a hurry, kicking pieces of blown nosewheel tire out of the way. The family 172 looks only a little worse for the wear—nose fork missing, prop bent. After asking the usual question ("Are you okay") Dad wants to know why Jill didn't get the nose up.

Her answer? "I couldn't see where I was going." Of course she couldn't. Jill sat so low in the saddle that she never had a chance to establish a good pitch attitude reference. If Dad had ever looked to the left while "instructing," he would have realized that his eyeballs were level with the top of her head—Jill could not possibly see the pitch attitude that Dad was referring to. What does Jill need? An extra seat cushion might be all it takes.

The truth is never mentioned in a flight manual or flight school syllabus: By deficiency in design, some airplanes just won't accommodate the full range of different pilot sizes and shapes. With the seat full-up, Jill could have put three fists, one on top of the other, between the top of her skull and the cockpit ceiling. That's one or two fists too many. Perhaps one good, hard $5 boat cushion, plus maybe easing the seat forward a notch or two, would have allowed this young pilot to establish good attitude references in this overgrown 152.

And it would have been beneficial, too, if Jill's instructors had stressed flying by visual attitude reference. But there's not too much call for it when the Test Guides demand airspeed and altitude accuracy. Does anything in the Guides ask for proficiency in "airspeed-failed" flight maneuvers.? Does any checkout instructor ever show the pilot how to assess the correct eyeball height and the pitch and yaw references?

As we end this saga, Jake is still cussing his "squirrelly" six-place that can't make it out of short strips. Old Dad tells people that his "hot" 172 just takes too much muscle for young girls like Jill. For her part, Jill is still wondering just what went wrong, and has gone back to her old flight school for a few more lessons in the 152, then a real CFI checkout in the school's 172.

Hope someone tells them how to "watch their noses" in future lessons and checkouts!

Taildragger Takeoffs Can Be Tricky

Pilots are obliged to follow the directions of controllers—most of the time. The well-known catch-all clause in the FARs that allows pilots to do whatever is necessary to ensure safety allows another course of action, so long as the pilot can justify it. The problem is, at what point does the pilot decide that he's right and ATC is wrong?

One 18-year-old, 150-hour private pilot followed ATC instructions that ran against his better judgment and wound up groundlooping his family's Cessna 140 as a result. Fortunately, neither he nor his passenger was injured in the accident.

The pilot and his passenger (who was a 140-hour student pilot) were preparing to depart Pulliam Field in Flagstaff, Arizona, for a flight to Oklahoma City, Oklahoma. Ground Control told them that Runway 21 was active. After taxiing to the approach end of Runway 21 and performing an engine run-up, the occupants of the Cessna noticed that the windsock at the end of the runway was indicating a variable quartering tailwind.

The pilot called the tower and asked to use the reciprocal runway. According to the passenger, the pilot was not comfortable with the idea of taking off in a tailwind. "The tower responded with some numbers (I didn't understand because of the static) and he said he had his binoculars on the windsock and that runway 21 was indeed recommended," the passenger said. In fact, the winds were measured as being from 060 degrees at seven knots.

On takeoff, it soon became apparent that the airplane was behaving strangely. Normally the tail would come up at about 40 mph indicated, but it stayed on the ground despite full throttle and full down elevator. The Cessna began to veer to the right "due to P-factor," according to the passenger [in fact, both P-factor and torque would tend to make the airplane turn to the left], and the pilot tried to correct with full left rudder. The airplane swerved to the left, and the pilot applied right rudder, but by this time the Cessna was out of control. The right landing gear folded under the airplane, and it slid to a stop.

"After emerging from the airplane, I observed a steady wind blowing from the wrong direction. A direct tailwind," the passenger said. "It appears to me that is why the tail did not lift and also why the rudder was ineffective."

NTSB didn't see it that way, though. In pronouncing probable cause, the Board held the pilot responsible, naming his inadequate compensation for the crosswind and his failure to maintain directional control and proper alignment as the reasons for the groundloop. The actions (or inactions) of the tower controllers were not mentioned.

Rather underscores the point that the guy in the left seat *is* the pilot in command, doesn't it?

Just Barely

Sometimes a quick decision can backfire and lead to an accident—even if it's the "right" decision for the situation. One pilot who made such a choice was involved in an accident in which his Cessna 140 (taildragger again!) just barely missed clearing an obstacle during takeoff. The pilot and his passenger suffered only minor injuries, and the Cessna suffered substantial damage when it plunged into a ditch and nosed over during the accident.

The pilot was practicing stop-and-go landings at the Oroville, California, airport and demonstrating the handling characteristics of the Cessna to his passenger, who also held a pilot's license. The pilot was in the right seat.

During one landing, according to the pilot, he heard a squeal as if one of the brakes was engaged and the airplane swerved to the right. The passenger said that the airplane was going to the right at a speed too low for effective use of the rudder, and that it abruptly swerved once the brakes were applied. The airplane went off the runway, and the pilot applied power to straighten it out and go around.

The Cessna was now on the right shoulder of the runway as the pilot accelerated to take off again. The airplane became airborne at about mid-field. The pilot, being careful not to stall, leveled off to let the airspeed build before climbing. That's when he saw an approximately 4-foot high barbed wire fence in his path. The pilot judged he had enough altitude to clear the fence and continued the go-around. In his accident report he wrote, "I thought, 'If we clear the fence, we're okay—if we hit it, I'll shut down and land.'"

The Cessna's main gear cleared the fence, but the pilot heard an unusual "twang" noise as the fence passed under the airplane. Assuming (correctly) that he had struck the fence, he closed the throttle and landed.

The pilot wrote, "While we were going along the ground I thought we were safe—then I saw the ditch...."

The Cessna went over the lip of the 10-foot-deep, 30-foot-wide ditch, and ran into the other side, nosing over in the process. Afterward, the top strand of the 42-inch-high barbed wire fence was found entangled in the tailwheel of the plane.

From "Big Six" to Tiny Trainer

Sometimes flight instructors climb in and out of so many airplanes that they lose sight of "details" which can make all the difference in a safe flight. It then becomes a question of what the student is supposed to be learning—the right way or the wrong. That question may have been raised for a seven-hour student as he hiked with his instructor back across the airport from their demolished Tomahawk.

On an instruction flight originating in La Porte, Texas, the CFI decided to land the Tomahawk at Pearland Airport, a local uncontrolled field. The 36-year-old CFI had 1,017 hours, 91 of which were in Tomahawks, and held both single and multi-engine instructor ratings. According to his accident report, he had made one earlier flight that day to Houston's Hobby Airport as PIC in a Piper Warrior.

Instructor and student arrived over Pearland shortly before 4 p.m. and after overflying the field to check the windsock, the CFI landed on Runway 35. Winds were 360 and light at about five knots, a witness reported. The two spent approximately 25 minutes on the field and it appears that the CFI spent at least part of this time considering runway options for takeoff. He had landed on the rather narrow Runway 35, 1,800 feet long by 15 feet wide. Another choice was Runway 29, 2,400 by 30 feet. Both are paved, although the pilot reported Runway 29 was pot-holed.

Before taxi, the CFI consulted the Texas Airport Directory and opted for Runway 29 due to its greater length and width. The student taxied to the threshold, at which point the CFI took the controls and consulted his checklist. According to the CFI's report, he considered the wind to be out of the north at five knots. In fact, investigators found that at the time of the attempted takeoff, the wind had swung to 120 degrees at eight knots—creating a tailwind for Runway 29.

The CFI decided on a short-field takeoff. The run-up was normal and as the instructor stated, "At this point I selected two notches of flaps (34 degrees), held the brakes firmly and applied full power. I have no rational explanation for this." By mistake, the CFI had selected full flaps.

The Tomahawk chugged dutifully down the runway with full flaps and a following wind, accelerating very slowly, while the instructor's attention was reportedly focused on maintaining directional control with the rudder. The controls were "mushy." As the airspeed reached 50 knots, he rotated and immediately sensed an oncoming stall. He lowered the nose to try to pick up speed and "take advantage of ground effect."

The instructor estimated his height at 20 feet and when the controls remained mushy he decided to abort the takeoff. He closed the throttle but was unable to maintain a level glide. The left wing impacted the slushy ground along the runway with the Tomahawk in a slight nose-up attitude. The airplane then swerved and slid to rest in a pool of water. The airplane sustained a severely damaged left wing, landing gear and prop, and was considered destroyed by investigators. Both occupants exited the plane unharmed and walked to a helicopter company on the airport.

In the portion of his accident report where he was invited to recommend ways to avoid the accident, the pilot cited his inadvertent selection of full flaps as directly contributing to the accident. Having flown a Piper Warrior earlier in the day, it was the CFI's opinion that he was mentally lowering the Warrior's flaps for the short-field takeoff in the Tomahawk.

NTSB investigators felt that the flap mistake was only a part of the problem. Mushing to a stall was considered the instructor's second gaffe, while the uncontrolled swerve on the ground rounded out the list of probable causes. The student's opinion of the events was not recorded.

Multi-Engine Pilots Have More Options, But...

Pilots of twins often steel themselves to the notion that, on takeoff, if power problems arise and speed is decaying, they will not have the option of continuing the takeoff, but must "land straight ahead." And it has been generally taught that the aborted takeoff may be made wheels-down if room permits on the runway, but with terrain a deciding factor, wheels-up when the plane is sure to go into the boondocks.

In this context, the pilot of a Cessna 411 had a novel approach when he aborted a takeoff at Panama City, Florida. He chose gear-up as a mode of staying on the runway.

The 4,900-hour commercial pilot, with 412 hours in type, was making a takeoff from the 4,828-foot long Runway 4. On an earlier flight, he had noted the engines had surged on takeoff in the Cessna twin, and this problem had been traced to a sticking turbocharger wastegate.

On this takeoff, as the plane accelerated down the runway the pilot again noted a surging, as if one engine were overboosting or the other were cutting out, he told investigators. (This alone would be grounds to abort the takeoff, in our opinion.) He retarded the throttles slightly and the engines evened out. At V_{mc}, he rotated and began to climb, bringing in full power on the throttles again. But the engines immediately began surging as before. He now elected to abort the takeoff, intending to land on the runway.

He now tried a new twist. In his accident report, he wrote, "Until this point I had not raised the gear. Was going pretty fast and running out of runway. Elected to raise gear to slow down aircraft." And it did. The twin came to a stop at the end of the runway. The pilot emerged uninjured.

Which raises a question: Was it a smart move for the pilot to raise the gear? Does a lightplane belly-skidding on a runway create more friction than one still on its tires with the pilot standing on the brakes? In our opinion, no. A plane on the runway is always better off when its pilot uses brakes to slow down, for several reasons. First, rubber on pavement is superior to belly friction. Second, the plane is under control for other maneuvers, such as guidance around obstacles or even an intentional ground-loop. Third, even if the plane does go off the end, it will leave the runway at a much slower speed.

But fourth, if it works, the plane comes to a stop totally unscratched. To raise the gear while still on the runway is to accept belly, prop and potential engine damage. To wait and see whether the brakes do the job, is at least to postpone it.

Abort! Abort! Whoops, Too Late

One useful trick that's not found in private pilot course books is the practice of picking an "abort" point on the runway when departing. The idea is that if the takeoff is abandoned at that spot, there will still be enough room left to stop the airplane. By essentially making the abort decision before the airplane starts to move, the pilot has made the task of aborting that much easier.

Many a takeoff overshoot has occurred because the pilot failed to make the abort decision in time. Just that happened to an 88-hour private pilot trying to take off from a 2,160-foot turf strip in Delft, Minnesota. In this case, however, there was twist: The airplane, a Piper Warrior, was bounced into the air before it had reached flying speed. The pilot wound up putting the airplane through the airport fence, but neither he nor his three passengers was injured.

With four aboard, the Warrior was heavily loaded. However, it was both below maximum gross weight and within c.g.

limits. Faced with a heavy load and a down-sloping runway, the pilot elected to use short-field takeoff techniques.

The Warrior didn't accelerate as fast as he had expected. Fairly far down the runway, it ran over a rise in the turf strip and became airborne. "I decided that if I could continue to fly, fine," the pilot recalled. "If not, I'd abort the takeoff."

As it turned out, the airplane started to settle, and the pilot immediately cut power and hit the brakes. But it was too late. Had the pilot set a realistic abort point before the takeoff, he probably would not have gained enough speed to be bounced into the air by the hump. As it was, he got himself into a corner from which there was no escape—not enough power to go, and not enough runway to stop.

Stalls and Spins

Sheer magic...that's what most people conclude when they contemplate the forces that keep an airplane aloft. Some education is required before anyone is able to understand that it's the motion of invisible air over and around a wing that provides lift; and even then, there remains a large body of non-believers.

But there's one thing that all of us pilots know for certain; when the flow of air ceases or is disrupted, the magic ceases and the airplane stops flying. There's nothing more fundamental to operating an airplane properly than knowledge of the aerodynamic stall and its first cousin, the spin, yet the stall-spin accident continues to be one of the most frequent causes of aviation accidents. In this section, we'll present some vital information dealing with stalls and spins, beginning with statistical proof that the problem does indeed exist.

Stall Accidents Persist Despite Training, Experience

A flight instructor watches closely as the throttle is drawn back and the airspeed decays. The aircraft begins to buffet lightly, the stall warning horn shrills, and the nose starts hunting up and down. The throttle is pushed home, the airspeed builds, and the aircraft resumes normal flight.

Flaps up, flaps down, power on, power off—everyone who has made it past first solo has practiced stalls just like this. Flight instructors warn and cajole pilots about airspeed and the effects of angle of bank on stall speed. The FAA written tests contain question after question regarding stalls and stall speeds. From the start of primary flight instruction to the awarding of the certificate, pilots are taught how to avoid stalls and how to recover from them if one should be encountered inadvertently.

Yet, for all this emphasis and training, the stall-related accident is still killing people at the rate of about 270 per year. Ever since the stall accident was discovered, pilots with experience ranging from zero time to 25,000 hours, flying everything from homebuilts to DC-10s, have found themselves on the losing side of a stall.

It is widely known that the "stall" type of accident is a perennial killer. (Actually, the "stall" category is filled with several variations. Under the NTSB's scheme of classification, there are the "stall/ mush," the "stall/spin" and the mere "stall" subgroups of accidents. For our purposes, the latter will be called "straight stall" here.) The NTSB, in one of its annual reviews of accidents, ranked the stall/ mush accident as the fourth most prevalent accident for single-engine fixed wing aircraft, among all the mishaps such aircraft fall heir to. The stall/spin was listed as the fourth most common *fatal* accident, while the straight stall accident was sixth on the list of killers. This only continues a sordid history of stall accidents.

As far back as 1972, the Board issued a special study in which it was stated that "stall/spin accidents...have historically accounted for more fatal and serious injuries than any other single type of accident." The Board's in-depth study provides a benchmark on which to judge the progress of the efforts of the last decade toward reducing the incidence of stall-type accidents.

Aviation Safety examined the stall accident a full decade after the Board issued its report. By building a database composed of all the stall accidents during the years 1980 and 1981, we have been able to analyze in detail the three types of stall accident. Comparison of the results of this study with those of the Board's 1972 study shows some interesting trends—some encouraging ones, and some that perhaps are distressing.

The Way We Were

While things have generally gotten better with regard to the *rate* of stall accidents, many facets of the stall accident picture appear to be worse than before.

In its 1972 study, the Board found in the three-year period covered (1967-69) there were some 1,261 stall-type accidents, or about 420 per year. During the two-year period of *Aviation Safety*'s study, there were 841 stall accidents, averaging out to about 420 accidents per year. Thus, the average number of stall-type accidents per year has not changed. The number of people killed in stall accidents did decline significantly, from about 332 yearly in the NTSB study, to 272 yearly in the *Aviation Safety* study.

Although the constant burden of stall accidents yearly could be considered depressing, what normally matters is the rate of these accidents, based on a measure of exposure, such as aircraft hours flown. Using this measure, there is a significant improvement between the NTSB and *Aviation Safety* results. In the Board's study, the rate of stall accidents was found to be 1.76 per 100,000 hours flown, with an associated fatal stall accident rate of 0.60 per 100,000 hours. For the period of *Aviation Safety*'s study, both of these parameters showed significant declines, with the total stall accident rate dropping to 1.15 and the fatal stall accident rate falling to 0.40.

While this points to modest improvement regarding stall accidents, the gain was not as great as the decrease in the over-all general aviation accident rate. For the period in NTSB's study, there was an average 22.15 total accidents per 100,000 hours, and 2.71 fatal accidents per 100,000 hours. In our study, the rates were 9.70 and 1.74, respectively.

In a nutshell, although general aviation's rate of stall accidents has dropped, the "hard core" of stall accidents has not been cracked, and the ratio of stall accidents to all general aviation accidents is actually rising.

How often is the result a fatal one? The ratio of fatal stall accidents to all stall accidents has not changed appreciably. For the period 1967-69, there were some 1,261 stall accidents, of which 427 (34 percent) were fatal. For the period which *Aviation Safety*'s study covered, there were 841 stall accidents, only 294 of which were fatal (35 percent). Additionally, the Board's study found that about 24 percent of stall accidents occurred during the takeoff phase of flight, 36 percent during the landing phase and some 40 percent during the in-flight phase.

More recently, the distribution showed some remarkable changes. For the recent period, the takeoff phase of flight accounted for some 36 percent of all stall accidents. The landing phase now accounts for 31 percent, and the in-flight phase for 33 percent of all stall accidents.

As later discussion will detail, we believe this may belie a shift in stall accidents away from the "buzz job" and "flat-hat" circumstances that might have been more relatively common in such crashes years ago, to a more "unintentional" kind of stall circumstance nowadays, such as during a normal takeoff or landing.

With the wreckage contained within a very small area, this accident shows the classic stall-spin scenario; a near vertical descent with very little forward speed.

The Board also noted in its report that in the three-year period immediately following World War II, the stall-type accident accounted for almost half (48 percent) of all fatal GA accidents. For the period of the Board's 1972 study, the stall-type accident had declined to the point were it accounted for only 22 percent of all fatal accidents. By our most recent data, the stall accident currently accounts for about 23 percent of all fatal GA accidents. Again, the data may be pointing to a "hard core" of stall accidents which only great added effort can overcome.

The Amateur Hour?

One of the surprising results of our study was the average flight experience of pilots involved in stall-type accidents. While it might be expected that pilots with a low number of total flight hours would be the most likely to have a stall-related accident, this would not seem to be the case. Pilots involved in stall-type accidents were found to average more than 2,000 total hours. Obviously, these are not the inexperienced tyros that many would expect to find stalling around.

It might also be expected that pilots involved in stall-type accidents would have a low number of hours in the type of aircraft which they crashed. Our computer study shows, however, that these pilots are averaging almost 300 hours in type.

The computer analysis also found that, while some certificate groups were involved in stall-type accidents by percentages which mirrored their distribution in the pilot population, certain others did not. Private pilots, for example, were involved in about 43 percent of all stall-type accidents. This is consistent with their distribution in the over-all pilot population, which is about 43 percent. It is interesting to note that the NTSB 1972 study also found private pilots involved in about 42 percent of all stall-type accidents.

Student pilots, on the other hand, would be expected to show up far more often than would be consistent with their distribution. The computer found, however, that student pilots, while comprising about 25 percent of the pilot population, were involved in only 11 percent of all stall-type accidents. This is somewhat lower than the figure given by the Board in its 1972 study, which found students involved in about 16 percent of all stall accidents. The lower rate of involvement of student pilots in stall-type accidents today may be due to better training, perhaps, or to their recency of experience regarding stalls. For student pilots tired of hopping around the patch, practicing stalls is one of the few maneuvers approved in their limited repertoire. Thus, it's at least possible that a student pilot might be in a better position than some if it comes to an inadvertent stall.

An even more surprising finding in cur data is that student pilots involved in stall-type accidents are, on the average, well past first solo. We had to discount the inflationary effect of having a handful of "career students" in our group (people who had up to 1,300 total hours, but still only a student license). When we did so, our students still averaged about 51 total hours at the time of the stall accident.

Holders of the Airline Transport Pilot Certificate, who account for about 8 percent of the pilots in the U.S., were involved in about 5.5 percent of the stall-type accidents. Holders of the commercial and flight instructor certificates, who account for about 22 percent of the total pilot population, were involved in only 28 percent of all stall accidents. To some extent this may reflect the predominance of commercial license holders in agricultural aircraft which often show up strongly in stall accident statistics.

Ordinary People

Since the pilot's license and experience does not seem to change the likelihood of a stall accident, is there anything about the airplane which has any effect? The answer appears to be "yes".

During the two-year period studied, there were 841 stall-type accidents. Excluding those related to aerial application operations (to be discussed later), there were 732 "ordinary" aircraft involved in stall-type accidents. The accident database was broken down further and examined on a fleet and even a model-by-model basis. In this way, it is possible to draw some comparisons among the various manufacturers and their aircraft. Some 91 percent of stall accidents in our study (and 92 percent in the Board's study) involved single-engine aircraft, even though single-engine planes occupy only about 80 percent of the nation's fleet.

This may indicate where the majority of stall prevention efforts ought to be concentrated. Whether by virtue of the circumstances under which they are flown, the high likelihood of having a current pilot at the helm, or because of the extreme reluctance of a twin to stall with both engines running, it appears multi-engine aircraft stay out of stall accidents, in the total picture. However, twins have a higher rate of fatal stall accidents than singles; wherever we've seen this effect, it seems to be linked with speed—both a higher stall speed, and a higher speed at impact. In any event, it is in single-engine aircraft where all the stall "action" is.

By way of comparison with the Board's 1972 study, single-engine aircraft at that time had a total stall accident rate of 1.97 per 100,000 hours. *Aviation Safety*'s study showed a rate for singles of 1.10, a significant decline. Twin-engine aircraft, during the Board's study, had a total accident rate of 1.52, which today has dropped to 0.46. The Board did not report fatal accident rates. The current associated fatal accident rates are 0.33 and 0.28, for singles and twins, respectively.

Interestingly, when taildragger singles are segregated and examined separately, the accident rates show a striking difference. Using the Board's 1972 data, the taildraggers identified in the study had a total stall accident rate of 5.37. Our study shows that this number has dropped to a value of 3.06. While showing an improvement, this rate is still egregiously high for "conventional" airplanes—more than four times higher than tricycle gear aircraft, which showed a rate only 0.73 in our study. The current fatal stall accident rate for the single-engine taildraggers is also quite high, weighing in at 0.86, as compared to 0.23 for tricycle gear aircraft.

There is no way to over-emphasize the lesson to be learned from these figures. Whether because conventional-gear aircraft find themselves in the classic "low and slow" kind of flying that has traditionally been a prelude to stall accidents, or because of the age of the designs (which may lack certain aerodynamic refinements or preventive stick loadings), the taildragger single is the "Stall King" of the skies.

One interesting explanation offered by some experts is that these ancient taildraggers generally lack any stall warning system. It is argued that retrofit of stall warning devices on taildragger aircraft would vastly reduce their incidence of stall accidents.

There are some interesting distinctions that can be made among the major manufacturers' aircraft. Dealing with the "Big Four" on a fleet basis, the manufacturer with the highest overall stall accident rate was Mooney aircraft. Next highest was Piper, followed by Cessna and finally Beech aircraft, which were best among the majors. Comparing these figures with the 1972 NTSB study, there has been an overall decline in the stall accident rates for each of the four major manufacturers.

Comparisons of individual models also are possible.

Among training aircraft, the Cessna 150 series (including the C-152) and the Piper Tomahawk were quite different in stall accidents. The C-150 was involved in 64 stall-type accidents during the period studied. Of these, only 19 were fatal. This gave the C-150 a total stall-accident rate of 0.72 and a fatal accident rate of 0.21.

The Piper Tomahawk stalled and crashed 18 times during the period. Six of these accidents were fatal. Thus, the Tomahawk produced a total stall accident rate of 1.65. The associated fatal accident rate was 0.55.

A similar comparison of the two most popular four-place fixed gear singles was not as easy. The Cessna 172 was involved in 69 stall-type accidents, 23 of which were fatal. These gave the C-172 a total stall accident rate of 0.77 and a fatal stall accident rate of 0.26.

The Piper PA-28 series were involved in 37 stall accidents, eight of which were fatal. Thus, for the PA-28 series, the total stall accident rate was 0.47 and the fatal stall accident rate was 0.10. These figures are somewhat distorted, however, by FAA's lack of distinction between the various types of PA-28s. Everything from the Cherokee 140 (the proper comparison to the Skyhawk) all the way up to the Turbo Arrow IV are lumped together in FAA's hours flown estimates. This produces a greater number of estimated flight hours for the PA-

28 series than can be attributed to the plain vanilla Cherokee alone, thus lowering the accident rates.

The Beech model 35 series fell victim to stall-type accidents 14 times during the period studied. Nine of these accidents were fatal. This produced a total stall accident rate of .79 and a .51 fatal stall accident rate. It is interesting to note that 63 percent of these accidents occurred during the landing phase of flight.

A surprise "worst place" for Beech aircraft was the Queen Air 65. Accumulating 4 accidents in 54,895 flight hours, this high power twin showed an overall stall accident rate of 7.29 and a fatal rate of 3.64.

Another surprise which our study revealed: even a supposedly "stall-proof" aircraft such as the Ercoupe showed up with some fairly high stall accident rates. In the case of the Ercoupes, the rates were 3.65 total and a fatal rate of 1.04.

The Homebuilt Factor

It was also possible to look at homebuilt aircraft and their pilots as a special subset in our study, although hours-flown figures were not available. The computer found a lack of experience on the part of the pilots of homebuilt aircraft involved in stall accidents. In the two years which our study covered, 86 homebuilt aircraft were crashed in stall-type accidents. While the pilots had times in type ranging from zero to about 800 hours, the average time in type was less than 50 hours. Even this figure doesn't tell the whole story, however, as a significant portion (42 percent) of homebuilt pilots who stalled and crashed did so on the first test flight of the aircraft. Crashing in homebuilts also appears to have a relatively high likelihood of fatal results—36 out of 86 homebuilt stall accidents were fatal.

As might be imagined, building one's own aircraft creates myriad possibilities for disaster on the first flight. While the vast majority of homebuilt aircraft are no doubt assembled with the utmost loving care and attention to detail, some builders, mistakenly or intentionally, do not follow the plans as closely as the designer had intended. Even slight variations in construction can turn some designs into rampaging monsters in the air.

Usually, however, homebuilt aircraft crash on the first flight due to the pilot's lack of familiarity with the aircraft. Pilots who take these aircraft on the first hops are test pilots in every sense of the word.

Perhaps due to excitement and anticipation combined with impatience to see the fruits of their labor bearing them aloft, some homebuilders simply do not follow the recommended series of taxi and high speed ground run tests before embarking on the first flight.

Extraordinary Circumstances

What about the conditions under which some flights are conducted? Does this have an effect on the incidence of stall accidents? Almost certainly, the answer is "yes."

Certain types of operations are conducted under what could only be considered as extraordinary circumstances. The most prominent example is agricultural operations (such as spraying fields, spreading fertilizers and seeds, etc.).

Agricultural operations are conducted under conditions which might make pleasure pilots cringe. Flying heavily loaded (often overloaded) aircraft from strips which are often no more than dirt roads or cleared fields, ag pilots find themselves facing obstructions and hard maneuvering under sometimes hostile atmospheric conditions. Some 45 ag pilots (41 percent) stalled and crashed on takeoff under conditions like these.

Typically, ag pilots operate in high density altitude conditions. Since crop spraying is generally accomplished during the spring and summer months, the high temperatures create elevated density altitude conditions, which were a contributing factor in 19 ag accidents (about 17 percent). More than half of these accidents were takeoff accidents.

The types of maneuvers which ag pilots are called upon to perform also contribute to their record of stall accidents. The in-flight procedure turnaround, a maneuver which has the aircraft making a sharp turn while first climbing, then descending for another run at the spray area, figured in 41 agricultural stall accidents (38 percent).

The most remarkable aspect of ag operations, however, is the extremely low number of fatal accidents. Of the 109 total agricultural-related stall accidents, only eight proved fatal (less than eight percent). The majority of these fatal accidents were straight stalls, which claimed five lives. The low incidence of fatal accidents is probably due to the construction of ag aircraft, which could be compared to the proverbial brick outhouse. Also helping to lower the number of fatal accidents is the presence of five point harness systems, the forward location of the chemical hopper (which acts as a cushion on impact), and the protective clothing which the pilots usually wear (crash helmets, gloves, fireproof coveralls, etc.).

Just Leaving?

If the conditions under which the aircraft is operated contribute to the incidence of stall accidents, what impact does the phase of flight have on the likelihood of a stall accident? Are certain times in a flight more dangerous than others with regard to stall accidents?

Based on the findings of the NTSB report and our own data, there seems to be a correlation between the phase of flight and the incidence of stall accidents. As discussed earlier, the largest percentage of stall accidents now occur during the takeoff phase of flight—the infamous departure stall.

The departure stall as an exercise is found in every private pilot course. It is a required demonstration for the private checkride and usually is thrown in for good measure on checkrides for every other certificate as well. Because of the high power settings which are carried into the maneuver, it is generally the easiest to recover from (provided a spin doesn't develop). In most training airplanes, when the nose drops at all, the maneuver's over.

But the departure stall is the most common type which ends in an accident. During the period we examined, there were 297 stall-type accidents in the takeoff/initial climb segments of flight. This is more than 35 percent of all the stall accidents for the two years which our study covered.

Departure stall accidents were fatal in 72 cases (24 percent). This is probably due to the high number of stall/mush accidents. This produces very low forward speeds, reducing impact forces and allowing the aircraft structure to protect the occupants. Of the 297 stall-type accidents during the takeoff and initial climb portion of the flight, 153 (51 percent), produced a stall/mush back to the ground. Of these, only 14 produced fatalities.

The next largest group in the departure stalls is the straight stall accident. There were 99 straight stall accidents during the takeoff initial climb portion of flight. Of these, 31 were fatal (slightly more than 31 percent). Straight stalls tend to produce quite high impact forces, with the brunt of the impact coming almost directly on the nose of the aircraft.

Stall/spins accounted for about 11 percent of the departure stall accidents. Of 33 stall/spin accidents which occurred in this phase of flight, 27 were fatal. This gives the takeoff stall/spin the highest fatal ratio at almost 82 percent.

The data may be crying out for attention to a facet of departure stalls not covered in most training curriculums—engine failures just after takeoff. Engine failure figured in at least 34 takeoff stall accidents. As many as 50 other stall accidents which the NTSB listed in the landing phase were preceded by an engine failure during takeoff.

Typically, departure stalls are practiced with full power into and out of the stall. It is a rare instructor who will chop the power abruptly before the aircraft encounters the stall. It is a rare pilot who has practiced losing the engine during a steep climbout. Under such conditions, the margin for error decreases rapidly, and the amount and degree of stall warning is also considerably reduced.

When this happens in the real world, pilots may have an enormous amount of difficulty coping with a situation which training has not prepared them for. This is particularly true when the power loss is not complete. Such partial power situations may tempt a pilot into trying to return to the field, or even attempting to continue the climb, leading to a stall accident.

A Case in Point

Both occupants of a Beech Skipper were killed when the plane apparently stalled while attempting to return to the runway after losing power on takeoff at Renton, Washington.

In the wake of the crash, investigators found evidence that the locknut on the exhaust valve rocker arm of the No. 1 cylinder had loosened, allowing the adjusting screw to back fully out, effectively preventing the valve from opening. This would have the effect of decreasing engine power as the adjusting screw loosened, and cutting power to virtually zero when the valve could no longer open.

The pilot in the right seat was a certified flight instructor with about 400 total hours who also was a mechanic and had been in charge of maintenance for the FBO. The left seat occupant was a young mechanic who had graduated from mechanic's school about five months earlier.

The NTSB investigator said the aircraft was being returned to service after a top overhaul of the engine. The engine was left on the airplane while the cylinders were removed and sent to a repair station for overhaul; the younger mechanic likely reassembled the engine, under the tacit supervision of the CFI-mechanic.

The two had conducted an engine run-up and other checks, but probably had not called for sustained full power from the engine, and therefore might not have caused enough vibration to back off the valve adjusting screw.

Upon takeoff from runway 34, the plane climbed poorly and tower personnel said they could hear the engine sputtering as it passed by. The Skipper got no higher than about 70 feet and began a turn that, under partial power, might bring it around for a landing on the airport. However, it appeared that the engine power went to zero in the middle of the turn, and the plane stalled and dove into the runway nearly vertically.

...Or Just Arriving?

Stall accidents in the landing phase amounted to 263 for the period studied (about 31 percent of all GA stall accidents). The largest single group of these—122, or 46 percent—occurred during final approach. Of 91 fatal crashes during the landing phase, 45 of these, or some 49 percent, were on final approach. Thus the final approach may be more conducive to stalls than other portions of the landing attempt.

The straight stall was the single most common type during this phase, racking up 63 accidents (about 52 percent of all stall accidents during final approach). These 63 accidents produced 18 of the 45 fatal accidents which occurred on final approach (40 percent).

Following the straight stall accident was the stall/mush. Thirty aircraft stall/mushed into the ground during final approach (about 24 percent of all stall accidents during final approach). Once again, the stall/mush produced the lowest number of fatal accidents, accounting for only six of the 45 which occurred during final approach. Typically, many of these accidents were the result of "low and slow" approaches with the pilots raising the nose to try to extend the glide without increasing the power settings to compensate.

The greatest killer, once again, was the stall/spin on final approach. While only 24 aircraft were identified as having entered a spin during final approach, 21 of these accidents (87.5 percent) were fatal. These accounted for almost 47 percent of all the fatal accidents during final approach.

The go-around from a balked landing resulted in 63 stall accidents. Less than 25 percent of these were fatal. Of the 15 fatal accidents which occurred during go-arounds, six were stall/spins. The straight stall produced another five fatal accidents, while the stall/mush accounted for the remaining four.

Stalls in the pattern amounted to 49 accidents, 24 of which were fatal. Some 13 of the fatal accidents were stall/spins, while straight stalls accounted for 10 of the fatals. The stall/mush was responsible for one fatal accident in the pattern.

For many years it has been theorized that stalls in the landing pattern were mainly the result of the pilot attempting to tighten up his turn from base to final and stalling out of it and into a spin. The record of actual crashes does not lend much support to this theory, since 25 of the 49 stall accidents were straight stalls at various points in the pattern. The stall/spin accounted for 18 accidents, and these too were scattered around the pattern. The stall/mush accident occurred eight times in the pattern, but claimed a life in only one instance.

The remainder of the accidents in the landing phase (some 23 accidents) accounted for seven fatal accidents. These landing accidents covered the areas of landing which included the leveloff and touchdown phase, and a group identified by the Board as "landing, other." Three of these fatal accidents were stall/spins. The remaining four were straight stalls.

Putting all this in perspective, it appears the "base to final" bugbear isn't the real villain, nor is most of the maneuvering which precedes final approach. Stall prevention efforts could be concentrated, again, in areas of improving the warning as a final-approach stall develops.

Progress Report

It is evident that inroads are being made in terms of reducing the rate of stall accidents, but there remains what might be called a "pocket of resistance." The total number of stall accidents has remained virtually unchanged since the late 1960s, and the proportion of stall accidents relative to all accidents has shown a significant increase.

In its 1972 study, the Board had recommended reinstating the requirement for spin training as a part of the certificate curriculum. This debate regarding the merits of spin training has raged for years. Considering that the stall/spin accounted for slightly more than 50 percent of all fatal stall accidents, it may be that requiring spin training and proficiency could have a positive effect in reducing the number of fatal stall accidents. This may be worthy of further investigation in view of the increase in the ratio of fatal stall accidents to all stall accidents.

Also, expanded training regarding power loss during takeoff and initial climb might be examined as a way to reduce the number of stall accidents which followed engine failure during the takeoff phase. In this way, pilots could gain experience under controlled conditions with a situation which figures in as much as 10 percent of all stall accidents.

Improved stall warning might also have a significant impact on reducing the number of stall accidents. While most modern production aircraft are equipped with some form of stall warning, these devices may not be the most effective available. In its original study, the NTSB commented on stall warning. At the time, the Board had reached the determination that, based on FAA tests conducted during the late 1960s, a tactile stall warning such as a stick shaker or pronounced pre-stall aerodynamic buffet was 99 percent effective in eliciting pilot response to stall situations. The same study showed that interrupted aural warnings (such as a beeping sound or on-off horn) were 84 percent effective, while a steady sounding warning horn was only 64 percent effective.

Despite such findings, the vast majority of light aircraft that have stall warning systems are still equipped with steady sounding horns. In some of these aircraft, the warning horn is electrically operated, opening the possibility that it may not function at all, leaving the pilot with only those aerodynamic warnings which the aircraft itself provides. In some aircraft, these aerodynamic warnings are only marginally sufficient for the pilot to react and prevent a stall, while in certain other aircraft the only aerodynamic clue may be the stall itself. This is particularly true of aircraft that experience engine failure while executing steep climbs just after takeoff. The sudden drop in airspeed may eliminate the aerodynamic stall warning which would normally be present.

One further lesson that is evident from both the older NTSB data and our current data is that the taildragger single—commonly found with no stall warning system and often no strong aerodynamic buffet—is the most likely to be involved in stall accidents, among all aircraft. This finding does not seem to be affected by pilot experience. Thus, if a pilot wishes to avoid injury or death in a stall accident, his best move would be to avoid these old taildraggers.

The stall-type accident has been a part of flying since its earliest days. While significant progress was made in reducing the number of stall-type accidents during the 20 years following World War II, the same can not be said of the last 15 years. Recent advances in aerodynamics, electronics, and learning behavior, however, hold out hope that further reductions in the incidence of stall-type accidents are possible.

HOWEVER, THE ACCIDENTS CONTINUE

The pilot of a Mooney 201 was killed when he crashed executing a tight turn to final at St. Petersburg, Florida. According to records provided to the NTSB by the pilot's company, he had a commercial license with multi-engine and instrument ratings, 2,247 total hours and about 48 in type. Despite this experience, he apparently stalled in a steep turn to final.

NTSB investigators said the pilot, working for a firm which does long- distance ferrying, had left Lakeland, stopped at Tampa and was arriving at St. Petersburg to pick up a ferry permit that would allow the plane to be flown to South Africa for delivery. The pilot was instructed by the tower to enter a downwind "close in" to Runway 9 and was advised he was number one to land. The pilot radioed "38K will tighten it up."

Witnesses said the plane was descending on the downwind leg very close to the runway, then began a steep left turn that if continued 180 degrees would have brought it onto final. The bank steepened to between 45 and 60 degrees, according to the witnesses, then the nose dropped through and the Mooney hit the ground. The tower controller told the NTSB he was so sure of the impending crash when he saw the nose drop, that he reached for the alarm to call out the crash trucks before the Mooney struck the ground.

The NTSB investigator said the plane had gear and full flaps down when it crashed.

A Primer on Spins

Although spin training has gone by the board in recent years (it's not required for the private certificate, and even instructors can get their tickets by demonstrating recoveries from "spin situations," not developed spins), the prudent pilot sometime in his career will seek out a spinnable airplane and a spin-comfortable instructor and learn this arcane maneuver.

We'll assume the pilot goes to a standard text to lay the groundwork for spin training (FAA's *Flight Training Handbook*, AC 61-21A, for example). This or something like it may be the extent of book knowledge for many pilots and instructors, but it is not sufficient. We'll outline here a handful among literally dozens of things the prospective spinner should know before he climbs into the airplane.

Certification

If an airplane is placarded against spins, believe it and abide by it. Airplanes certified in the Normal category had to be recovered within one additional turn after a one-turn "spin." There is virtually unanimous agreement among experts that a one-turn "spin" is not really a spin at all, but only the entry, or incipient phase; the second and subsequent turns will reveal the airplane's true spin characteristics. Manufacturers may not investigate the second, third and subsequent turns of the spin for the Normal category; there may be an unrecoverable mode there, and indeed some airplanes are known to have this behavior.

Certification in the Utility category sometimes means that the airplane has been demonstrated to recover within 1-1/2 additional turns from a six-turn spin. However, an option allows the manufacturer to certify an airplane in the Utility category, but only do the spin testing required in the Normal category. Therefore, Utility category alone is not enough to prove that the airplane is legally spinnable.

Further, as the NTSB recently pointed out after several spin training accidents, certain airplanes that are certified in both Normal and Utility categories (e.g., the Piper Cherokee) cannot be spun unless the restricted c.g. envelope of the higher category is respected. Twins have no spin certification requirements and may be unrecoverable after the first turn. The presence of a spin recovery procedure in the manual of a spin-placarded single or twin does not imply that the procedure has been proven to work every time. The manufacturer provides this information with his best wishes, but no guarantees.

Above all, one should remember that the certification pilot was spinning a brand-new prototype airplane, was ready for any conceivable behavior when he set the spin in motion, had no trouble recognizing the spin and applying correct recovery controls, and probably had both a spin chute for the airplane and a parachute for himself in the event an unrecoverable mode appeared. The lay pilot will never have all these advantages on his side.

Different by Design

Many spin discussions are predicated on the notion of a "standard" spin recovery procedure. This has been shown to be a fiction, since with spins, there is no such thing as a standard airplane.

The "standard" procedure involves idle power, full opposite rudder until rotation slows, then brisk forward elevator ("forward of neutral"), holding these inputs until rotation stops, neutralizing the rudder to prevent excess stress on it in the dive, then a pull-out to level flight. It's assumed that ailerons will be neutral throughout.

In fact, many airplanes will recover better with ailerons into the spin; others with ailerons against the spin. In some airplanes, it is more important that the rudder be moved first; in others, the elevator. Sometimes these control moves are regarded as more important than getting the throttle to idle, which has always been considered the *sine qua non* of spin recovery. Some manuals for twins suggest reducing power immediately, but then adding some on the inboard engine to slow the rotation.

The amount of delay between rudder and elevator movements varies widely. Some manuals call for waiting up to one-half turn; others want the movements as nearly simultaneous as possible.

The amount of control movement also varies. Full rudder is almost always suggested, but elevator movements vary from relaxing back pressure to briskly shoving it full forward, and points in between.

Hardly any manual talks about pitch attitude and rotation rate, both of which vary widely. It is common for the novice to think he is going straight down in the spin, only to find out he is going "straighter down" in the recovery. It will require discipline to put the wheel full forward, instead of just relaxing back pressure. Rotation rates might vary from about 180 degrees a second to 360; sometimes this varies within the developed spin. Because the spinning airplane is quite a good gyroscope, where a resultant change comes at right angles to the input force, elevator forces used to recover actually increase the rate of rotation.

In the developed spin, the airplane may wallow in roll, pitch, and yaw. It may also have a pronounced buffet or shudder due to its stalled condition. The combination of effects can be disorienting.

While it is rare in spin-certified airplanes, there may be more than one spin mode, usually discovered by aggravating a control (extending flaps, adding power, ailerons against, etc.). The new mode may be flatter or steeper than the old.

Test pilots greatly respect the flat spin mode if it is encountered. It is often unrecoverable; the airplane has transitioned into an autorotative gyration so powerful that none of the flight controls can break it. Carrying power into the spin is often the way to get into the flat spin mode; retarding power may not help after it stabilizes. At this point, the test pilot deploys the spin chute. The lay pilot does not have this luxury.

Individual Airplanes

All of this is based on the generic airplane design. But individual copies of the design do not always behave the same as the prototype. Center of gravity, for instance, is critical. A pilot spinning an airplane that is loaded outside of prescribed c.g. limits may be inviting an unrecoverable spin. Generally, the farther aft the c.g., the longer the spin takes to stop when recovery controls are applied. In some rare cases, a grossly forward c.g. could make the spin unrecoverable.

Load distribution is of concern. In a milestone NASA study, researchers found that taking 20 pounds from one wingtip and adding it to the other produced a marked asymmetry in spins. The spin toward the lighter wing was flatter and faster than toward the heavier wing, and took more than three turns to recover, as opposed to slightly more than one the other way. This has serious implications for a pilot contemplating a spin in an airplane with one fuel tank full and the other empty.

Various anti-spin devices have been attached to some airplanes, and those devices must be present to insure positive spin recovery. They may include tail skegs, dorsal strakes, flow fins along the fuselage, and the like. We are told on one model, the little fin on the back of the nosewheel pant is a required part of the spin-recovery controls; remove the wheel pants and recovery is not so positive.

Each individual airplane probably differs from its stablemates in wing angle of incidence, washout, placements of stall strips, tail angles and rigging. Any of these could have a significant effect on spin characteristics.

Airplanes in service get little dings and dents in the wings, sometimes develop skin ripples and often have lots of bugs and dirt on the leading edges. These could affect spins.

The moral here is, a pilot should make sure his airplane is as close to the original design as possible if he expects to get the advertised spin behavior.

Recovery Techniques

Even though every pilot may attempt to follow the book precisely, each pilot's execution of the technique may be different. "Brisk" movement of the controls is open to a lot of interpretation. However, all experts agree that the main intent is to keep the movements positive, not half-hearted. Often, the rudder-elevator sequence is considered important so that the elevator doesn't blank out part of the rudder.

Experts also point to several common errors in spin recovery. Because the nose is already steeply down, a pilot may be reluctant to put in full forward elevator. And during recovery, he may be eager to raise the nose, causing an accelerated or even a new spin. The pilot may have a mechanical mind-set about the rudder, keeping it full-over too long; this will certainly add to stress on the rudder in the recovery dive, or could even send the airplane through recovery into a spin in the opposite direction.

But perhaps most common, a pilot may not be willing to hold recovery controls long enough. His one-turn, incipient spins may lull him into expecting quarter-turn accuracy in the recovery. When he goes to three-turn spins and the recovery takes more than a full turn, he may think something is wrong. If he backs out of the recovery and tries again, he may become even more convinced that things have gone awry.

Altitude

That's why it pays to have plenty of altitude. Many spinnable airplanes will recover in less than 1,000 feet for a one-turn spin, and 500-700 feet additional per turn. However, delays and mistakes in recovery can add enormous altitude losses.

While manufacturers often don't mention an altitude loss figure, Mooney notes its spin-placarded 201 and 231 may lose 2,000 feet in a one-turn spin. Cessna's 152 manual advises allowing 1,000 feet for a one-turn, and 2,000 for a six-turn spin. Piper's Tomahawk manual has the highest estimate we've ever seen. The revised edition says a one- turn spin could cost 2,500 to 3,000 feet of altitude.

The manuals advise having enough altitude to recover by 4,000 feet AGL. This is not excessive. Professional test pilots often use 3,000 feet as their jump decision height.

Punching Out

Considering that an airplane might be losing 500 feet per turn and rotating at a turn per second, 3,000 feet gives about six seconds until ground impact. This lesson is not lost on test pilots, who will often study the airplane's door latches and seatbelts with more than casual interest before spin tests.

Although there is a decided lack of parachute-wearing in spin training these days, we'll assume the occupants are wearing chutes. If they do not have an aerobatic trainer, they will not have the luxury of pulling hingepins and getting rid of the doors instantly. Rather, they will have to operate the door latches, unfasten their belts and harnesses (without unfastening the parachute harness), find a way to open the door wide enough, find a push-off point, jump and pull the rip-cord, all in about four seconds. It's easy to see how this procedure could be botched if the pilot hasn't thought about it ahead of time.

Unrecoverable?

Somewhere around the second through fourth turn after recovery controls have been applied, the pilot may conclude that the airplane is not going to recover. He is now a fledgling test pilot undergoing initiation rites. Still holding other recovery controls, he may want to try ailerons in the direction of the spin, pumping the elevator, or ailerons against the spin.

Since c.g. is so often a culprit in the flatter, more unrecoverable spins, one aerodynamic expert suggests sliding one's seat forward; this would be difficult to do, but might just work. Shifts in c.g. or load distribution have remarkable effects, as witness military pilots who have opened the canopy and stood up to jump, only to find the airplane recovering from the spin.

An experienced banner-towing pilot and his 1,100-hour CFI student, practicing a banner pickup, were killed when the plane apparently stalled and spun from an altitude of about 300 feet.

The pilot in command, in the rear seat, was a 4,960-hour CFI with an estimated 2,000 hours in type and a long career in banner-towing operations. He was 52 years old. As the banner-towing company's check pilot, he was instructing a 45-year-old CFI who had been recently hired. The accident flight was the trainee's second flight in banner-towing work.

The two had completed one banner-towing run when they made a low pass, dropped the first banner and picked up the second on the same pass. The plane began a steep climb characteristic of banner flights, when it wobbled, stalled and spun. Just before impact, the spin ceased, but not in time for recovery, witnesses said.

Investigators said a one-gallon thermos type container was found loose in the area of the rear seat. In addition, the rear-seat pilot's seatbelt was found unfastened. Witnesses who knew the pilot said he was extremely safety-conscious and would never have flown without a fastened seatbelt.

The "Deep Stall"—
If You Get Into a Real One, You're in Deep Trouble

Naturally, all of us have practiced stalls from time to time. Some of us may even think we've experienced deep stalls. But after you've read this harrowing story of Bill Kelly's experience on a test flight, you'll realize that the deep stall is, thankfully, almost impossible to get into without a lot of effort.

Recently, I overheard a local commercial pilot (amateur/ professional, that is—not really a working pilot) describe to his buddies how he had been up looking at deep stalls in his Cherokee Six. I turned sheet-white at the mention of "deep stall" but didn't break into his tall flying tale.

After hearing a few more words about his airborne episode, it was obvious that he was just describing full stalls. He had glowing praise for his old bird and how he could hold the control wheel full-back, with heavy buffeting and a glowing red stall-warning light, and still keep the wings relatively level with coordinated rudder and aileron. Deep stall, he called it—but he was wrong.

It's unlikely that he could have prodded that benign behemoth into a true deep stall, especially flying solo. It's possible, though: He could have loaded a baby elephant into the back bench seat, which would have moved the c.g. far enough to the rear to allow this unallowed maneuver. But then, it's unlikely the pilot or the elephant would have survived the consequences of the uncontrollable and unrecoverable stunt.

To me, a deep stall is one in which you cannot push the nose back down to an unstalled angle of attack, even with full-forward control wheel or stick. The wing has probably reached an extraordinarily high angle of attack (AOA), well beyond the normal AOA for maximum coefficient of lift. The high AOA was probably preceded by a sudden, unstable pitch-up right into and past stall AOA. Immediate application of full-down elevator didn't do much to arrest the AOA increase, and the resulting drag probably pegged the VSI on its rate-of-descent limit. As the control wheel or stick deformed the nose-down control stop, you probably voiced a suitable expletive.

In 40 years of flying, I've experienced only one deep stall.

My verbal comment, recorded on the unerasable voice channel of the instrumentation tape, was, "Oh, s—t." Right before that was a crunch and tinkle—the sounds of the control wheel column hitting its stop and the glass face of the DG shattering from the impact.

Flight Test Traces

Let's take a look at the airborne instrumentation traces from that scary test flight, which was done in a prototype twin-turboprop airplane—a larger, T-tail follow-on to an already certified airplane with a conventional (low) tail. The engineer on the project wasn't too happy about going to a T-tail empennage, but the configuration had been dictated by corporate management.

I had had the "honor" of performing the initial checkout flights at forward c.g. and was ready to start exploration of mid-c.g. loadings. We already had noted rather poor static longitudinal stability—very light control wheel pull-forces as airspeed was decelerated from a low airspeed trim.

I had installed a heavy rubber bungee "downspring" on the control column to provide sensible control forces. The downspring gave reasonable increasingly heavy wheel pull-force as speed was slowed. Unfortunately, it probably fooled me and delayed my recognition of an approaching trouble area. The purpose of this particular test was only to record static longitudinal stability data—*not* to explore deep stall. With gear and flaps up and power near idle, I did a reasonable job of slow deceleration for the first 30 seconds or so; airspeed decayed smoothly, and AOA increased as expected.

Then, in a matter of just a few seconds, the AOA headed for the moon—way past the approximate 22- to 24-degree reference angle for stall! Probably because of the low power, the pitch attitude didn't shoot upwards—the airplane was just starting to fall due to rapidly increasing drag and loss of lift. The on-board recording equipment showed that the AOA peaked at about 43 degrees, then held above 30 degrees for several seconds. Now, this is really "deep-stalled," and the airplane was falling like a brick.

The recording traces show 75 pounds of *push* force—and add to that about 25 pounds of down spring force. There are little "joggles" in the traces for control wheel force and elevator position—probably where I didn't believe this was really happening to me—and I just released most of the pull force I had been holding. That's also about where my expletive was recorded. When the control wheel started moving forward, AOA continued to increase for several more seconds!

But then I *pushed*—and pushed hard. The glass face of the DG probably shattered when the control wheel shaft hit full-forward. I still vaguely recall straining my elbows and watching the nose staying level on the horizon. The project engineer was riding herd on the instrumentation in the back end of the airplane, but he heard my exclamation and the thud and tinkle as the control wheel went full-forward. He couldn't see outside, but he sure knew that something was wrong!

The airspeed trace showed an increase after I shoved the elevator full forward, but this came from a swivel-head pitot/static boom and was really *downward* airspeed. We were falling, wings-level and nose-level, in about a 40-degree angle of descent. The AOA didn't really reach "flyable" angles until almost 45 seconds after the exercise began.

I remember (vividly!) feeling locked into this level fall, then discovering that the ailerons and rudder were still effective. I started a very slow coordinated roll to the right, and as the bank angle steepened, the nose slowly dropped. The wheel remained full-forward. Finally, in a very steep bank and pointing nearly straight down, the AOA relaxed, IAS came creeping upwards and the elevator finally took hold.

We had lost almost 10,000 feet before getting back to controlled level flight!

Watch Your Tail

Whew! Never again, please. Later investigation, at a much more forward c.g., showed that the inboard wing was stalling completely and shedding such a large zero-velocity wake that the horizontal stabilizer/elevator was getting zero-velocity airstream. At our loading, the horizontal tail load needed to be positive (upward lift) for stability at high AOA. We had lost all of that tail lift, and the result was a pitch-up.

Moral: You don't ever want to lose your tail. That horizontal part of the empennage provides stability and pitch control. Just let it stall or lose the air velocity it needs, and you are in deep trouble—*deep stall* trouble if the tail is providing upward lift, which is likely at low airspeed with a c.g. aft of about 25 percent mean aerodynamic chord (MAC).

Now, this particular airplane (let's call it "Old Greenbird," since it was still painted in zinc chromate) *did* finally make it to FAA certification, but only after wind tunnel tests and extensive modification. The tail cone was lengthened about three feet to move the empennage further rearward. The vertical tail got taller by about two feet to put the horizontal tail higher, and stabilizer/elevator area was increased by almost 40 percent. Greenbird is an easy-to-fly "kiddy-cart" nowadays, but it never did reach its projected rear c.g. limit.

Moral 2: Unless you want to play test pilot, don't mess around with your own airplane at loadings behind the aft c.g. limit. You may not "stall" the tail like I did, but you may well experience the same effect if the tail cannot support the needed loading to give you control. Hopefully, long before you lose control, you will experience complete lack of longitudinal stability—which is almost as bad as lack of control.

Moral 3: Don't mess around in icing weather with an un-booted airplane. Sure, we all worry about ice on the wing leading edges and loss of lift accompanied by a big drag increase. But you should be concerned also with what a "trace" of ice on the horizontal stabilizer's leading edge might do to your longitudinal control.

Suppose the trace is right smack on the front edge of your horizontal stabilizer—and in a triangular shape. Yeah, tri-angular—like one of those short "stall strips" on some wing leading edges. What if that ice "trips" a stall? If the tail is carrying a download and stalls, you are going to nose down right now.

Have you ever noticed the slots in the "stabilators" on some airplanes? They're there, in a few cases, to cure sudden nose-down problems found in earlier versions. Even air-planes with fixed horizontal stabilizers and elevators can have problems if the tail stalls. One venerable commuter airplane allegedly has problems if a full-flap approach is flown at too high an airspeed; downwash over its super-effective flaps may cause a stall AOA over the horizontal stabilizer with even a trace of ice on the leading edge, setting up an uncommanded and uncontrollable nose-down pitch. A well-known crop-duster, now out of production, had a similar problem *without* ice on the tail. Not quite the same as a deep stall but similar, in that pitch control can be lost due to a loss of tail feather effectiveness.

A final note for you pilots with the tail feathers on the wrong end—you canard aviators. Don't mess around with modifications to your canard homebuilt without some really expert engineering advice. We had a canard deep stall incident last year. The main wing stalled before the canard, and the airplane pitched up into a locked-in parachute descent. The pilot was lucky: He rode it all the way to a belly landing in the ocean and wasn't injured. But, he could not get the nose down—could not recover. No, it wasn't a Burt Rutan design—but the pilot should have talked to Burt first. Don't mess with "front-wing" mods that might make the front wing hang on and provide lots of lift *after* the rear wing stalls. That's just like losing your tail in a conventional airplane.

Multi-Engine Proficiency

4

The multi-engine airplane presents its own brand of pilot-proficiency problems, perhaps the most obvious being the loss of power in one engine and the requirement to continue flight in a rather abnormal condition. With the exception of the Cessna Skymaster (a great idea that bloomed, then died for lack of acceptance), a multi-engine airplane suffers from a severe, sometimes terminal case of yaw, roll, and loss of control. And because twins are generally heavier and faster than singles, out-of-control impacts are usually more likely to be fatal. There's obviously a lot to be said for good training and maintenance of pilot proficiency when one is flying a twin.

The alleged difficulties of twin-engine piloting are probably a big factor in many aviators' decisions to stay with a single. (True, twins are more expensive to buy and operate, but they also offer a lot of advantages; speed, comfort, room, operational capabilities, and perhaps most important, two of everything—vacuum pumps, generators, etc., the appliances that can get you out of a lot of trouble if you've got a spare.) But as with everything else in this world, there's a price to be paid above and beyond the money involved; more rigorous training, and a lot more continued training if one is to maintain the edge that's required to handle anything that comes along. Let's face it, with a bigger, heavier, more complicated piece of machinery, there's more to go wrong.

Proficiency training can remedy that situation, and in this section of *Command Decisions* you'll find reports of mishaps that might have been prevented by better training ("better" means more quality as well as quantity), and better implementation of basic multi-engine piloting techniques. We must learn from the mistakes of others—we'll not live long enough to make them all ourselves.

For openers, just to prove that non-proficient pilots can get themselves into trouble with a twin even when the difficulty has nothing to do with the number of engines installed, let's begin by examining how multi-engine pilots are trained.

Puzzle Palace

It's drilled into a pilot during multi-engine training and subsequent check flights that an engine failure on takeoff must be handled quickly and methodically. One point given special emphasis is the importance of feathering the propeller to reduce drag. Most piston twins will neither climb nor maintain altitude with the prop on the dead engine windmilling.

But to accomplish this critical task, the pilot first has to determine which engine is the dead one. It's easier said than done. In a textbook scenario, the pilot will by reflex be holding full rudder to counter the yaw produced by asymmetric thrust from the good engine and by drag from the bad one, and use the mnemonic "dead foot, dead engine" to identify the one that's failed.

It works just fine most of the time when an instructor or check pilot simulates an engine failure. But it isn't always that simple in the real world, where a pilot probably isn't expecting an engine problem, where an aircraft being bounced around in turbulence can make identification of the dead engine a conundrum, where a propeller overspeed could fool a pilot into thinking a perfectly good engine has given up the ghost.

Meager Rewards

The rewards of even flawless handling of an engine failure in a piston twin are generally meager. Take the Piper Chieftain for example. Under standard conditions, the aircraft's single-engine climb rate is 230 fpm—not all that bad for a piston twin. But look at this twin's engine-out performance a couple of different ways: It has 350 horsepower per side, but when one quits there are only about 50 excess horsepower available for climbing. While 230 fpm doesn't sound too bad (for a piston twin, that is), consider that at the Chieftain's best single-engine ROC speed (106 knots), we're talking a gain of only about 125 feet of valuable altitude for each mile the aircraft travels over the ground.

While twin pilots are trained and checked in their ability to cope with a dead engine, it's just as likely that when the real thing occurs, it may involve a partial loss of power and the pilot must decide whether to shut down and feather or try to shepherd what he's got left. When something goes amiss on takeoff, a light twin can become a veritable puzzle palace, and solutions don't come easy.

Such a puzzle confronted an experienced commuter pilot two days before Christmas. The day had started early for the 54-year-old ATP. During three separate weather briefings in the wee hours, he learned of SIGMETs for moderate to severe icing conditions and turbulence along his route from Kenai, Alaska, to Anchorage.

But the pilot didn't let that dampen his habitual good humor. He joked with a company pilot about the weather, saying, "It looks like another great day for flying." Actually, with 14,500 hours of experience, including nearly 10,000 in twins, the pilot probably had encountered many similar "great days" before. What he didn't know was that the weather would be the least of his worries that morning. He would soon be confronted by not one, but two sick engines on takeoff.

WHICH ONE?

It was still dark at 6 a.m. when the pilot and his six passengers taxied for takeoff from Runway 1 at Kenai Municipal. The weather there was cruddy VMC, with scattered clouds at 300 feet, a measured 1,500-foot overcast and six miles of visibility in light rain and fog. The flight was cleared IFR direct to Anchorage at 3,000 feet.

Shortly after takeoff, the pilot radioed "We've lost an engine and we're circling for Runway 1." Witnesses saw the aircraft turn onto downwind and begin descending from an altitude of only 300 to 600 feet. One of the surviving passengers would later recall hearing the left engine backfire loudly on takeoff. The other survivor would say he heard a sound he thought was an engine blowing up but could not say for sure which one it was.

The Chieftain descended wings-level into trees and then crashed inverted into a house about a half mile west of the airport, where it exploded and burned. There were two people inside the house, but they escaped with minor injuries. Only two of the seven people aboard the aircraft survived.

The flaps were found nearly fully lowered, and the NTSB

report indicates that investigators explored the possibility that the pilot may have taken off with full flaps. The Board concluded, however, that he most likely took off without flaps but lowered them at the last moment in an attempt to cushion the impact.

The investigation also disclosed that although the Lycoming TIO-540 engines were producing power when the aircraft crashed, both of them had mechanical problems. The left engine had severely worn camshaft lobes, a condition that would sap some power. However, neither the NTSB or Lycoming was able to determine how much power actually would have been lost.

CRACKED HEAD

The right engine was in worse shape. The NTSB said there was a pre-existing crack in the cylinder head that stretched halfway around the barrel of the number three cylinder. This crack opened up during the ill-fated takeoff, causing the intake manifold to separate and vent the compressed air supplied by the turbocharger. The Board determined that this rendered the right engine capable of producing only 193 of its maximum rated 350 horsepower.

It appears, then, that although the left engine had lost some power, it was in fact producing substantially more power than the right engine. The Board believes, however, that the pilot—like one of the surviving passengers—may have thought it was the left engine that was backfiring and purposely reduced power on the left engine "in a mistaken effort to control the engine and lessen the damage." With the right engine able to produce only 55 percent of its maximum rated power and the left engine throttled back, the aircraft was no longer capable of maintaining altitude.

The Board's theory is supported by the position of the rudder trim tab. With the right engine producing some power and the left one throttled back, the Chieftain would have yawed to the left and the pilot would have needed right rudder to counteract the yaw. The trim tab was found fully deflected to a position that would have helped the pilot maintain right rudder.

The NTSB concluded that the cracked cylinder head on the right engine was a probable cause of the accident. In its own formal terms, the Board also determined that during the

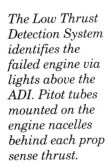

The Low Thrust Detection System identifies the failed engine via lights above the ADI. Pitot tubes mounted on the engine nacelles behind each prop sense thrust.

few seconds that elapsed between the pilot's takeoff announcement and the Chieftain's descent, the pilot was presented with a puzzle he was unable to solve.

A New Way to Skin the Cat

One of the aircraft industry's most glaring failures is its willingness to leave pilots of piston twins with only their feet to point out a power loss. Except for an aborted attempt by Cessna to provide an alerting system in the original Skymaster, multi-engine pilots have had to rely primarily on the specious "dead foot, dead engine" ritual to identify a sick powerplant.

The accident record shows that the ritual doesn't work very well. Power outages during the critical seconds of takeoff and landing too often are met either with inaction or improper action. The margin for error is too small.

Spotting the Need

Several years ago, an enterprising designer named Sherman E. Hall decided to try to expand that margin. At the time, he was vice president of engineering and development for Robertson Aircraft and was getting much more than his fair share of single-engine experience while testing piston twin modifications.

"It's there that I realized the downfalls of the piston twin, and I always had in the back of my mind an idea to help pilots out," said Hall, whose credentials include flight instructor and mechanic ratings. Eventually, Hall left Robertson and formed his own company,

Advanced Aero Safety, to pursue his idea. In 1982, he patented the low thrust detector system (LTDS).

Basically, the LTDS compares the amount of thrust being produced by each propeller and provides aural and visual warnings whenever there's a major discrepancy. The system is beautiful in its simplicity; the whole thing weighs only about one pound.

The sensors are small, heated pitot tubes that are installed on the sides of the engine nacelles where they'll protrude into the slipstream behind the descending propeller blades. The sensors are plumbed to a transducer that converts the ram air pressures into electronic pulses. A printed circuit within the transducer constantly compares the measurements of slipstream velocity behind each propeller.

Lights and Horns

Should the system detect a significant difference in thrust, the pilot is provided with three separate advisories. A flashing arrowhead on a thin, rectangular bar mounted above the attitude indicator—or elsewhere in the pilot's line of sight—literally points to the engine that's losing power.

At the same time, tone generators emit either high-pitched beeps to signify a power loss from the left engine or low-pitched tones to warn that the right engine is losing thrust. Either way, the aural alert sounds only three or four times. Hall felt, rightly, that continuous noise would be more of a distraction than an aid.

The system also includes two light-emitting diodes fastened to each propeller control lever. Should slipstream velocity behind one prop fall more than roughly 15 percent below the other prop (the preset differential actually is 1.5 inches of water pressure, or about 55 mph), an amber light flashes on the corresponding prop control. If the differential drops to more than about 50 percent (3.0 inches or 85 mph), a red light also begins to flash.

All of this happens at once, of course. When power starts dropping off, the pilot hears a tone and sees both an arrowhead pointing at the culprit engine and flashing lights on its propeller control.

No Guessing

The LTDS can eliminate much of the time and guesswork involved in detecting, identifying and verifying a dead engine. Should the system activate during the critical moments of a tight takeoff, the pilot could quickly firewall the engine controls, clean up the airplane and then pull back the prop control with the flashing amber and red

As a further indication of lost thrust, small LEDs mounted on the prop controls also illuminate.

lights to feather the prop on the dead engine. Hall tells prospective customers that his system can save three to five seconds of identification time during an actual engine failure on takeoff. That doesn't sound like much, but it could mean the difference between salvaging the takeoff or becoming a statistic.

We have flown two LTDS-equipped airplanes, a Beech 56TC Baron and a Piper Seneca, with multi-engine flight instructors in the right seats to simulate engine failures. We noticed during these flights that the tones and flashing lights alerted us to a power loss before the onset of asymmetric thrust.

The aural alert is the weakest part of the system. The cockpit clamor in both the Baron and the Seneca often drowned out the low-pitched tone for the right engine. We also found that even the left-engine's high-pitched beep could not be heard while wearing a headset. Hall says the system can be modified to pipe the aural alerts through headsets, but he doesn't think it is worth the expense. We disagree. The LTDS normally works very well with the lights, alone, but the lights can be washed out in direct sunlight. We would want to be able to hear the horns during a takeoff out of the rising sun.

Question of Balance

One problem discovered while flying the Seneca was that the system was not balanced properly. It had been installed only a few days before we flew the aircraft, and tests on takeoff, cruise-climb and landing showed the system responded to a power loss from the right engine much more quickly than from the left.

For example, during a full-power climb at the best single-engine rate of climb speed, the amber light on the right prop lever began flashing when the throttle was reduced to 22 inches. But the amber light on the left prop lever didn't start flashing until power was reduced to 16 inches on that side.

Hall told us the systems are calibrated at the factory and should provide a maximum variance of only 20 percent when installed. Anything more indicates a possible leak somewhere in the system or a damaged diaphragm, which can be caused merely by blowing into one of the pitot tubes. He noted that installation instructions include a final check for calibration.

Simple System

Hall maintains that the LTDS is a simple system that can be installed by any competent AP mechanic. Hall estimates 16 to 35 man-hours for installation, depending on the aircraft. The kit includes two switches—one to turn the system on, the other to direct a couple of amps worth of electricity to deicing filaments within the pitot tubes.

Hall says supplemental type certificates have been obtained for most light piston twins. Some notable exceptions include the Beech 18 and the Cessna Skymaster, though Advanced Aero Safety is currently developing a kit for the centerline-thrust twin. However, the STC list includes some relative oddballs, such as the British Beagle and the Rockwell/Fuji 700.

A few owners have taken the system one step further by having it wired to the Bendix/King radar graphics systems in their airplanes. When the LTDS activates, it causes the engine-out emergency checklist to be presented on the weather radar screen.

But Hall recommends a far more modest supplement that dates back to the Wright brothers—a yaw string. Though it may look a little silly on an expensive aircraft, a length of yarn taped to the bottom center of the windshield is an excellent guide for establishing an attitude that will result in zero sideslip, an important factor in managing an engine failure.

Testimonials

There are about 25,000 piston twins in the U.S. and, to date, low thrust detector systems have been installed in about 600 of them. Advanced Aero Safety has received some glowing reports from its customers, ranging from one who noted that an early takeoff abort may have precluded some expensive engine work to another who bluntly stated that "immediate confirmation of right engine failure by your zero thrust indicator probably saved my ass."

We think anyone who owns a piston twin should consider installing an LTDS. We hasten to note, however, that although the system can help a pilot detect a power loss and point to where it's occurring, an LTDS is merely an aid; it cannot take the place of maintaining the readiness and proficiency required to handle an engine failure on takeoff or landing.

The Multi-Engine Training Dilemma

If a pilot is to achieve proficiency, training and practice are required. The instructor's task is to provide training that's as realistic as possible, in an environment that considers safety above everything else. Sometimes a CFI permits his zeal for real-world training to overcome the performance capabilities of the vehicle.

A 58-year-old CFI and his student were killed when the Apache crashed during an attempted single-engine go-around. The CFI held an ATP and various type ratings, and had logged 21,560 hours, according to FAA records. His "student" held no license. Investigators said the pilot under instruction had held a student certificate at one time, but it had expired; he claimed to have logged more than 100 hours.

The CFI had departed Fort Lauderdale alone in the Apache, which was next heard from on the Unicom frequency for Avon Park airport. Pilot witnesses, one of whom was a flight instructor, heard the flight report over Unicom that they were going to conduct a simulated single-engine approach to Runway 9. One witness said the flight made this call twice.

The witnesses stepped outside and observed the Apache on final approach at about 200 feet. They noted that the left engine was shut down and the prop was feathered. The landing gear was extended and the flaps were full down.

Witnesses stated the Apache could have safely landed from its position, but instead the pilots attempted to go around. The witnesses heard the right engine go to full power as the go-around was begun.

The Apache was able to maintain runway heading, but it was slowly losing airspeed and altitude as it flew down the runway. It got about a quarter mile from the departure end of the runway when witnesses saw the nose rise and the Apache rolled to the left. It completed about one-half turn of what witnesses described as a "classic V_{mc} roll." The nose was pointed down at an estimated 60-degree angle.

Witnesses then heard an abrupt reduction in engine power and the spin was stopped, but there wasn't enough altitude to recover. The Apache struck a utility pole and some junked cars and exploded.

Investigators examined the wreckage after the crash and found no evidence of any malfunctions. It was noted that the mixture control for the left engine was all the way aft in the idle-cutoff position and the propeller control was in the feather position, corroborating the reports of the witnesses.

There's a Much Better Way

The instructor in that just-related episode made a total commitment to his airplane's performance on one engine, and found the machine wanting—badly. A strong case can be made for exposing multi-engine students to an actual engine shutdown (a pilot shouldn't experience his first "feathered" landing all by himself), but it must be done under carefully controlled conditions, and one of those conditions should be "no go-around."

That kind of training, in which a student can build a reservoir of experience and knowledge about the performance limitations of himself and his airplane, is the best kind. It provides a base from which he can develop his proficiency further, but equally important, it enables him to recognize an actual situation that has the potential of taking him "outside the envelope"—in other words, into an environment with severely limited options.

In the interest of your multi-engine education, consider these words from veteran flight instructor and test pilot Bill Kelly, as he shares his thoughts on the subject of "real" multi-engine training:

WORDS OF WISDOM

I recently wrote a magazine article on the subject of engine failure training, mostly concerned with failure on one side of a two-motor airplane. The double-spaced "rough" covered a lot more pages than the editors usually want for a column, but it was excusable, because I had just finished a couple of multi-engine students, and had just completed a CFI Refresher Course. I had lots of ideas after all this exposure to training, but really didn't intend to write about multi-engine emergencies right now, but something happened just this morning that makes the subject quite timely.

Imagine this situation: During the previous several days, the instructor and his low-time multi-engine student had run the gamut of initial training in a light twin. Included were the usual slow-flight, stalls, V_{mc} demonstration—and a look at various drag items while flying on only one of the two engines. Included in the "drag demo" were the effects of a windmilling prop, gear down, and flaps extended.

Unexpected "engine failures"—throttle cuts only—were pulled on the student at high power, at low power, after takeoff, in the landing pattern, in cruise, in turns, etc. This student was good. With less than 400 hours total time, he was able to handle this underpowered trainer: He *flew the airplane first*, then proceeded with the checklist.

This sharp student made a few mistakes during his training—but he made each mistake only one time. Once, after an engine cut in a low-power turn, he was slow in getting the wings level (*"fly the airplane first"*), got the power up while still in the turn, then *really* had trouble getting back to level flight. Another time, at low power in gliding flight, he skipped the "mixture rich, props forward, throttles forward" steps after getting the wings level, but went ahead with the drag-reduction items, gear and flaps. This trainer has very light rudder forces, even at V_{yse} with full power. And of course, rudder forces are even lighter if the "good" engine is still at low power. With the power still way back, he tried to "identify and verify"—and selected the *wrong* engine as the "dead" one. If this had been a real engine failure, and if he had feathered the wrong engine, that light twin would have become an unpowered glider.

This student learned rapidly from his mistakes: Fly the airplane to wings-level. Always go to full power. The high power isn't just to stop a descent rate; more important, it's to insure that the airplane yaws into the dead engine so that you can decide for sure which is the dead engine.

And, of course, in a *real* emergency verify the dead engine by retarding the throttle on the dead engine and observing no change in yaw tendency. Also, by leveling the wings and noting the aileron control force and displacement, you will also know which rudder pedal to push forward: if it takes right wheel rotation to hold wings level, it should also require right rudder. Believe it or not, pilots often try to handle a left engine failure by holding right aileron and left rudder, especially if they don't go to full power after getting the bird under control in wings-level flight. Those are just about the perfect control inputs for a rapid spin entry if the wing is nearly stalled.

Let's get back to the particular emergency that got this subject going. The student was a "natural pilot"—not just because he was a good "stick jockey," but also because he had read all the books, had attended a very good ground school, and understood the basic problems before he started to fly this course. I can't take credit for the ground training—he got that elsewhere—but I was the flight instructor concerned.

Yes, we had a *real* engine failure. It came during a set of clearing turns for a stall series. It was not just the usual sudden reduction in noise level, and yaw/roll. This one started with about two seconds of very heavy vibrations, and a suddenly stopped right propeller; an airborne sudden stoppage, with the prop still in flat pitch, not rotating, and not featherable. The engine "blew."

But the student reacted properly: "Level the wings," and "mixture rich, props forward, throttles forward". The right prop was stopped dead (would not even rotate with the starter). He brought the nose up to V_{yse} attitude, and held a steady heading. From here on it was sort of easy; student to fly, me, the instructor, to troubleshoot and finish the "Secure Checklist" by turning off fuel, ignition, etc.

But there was a dilemma developing. We were at 3,500 feet AGL right overhead a good three-runway local airport with an operating tower, and only about 10 miles from home base. But home base has only two runways, each a thousand feet shorter than the three macadam paths below, and with no tower, only Unicom. Also, home base has lots of glider and ultralight operations, and there's a lot of densely-populated suburbs between present position and home base.

Sounds like an "iffy" trip back home, doesn't it? There also is about a 20-knot headwind to get there. Also, the airport below is *right below*. It's Bartow, Florida, known locally for a well-run city-operated tower, plus a rapid-reaction airport fire truck.

The deciding factor was a quick check of level flight performance at V_{yse} as we tried to level at 2,500 feet AGL: We really were descending—getting *no* level performance— but rather, a 200 fpm descent. That flat-pitch prop was creating mucho drag.

That did it. To heck with home base. Even the FARs say "land at the nearest suitable airport," and Bartow, below, was very suitable. The control tower was a big help; they got all of the C-152's and the Cherokees out of the way. Within a minute of our first call, the little red fire wagon (complete with foam and asbestos suits) was at the runway intersection. Very comforting, especially when I had not even asked for priority or declared an emergency. (I should have done this, just to be sure of a clear runway. Also, who knows—a sudden stoppage in the air often means a cracked crankcase from broken rotating and reciprocating parts, and a good chance of oil fire).

The student flew it all the way to touchdown. That was a real good lesson for him, and a good lesson for me, too: I knew the airplane systems better than he did. He was a real good "attitude/airspeed/power" pilot. Between the two of us, we got down in good shape. Later, when he asked "How did I do?" I found one item to complain about. We had a strong north wind, and were flying a left pattern to Runway 05. He let the downwind leg get blown in a little close. Had it gotten too close, we might have overshot final, and been in trouble making it back to the runway.

The owner and his mechanic would be happier to have plane on home turf, so why not proceed back to home base? It was only ten miles distant, and we had lots of altitude. But we could not *hold* altitude; there were many houses/wives/ kids/pets in between, there was no for-sure way to get priority at a Unicom field, and no fire truck at home. And of course, there's Murphy's Law, Corollary 13, quote: "If the other engine *can* foul-up, it *will* foul-up." I admit that I did not think about all of the above—I just saw a beautiful big airport below, and decided to land right there.

But maybe the judgment training at the last two CFI refresher courses helped a little. FAA, Transport Canada, and GAMA are working on improving pilot judgment, and even have a few textbooks out. The main thrust of this new judgment bit seems to be similar to the fault analysis done by airplane systems designers, i.e. "What could go wrong?"

In our case, with one powerplant inexplicably dead, what could go wrong if we continued on for another ten miles? Plenty: unable to reach the home-base traffic pattern because of headwind and descent rate; no-radio airplanes at home base, and no way to get priority; possibility of a small lingering oil fire, and no built-in fire extinguisher; and no fire truck at home base. And, of course, the possibility of Murphy deciding to enforce his Law on the left engine which was grinding away at maximum continuous power.

Now this started out as just another session on multi-engine problems, emergencies, and training. But it really applies to single-engine work also. Especially important is the idea of thinking ahead, and planning on what to do when Mr. Murphy gets nasty. In our case, we had not planned ahead on "what to do if one engine quits after takeoff, and the airplane won't climb?" All of the training indicated that, at training weight and with the dead engine feathered, it *would* climb. But our dead engine would not feather and, due to a misunderstanding at the previous refueling, we were 30 gallons heavier than the usual training-flight weight.

What if the left engine of this airplane had blown 15 minutes earlier, when we were shooting takeoffs and landings over 75-foot pine trees? Gentle descent to a hard crunch, that's what if. Well, you can't have an absolutely foolproof plan for every contingency, or you would never fly. But the odds against disaster can be improved considerably with some thought about possible consequences.

Like the pilot, all by himself in a big powerful single, who experiences a little engine roughness and slow loss of power while flying over high country in the deserts of the southwest. He has more than 30 miles to go to big Mount Metropolis Regional, his filed destination. There are three suitable small fields close to his course, but he turns down assists from Center and Approach for vectors to one of these strips, and continues on.

Meanwhile, his problem is getting worse: he sees it as a continuing loss of power, and inability to hold altitude. His dual magneto sees the problem as continued heat build-up from a broken exhaust pipe nearby, and finally succumbs to internal heat stroke. Now, past the three small strips, but still too far to glide to destination, he crunches the plane in a desert landing.

Another corollary to Murphy's Law states "What is bad now will only get worse." Better to land under power at an unattended strip, than to press on toward good facilities— but never make it there.

A little thinking ahead, or "judgment," would probably also save a lot of the weather-related crashes. In wintertime, a little consideration of icing is appropriate. It shouldn't take an FSS briefing of "icing in clouds and precip" to convince the pilot of an unbooted airplane to cancel a flight. If the clouds and/or precip through which you are going to fly are at a level where the OAT is at or below freezing, *plan* on getting ice.

Consider the pilot delivering the "Cadillac" of big singles way up north in late autumn. He's flying in a thick layer of clouds when the ice first appears; but ceilings down below are averaging 3,000 feet AGL, and the predicted freezing level is about 2,000 feet. There are lots of good airports, motels and restaurants close by; but this pilot presses on.

A little thought here would have saved a crunch. The weather brief for his destination, still several hundred miles to the north, called for low ceilings, and a freezing level about 1,000 feet BGL. Now, if that ice continues to build, there won't be any warm air below to melt it before landing—and no VFR space below to maneuver while melting down, even if the OAT were a little higher. Result, an ILS approach that almost made it to the runway. With all that ice plus full power, the "Cadillac" couldn't quite make it to the macadam. How do you explain this to the new owner who is waiting to take possession of an expensive new bird?

A little "what if..." thinking several hundred miles back might have put this pilot into a comfortable hotel room with a good dinner, and a day or two wait for improving conditions.

What if that big, rough drop on the right magneto doesn't go away; and *what if* the left mag develops a problem too? Or, *what if* that "minimums" destination weather drops *below* minimums, and *what if* that marginal forecast for the alternate drops also? Got enough gas to get to good weather?

My problem the other day was easy—not much *what if*— with a good field below. It could have been a lot worse; the engine teardown revealed a broken crankshaft that had eaten up a lot of the innards, but no cracks in the case and no oil leaking onto hot exhaust pipes. But I'll sure do a lot more thinking ahead the next time I have even a minor problem.

Centerline Thrust Isn't Always the Answer

The Cessna 337 was touted from its inception as a much safer way to fly with two engines, that philosophy based on the fact that when one engine quits on a Skymaster, there is no asymmetric thrust, and the airplane continues to chug along under complete control, albeit more slowly or with less vertical capability.

Unfortunately, the push-pull Cessna didn't live up to its expectations, but it wasn't because of where the engines were placed; most of the problems that caused the 337's demise arose from pilots' attempts to make the airplane perform beyond its capabilities, or from operator errors that could have taken place regardless of the airplane type. That, too, speaks of less than total pilot proficiency.

Everyone aboard a Cessna 337B escaped injury when the plane crashed into the top of a tree and some rough terrain shortly after takeoff from the airport at Sedona, Arizona.

The pilot was just taking off from Sedona with three passengers when a tower controller informed him that his tow bar was still attached to the nosegear of the plane.

In an apparent attempt to avoid damage to the plane from the tow bar, the pilot not only chose not to retract the landing gear, but also now feathered the front engine of the centerline-thrust twin.

In this configuration, he maneuvered the airplane into a position to return to the airport. However, he said when the controller mentioned that if he landed as intended it would be in a tailwind, the pilot elected to go around.

The front engine now failed to restart, and the pilot said he noticed altitude was dissipating rapidly. He said he therefore chose an off-airport landing.

The elevation of the crash site was 4,827 feet and temperature was about 86 degrees at the time, raising the question of density altitude as a factor, investigators said.

In the recommendations section of the NTSB report, the pilot suggested, "Do not attempt a single-engine go-around in a two-engine airplane."

Forget About Vmc, But...

Although the centerline-thrust twin Cessna 337 does eliminate the potential for a kind of accident most lethal to multi-engine pilots—rollover due to V_{mc} problems after engine failure—certain peculiarities of the airplane historically have plagued pilots who fly the "Push-Me-Pull-You."

As a fleet gets older, its lore may be forgotten. No pilot should undertake to fly the 337 without knowing at least two things:

1. Many pilots have come to grief when the rear engine quit without their knowledge. But this led to a warning light being installed on the panel (besides the normal, well-placed gauges) just to call attention to the problem, and the handbook has always advised feeding in power from the rear engine first on takeoff, so that it will be obvious if the back engine isn't alive.

2. While almost every other twin benefits from prompt gear retraction, the 337 does not. Because of the significant drag created by the gear in transit, it is not advisable to retract the gear until the other problems of the engine failure on takeoff have been resolved.

A crash which sadly illustrates these points occurred at Greensboro, North Carolina, when two pilots undertook a flight in a Cessna 337G. The owner of the plane, a doctor, had a commercial license, an instrument rating and 815 total hours. He held a multi-engine rating limited to centerline thrust, and had flown 129 hours in type.

His friend was a retired airline pilot with 11,200 total hours and type ratings in DC-4s and Convairs. If he had any time at all in a Cessna 337, it was not reported.

After flying from Hilton Head Island, South Carolina, the owner suggested that the airline pilot take the left seat and fly the aircraft back to base, so the owner could "check him out" in it.

The airline pilot agreed, and began to familiarize himself with the cockpit. The two discussed the airplane systems for a while, and then were ready to start the engines. The left seat pilot tried starting the front and rear engines, but was unsuccessful on both counts. The owner, sitting in the right seat, said he would try. He told his companion to open the throttles and not use the boost pumps, whereupon the engines started immediately.

The aircraft was cleared for takeoff from an intersection which would give them about 3,100 feet for the takeoff. The left seat pilot, handling the radio, accepted the clearance. The Cessna was told to hold for a jet's wake turbulence.

During the hold, the two pilots discussed aircraft performance data and performed the engine run-up and before-takeoff checklists. They were shortly cleared into position and after a pause, commenced the takeoff.

At this point, ground witnesses looking at the plane realized the rear propeller was not turning. The witnesses would observe the plane using an "excessive" amount of runway in the attempted takeoff.

To describe the rest of events, we have only the NTSB investigator's paraphrase of what the left seat pilot told him: "The pilot said he released the parking brakes, taxied onto the runway and then sat there for about 15 seconds while he pushed everything forward (mixture, props), and then started bringing in the throttles.

"The left seat pilot said that the acceleration seemed sluggish. The right seat pilot said that everything was okay.

"As the aircraft speed reached 50-55 mph, the left seat pilot said it just did not feel right. But the right seat pilot said it was all right and they had plenty of airspeed.

"The left seat pilot elected to keep the aircraft on the runway as it was a hot day, and did not rotate until they were indicating about 90 mph. The aircraft came off fine, but the left seat pilot said it just did not feel right, and asked the right seat pilot if it was okay. The right seat pilot responded that they had plenty of airspeed.

"The left seat pilot retracted the landing gear and immediately the airspeed began to drop. As the airspeed decreased to 80 mph, the left seat pilot lowered the nose of the aircraft and both pilots pushed everything forward.

"The aircraft was nearing the approach lights to the opposite runway with the aircraft descending. The left seat pilot did not want to go into the steel support posts, so he banked the aircraft to the left. The aircraft was indicating approximately 78 mph, still descending. At about 10 to 20 feet above the ground the left wing stalled and the aircraft impacted the ground in a nose-low, left-wing-low attitude." The left seat pilot survived with serious injuries; the right seat pilot died.

In the wreckage, investigators noted that the three engine split gauges all showed indications that were lower, or zero, for the rear engine as compared with the front one.

They also noted sooted spark plugs on some of the rear engine cylinders, and sooted exhaust stacks. They put the engine on a test stand. It started and ran, but idled at 600 rpm (correct idle is 650).

Investigators found something quite interesting when they did magneto checks on the engine: First check: Left mag—225 rpm drop. Right mag—engine fell off as though quitting. Second check: Left mag—400 rpm drop. Right mag—125 rpm drop. Third check: Left mag—225 rpm drop. Right mag—75 rpm drop.

After a pause during the third check, the switch was returned to the right mag and caused only a 25-rpm drop. Finally, they rapidly ran the engine up to about 25 percent throttle and retarded to idle. The engine quit, but would restart if the throttle were advanced promptly.

Investigators found the engine's left magneto had been set to 23 degrees before top center, when it should have been 20 degrees BTC. "This was causing the left magneto to fire during the compression cycle of the number 1 cylinder," investigators said.

It is thus reasonable to conclude that, had the pilots conducted a very cautious run-up, they might have detected problems with the rear engine. Had they advanced the rear engine throttle first and monitored the gauges, they would have known the engine was dead. And had the left seat pilot been aware of the Cessna 337's unique gear-door characteristic, he might not have retracted the gear when he did.

Same Characteristic, Different Circumstance

Cessna's 337 Skymaster is doggy enough on one engine that a prudent pilot ought not to consider a single-engine go-around except at very light weights. But as the manual warns, the climb rate on one engine goes negative if the landing gear is cycled, since this involves the opening of gear doors that produce a massive increase in drag.

A pilot who got practical experience in this maneuver was alone in his 337A and returning to his home field at Madison, Mississippi; he had just entered the downwind leg when the rear engine quit. NTSB investigators later found that the main tank was empty, and even though the pilot turned on the boost pumps and switched the rear engine to the full auxiliary tank, power was not restored.

The pilot later told investigators he did not feather the rear propeller because it was "still surging." According to the pilot, he continued the approach and as he did so, the gear warning horn went off. He also stated that he now attempted a go-around at "about 300 feet," that the Skymaster "would not maintain altitude and stalled at about 25 feet AGL at 45 mph IAS."

That's not exactly how the NTSB summarized the accident. The report says, "The front propeller struck the runway 11 times at a point 1,530 feet from the approach end of the runway. At approximately 252 feet from the first propeller marks, the aircraft struck the runway again. This time there were 11 more propeller gouges along with a 10-foot-long gouge and white paint, indicating the fuselage struck the runway. The aircraft then climbed straight ahead until reaching approximately 200 feet near the south end of the runway, and the landing gear was then lowered. As the aircraft turned crosswind, it began a gradual descent which continued until striking trees and ground on downwind leg." The pilot emerged without serious injuries.

The investigation disclosed that the pilot had 229 total hours, but had logged only 7.6 hours of dual and 3.0 hours solo in his Skymaster. Said the NTSB investigator, "However, his pilot logbook was not endorsed for solo in this category and class of aircraft. His instructor had advised him not to fly solo because he was not yet proficient in emergency procedures."

Too Much Power

One of the emergency procedures taught in the Beech King Air simulator programs is known as an "unscheduled torque increase," and involves a rather sudden and totally unexpected power surge in one of the two turboprop engines. When this happens the first time, there's hardly a pilot around who can react rapidly enough to keep the airplane from running off the runway; after all, we've all been trained to close the throttles when something untoward takes place before an airplane is committed to flight.

In this situation however, the offending engine has "run away" and is not going to be stopped by anything short of closing the firewall fuel valve, and the very worst thing to do is to pull pack the power on the other engine. Talk about asymmetric thrust! This makes a V1 cut look like a walk in the park, and in the second or two it takes to sort things out, the airplane goes careening off the runway. The only damage is that visited on the pride of the student, who had been briefed to continue the takeoff and handle the problem in the air.

It's very difficult to override deeply trained responses, especially during that most critical of all phases of flight, the takeoff, but the truly proficient pilot is ready for anything.

Differential power due to an overboost was apparently involved in an accident that left three occupants of a Cessna 421 uninjured when the plane departed the runway surface during an attempted takeoff from Leech Field in Center, Colorado.

The Cessna 421 is equipped with Continental GTSIO-520 engines and Garrett turbochargers. The pilot-owner reported that on two previous occasions, he had experienced an overboost problem with the left engine on takeoff, but the problem was easily corrected by adjusting the throttle. He said the problem had apparently been corrected to his satisfaction by having the turbocharger wastegates lubricated.

However, on the accident takeoff, even though the engines were run up and stabilized at 30 inches of manifold pressure before brake release and then advanced slowly to full power, the left engine overboosted as it passed 35 inches, and pegged the manifold pressure gauge. The plane yawed to the right. The pilot now pulled the left throttle back to regain control. However, the manifold pressure dropped rapidly on the left engine, and the airplane yawed left and went off the runway. The pilot was using full right rudder and coming back up on the left engine power in an attempt to get back on the pavement when the twin struck a dirt bank to the side and off the end of the 7,100-foot runway.

Investigators found two discrepancies of interest regarding the left engine. First, the turbocharger wastegate was sticking, due to exhaust deposits on the butterfly valve and shaft. Second, the overboost relief valve was stuck closed, meaning that the normal protection against an overboost would not occur.

Right Down to the Wire

We've already looked into the problem of determining which of a twin's engines might have failed. This problem becomes even more difficult at low power settings and low airspeeds, such as exist on short final approach. "Fly the airplane" remains the watchword of the proficient pilot.

The pilot and his passenger escaped injury when their plane was ditched in Florida's Lake Okeechobee after a power loss that occurred on short final to Pahokee Airport. The 71-year-old commercial pilot told investigators he had more than 18,000 total hours, including 2,600 in Aerostars.

The Piper twin was landing at Pahokee after a flight of about an hour and a half from West Palm Beach. The pilot said because he was unfamiliar with the airport, he had slowed the aircraft while entering the pattern, and allowed room for traffic landing ahead of him. He was in approach configuration at 115 knots IAS on final, about 75 feet above a levee and 800 feet short of Runway 17, when he noticed a decay in airspeed and altitude. He applied a little power, then full power, but it didn't correct for the problem.

He maneuvered to the right to avoid trees and the levee, then applied left rudder, but noticed a lot of pressure on the rudder, as though the right engine had lost power. He considered retracting the gear and flaps for a go-around, but realized there was no time remaining, "so I determined to fly the airplane," he told investigators. He therefore intentionally ditched in the water, managing to raise the flaps but not the gear before impact.

FAA inspectors told the NTSB said they were unable to find a reason for the suspected loss of engine power.

Experience Doth Not a Proficient Pilot Make

The training exercises used to develop proficiency in a multi-engine airplane involve the operation of several systems; engine controls, wing flaps, flight controls, and landing gear. The latter is sometimes taken for granted, and failure to accomplish the most basic of all checklists—GUMPS—after a period of intensive training can result in considerable damage and/or embarrassment, as these pilots discovered.

Substantial damage was inflicted on a Cessna 320 at Carlisle, Arkansas, during a gear-up landing that occurred despite the presence of two experienced pilots in the front seats.

In the left seat was a flight instructor with 5,900 hours and an instrument rating, but no multi-engine rating. He was being given multi-engine training by the right-seat pilot, a flight instructor with 2,480 total hours and 355 multi-engine hours. Time in make and model was low for both pilots— seven hours for the left seat, eight hours for the right.

They had departed Little Rock and had done airwork, including several different single-engine exercises, alternating the simulated failed engines and cycling the landing gear up and down several times during these maneuvers. Upon arrival at Carlisle, the left seat pilot said he believes he mistakenly moved the gear switch from the "Up" to the "Neutral" position, instead of "Down." In addition, neither pilot checked the gear indicator lights.

As the propellers struck the runway in the landing flare, the right-seat instructor put the switch in the down position, but this had no effect. The instructor suggested to investigators that the accident might have been avoided by not setting up a prior situation where "a gear warning horn was constantly blowing" during the training sequence.

From Bad to Worse

Perhaps it's because we depend on them so completely, maybe it's due to their outstanding reliability; whatever, some pilots seem to think that airplane engines can do no wrong, and that the occasional glitches—rough running, starting difficulty, etc.—will somehow cure themselves.

But such is hardly ever the case. Airplane engines are nothing more, nothing less than mechanical devices, subject to mechanical problems which seldom, if ever, get better without being fixed. The pilot who encounters engine difficulties, who is provided ample warning of trouble ahead, and who presses on in the hope that things will get better does not exhibit a high level of proficiency. If at first you don't succeed, *don't* try again until you've fixed the problem.

Here's a situation in which a Piper Aztec crashed following a series of engine failures during a series of takeoff attempts. The pilot may have compounded his problems by inadvertently feathering the propeller on his only remaining engine.

The scene of the accident was Runway 16L at Fort Worth's Meacham Field. Tower controllers said that the Aztec had made two previous takeoff attempts, but aborted each due to failure of the left engine. After each attempt, the pilot was able to restart the engine and taxi back for another try.

On his third attempt, the Aztec became airborne, but the left engine failed shortly after liftoff. Tower personnel said the aircraft never climbed above 60 feet during this attempt.

The Aztec entered a descending steep left turn which continued until the airplane crashed in a field on the airport property. The pilot escaped unharmed.

Investigators examined the Aztec and found the right engine's propeller was feathered at impact. They also found water and other contaminants throughout the fuel system. Contaminants were found in the left engine fuel components, which investigators believe may have led to its failure.

Advice is Free—But the Cost May Be High

FAR 91.3 charges a pilot with responsibility for the safe operation of his airplane, and also gives him final authority to exercise that responsibility. And who should know better what to do than the person at the controls? But on occasion, a pilot permits someone else to invade his province of knowledge, responsibility and authority.

Extension of the landing gear during a single-engine go-around immediately preceded a roll-over into the ground by a Cessna 310 at Stapleton Airport in Denver, Colorado; the two persons aboard died in the crash and ensuing fire.

The NTSB report said the plane was arriving from Tulsa, Oklahoma, and had been cleared to land while on a right downwind to Runway 8L, when the pilot reported he had lost his right engine. He immediately started a right turn, as if to angle toward Runway 8R, but a Boeing 727 was in position on that runway; the controller pointed out the conflict, and also noted that the Cessna's landing gear was not extended.

The pilot began a go-around. Meanwhile, the 727 cleared the runway, and controllers now cleared the Cessna to make a right turn for another approach to either 8R or 8L, at the pilot's discretion. The controller advised, "Just continue around and lower the landing gear."

According to post-accident evidence, the twin was about halfway through its turn (roughly on the downwind again) when, just after the controller's instruction (suggestion?), the landing gear came down. Immediately thereafter, the twin rolled to the right and descended into the ground.

Investigators found evidence that the right propeller had been feathered prior to impact. The landing gear was down and locked, and wing flaps were at 15 degrees.

Investigators also found that almost every system in the right engine had been capable of operation prior to impact, but that the engine-driven fuel pump was out of limits (on the high side) and erratic when put on a test bench.

The pilot had a commercial license and about 900 total hours. However, he had obtained his multi-engine rating only about 11 months previously, and had logged about 67 hours of twin time, mostly in the 310. Prior to that, and for most of his total flying hours, he had flown a Mooney M20G.

During interviews with the two controllers on duty in the tower, the NTSB investigator determined that neither had a pilot's license, and neither was aware of the special concerns of multi-engine pilots about V_{mc} and the concurrent hazards of turning into the dead engine and lowering the landing gear at low airspeeds.

Ready, Set, Go

Making certain that an airplane is ready for flight is an all-encompassing activity, the responsibility for which is placed on pilots by FAR 91.103, to wit: "Each pilot in command shall, before beginning a flight, become familiar with all available information concerning that flight." There's more, but the rule-writers could have stopped right there and the point would have been made adequately.

Weather plays a big part in preflight preparation, as does aircraft performance with respect to runway length and obstacles to be cleared. Perhaps an equal-value consideration is that of aircraft loading; performance charts and flight characteristics are based on load configurations that do not exceed the limits of weight or c.g. location—anything else elevates you to test pilot status.

Finally, there's the matter of the pilot's ability to handle any abnormal situation that might present itself during the flight...by any other name, that's *pilot proficiency*. In our final example, something very unusual happened immediately before or after the Queen Air lifted off; the most likely explanation was a fire in the right engine, followed by a violent roll in that direction.

Pilots can't ordinarily be held responsible for equipment failures like this, but Rule Number One—fly the airplane—seems to be applicable in this case. There was enough runway to contain a rejected takeoff, and the roll toward the presumed failed engine may have been preventable. In any event, a crash landing straight ahead would have been better than what happened.

Almost forgot—you should also know that this Queen Air was nearly 700 pounds over its allowable takeoff weight, and the c.g. was at or slightly behind the aft limit.

> All six people aboard the Queen Air died when the twin crashed during takeoff from the Southwest Georgia Regional Airport at Albany.
>
> The crash came as the 43-year-old pilot was attempting to depart on a flight to Akron, Ohio. The pilot had several thousand hours of flight time and was well experienced in the accident airplane, having flown it exclusively for several months prior to the mishap.
>
> Witnesses on the ground, including tower controllers, said they saw the Queen Air lift off Runway 34 and roll to the right. The right wingtip then caught the runway and the Queen Air burst into flames, sliding on its back into a grassy area off the right side of the runway.
>
> Investigators located two other witnesses who gave different accounts of the accident. One witness, a pilot flying over the field at the time, said he saw flames coming from the right wing before impact. The other witness, who was located at a nearby factory, also said he saw flames coming from the right wing before the Queen Air hit.
>
> Preliminary examination of the engines and their components disclosed no catastrophic failures. However, the engines have been shipped to Lycoming for further examination and testing. It should be noted that the Queen Air has a history of exhaust system failures that led to in-flight fires and separation of the wing. However, an airworthiness directive calling for 100-hour inspections of the engines, exhaust, wiring, and plumbing was supposed to "prevent or reduce the possibility of in-flight fires."

In Closing

To paraphrase an aviation bromide, "a superior pilot (one who possesses outstanding skill and judgement) uses his outstanding judgement to keep him out of situations in which his outstanding skill is required." The same might be said for pilot proficiency, and in particular, for those flying multi-engine airplanes.

Given the fact that the most critical phase of flight is the takeoff, the proficient multi-engine pilot never takes the runway unless his airplane is ready, unless *he* is ready, and unless he has convinced himself that "this is the one where the engine quits at lift-off," and is fully prepared to *fly the airplane*, no matter what.

Emergency Procedures

Aviators begin to develop an emergency philosophy from the very first training session. As a matter of fact, a person who peruses aviation publications would have to conclude that, based on the number of articles dealing with emergency procedures and accidents, aviation is rife with hazardous situations.

Not quite true, as we all know; nevertheless, we do put ourselves at risk every time we slip the surly bonds of earth. It's the way we manage the risk that makes the difference, and effective risk management is certainly one of the hallmarks of a highly proficient pilot.

There's no panacea for emergencies in the air, no single procedure that can be brought to bear every time; but by reviewing and discussing some of the circumstances experienced by others, we can increase our own understanding and ability to deal with abnormal situations as they occur.

Defining an Emergency

Because there are few reported cases on the books involving disputes over invoking the emergency doctrine, it is difficult to provide criteria for determining what constitutes a legitimate emergency. As a general rule, the criteria should simply be that in the subjective mind of the pilot an immediate deviation from the regulations was required in the interest of safety due to an emergency not of his own making.

Inflight fires are easy, but how about deviation around weather, deviation from assigned altitudes, and deviation from ATC clearances? These would have to be tested by the general standard of the requirement for immediate action for the safety of the flight. Deviations from assigned routes or vectors for weather avoidance may not pass muster if the weather was forecast and the pilot elected to go anyway. If, on the other hand, the weather was not forecast, and not available from Flight Watch, Flight Service, ATIS, or some other in-flight source, then a good case could be made for an emergency "not of one's own making."

With the current abundance of real-time weather information, it is difficult to imagine a scenario where a truly unexpected thunderstorm appears dead ahead without some advance notice.

FAR 91.123(b) prohibits operating an aircraft contrary to an ATC clearance except in an emergency, and a June, 1988, U.S. Court of Appeals case provides some insight. In the case, Borden vs. FAA, the court discusses the general nature of the requirement to adhere to ATC clearances, but ends its opinion by upholding a violation for taxiing across an active runway.

Pilot Borden had landed at Lambert Field, St. Louis, on Runway 24 and was given taxi clearance to his destination with an instruction to "hold short of Runway 30". During the taxi, the controller told Borden to make a "left turn right there," which Borden took to mean he was now cleared all the way via the next left turn. Unfortunately the left turn took Borden across Runway 30, on which another aircraft was taking off approximately 4,000 feet away.

Borden unsuccessfully argued that the phrase "that left turn right there" was an amended clearance. The FAA argued that it was merely "informational" and thus not a clearance at all.

In its wisdom, the court of appeals held that the airman has a duty not to proceed without first clarifying any possibly ambiguous instructions or clearances. In its opinion the court said, "The lesson to be learned may be simply that, even in the face of confusing or inadequate instructions from the control tower, the pilot must, if he can, assure the public safety by requesting clarification before he proceeds." In another words, even if ATC goofs, if that goof is correctable by the PIC, the pilot is still held accountable—at least by this particular court.

The Pilot's Emergency Authority

A recent Administrative Law Judge's decision dismissing an FAA Order suspending an airman's certificate offers some interesting insight as to the extent to which a pilot may rely upon emergency authority when deviating from ATC clearances.

As background, a young insurance executive had recently purchased a new Piper Malibu. Although fully equipped, it did not have copilot instruments. The pilot had obtained his private certificate and instrument ratings from FAA-approved flight schools, but had logged less than 400 hours total time and only 20 of instrument time.

He filed an IFR flight plan from an east coast airport to Olathe, Kansas. Although he was current both with regard to his Flight Review and IFR currency, the purpose of this trip was to attend a Piper Malibu clinic and for an updated Flight Review.

The weather at the departure airport was at or just below the localizer-only landing minimums when the pilot was given his clearance to depart Runway 10 with a further clearance after departure to turn right to a heading of 290 degrees and climb to and maintain 2,000 feet.

After a proper clearance readback the pilot was cleared for takeoff. He later testified that shortly after lift-off he entered instrument conditions. Up to this point the flight was routine, but it quickly turned to worms.

Hand flying the aircraft, the pilot retracted the gear and throttled back to climb power. He contacted departure control when at 500 feet. Departure acknowledged radar contact and repeated the clearance to turn right to a heading of 290 and maintain 2,000 feet. The pilot acknowledged the departure clearance and shortly thereafter noticed that his attitude indicator showed him to be in a steep right descending turn, while his turn-and-bank and HSI indicated a wings-level climb.

In attempting to resolve this disparate attitude information, particularly when the attitude indicator was not equipped with a failure warning flag, the pilot delayed his right turn and inadvertently climbed through his assigned altitude to 2,800 feet. When queried by the controller as to his heading and altitude, the pilot responded in a voice several octaves above his normal frequency that he was "all screwed up." There followed approximately three minutes during which the pilot informed the controller that "I'm in trouble." The controller ignored the indirect plea for help and simply berated the pilot for not returning to his assigned altitude. During this period the Mode C readout reached a maximum of 2,800 feet for an approximate 800 foot deviation.

Ironically, once the pilot returned to 2,000 feet he was immediately cleared to 3,000 feet. By this time, he had resolved the attitude dilemma and was relying solely on the turn needle, altimeter, VSI and HSI.

The Malibu was then handed off to a different departure controller who cleared him to his requested cruising altitude. During this further climb he broke into the clear at approximately 4,000 feet. Within minutes the attitude indicator realigned itself and the remainder of flight to Olathe was in VFR conditions and uneventful.

The pilot had the attitude indicator and vacuum system inspected in Olathe. Other than some minor contaminants found in the vacuum lines, no other discrepancies were found that would have affected the proper operation of the instrument.

Shortly after this incident the pilot received a letter of investigation from his local FSDO, to which he responded without hesitation. He stated that the failed attitude indicator had so preoccupied his attention that he inadvertently climbed through his assigned altitude. He had thus exercised his emergency authority pursuant to FAR 91.3(b).

Next the pilot received a formal letter of investigation for an enforcement action. He was invited to discuss the matter with a representative of the FAA's Regional Counsel. Having been led to believe that this was just one of those friendly fireside chats, the pilot was surprised to be confronted with a meeting that could be more accurately described as an inquisition with both the FSDO representative and the attorney furiously taking notes on exactly what the pilot had to say in his defense.

FAA was not satisfied with the pilot's version of the incident. A formal suspension for a period of 30 days was issued for violation of FAR 91.13 for careless operation and a violation of FAR 91.123(a) for deviating from an ATC clearance.

At the formal hearing before an Administrative Law Judge, the FAA rested its case after introducing the transcript of communications and a tape recording of the communications in which the pilot acknowledged that he had violated the altitude clearance.

Under the rules for such hearings, and the precedent by which Administrative Law Judges determine who has the burden of proof, the burden of defense then shifted to the airman to prove that he in fact had a legitimate emergency and that the emergency was not of his own making.

The most persuasive evidence of course, was the pilot's very moving testimony as to the seriousness of losing his primary attitude indicator moments after liftoff and in close proximity to the ground. This testimony, of course, was corroborated quite emphatically by the rather excited communications on the tape recording.

In further support of the pilot's position, the definition of "emergency" in the *Airman's Information Manual* was introduced. The

AIM defines an emergency as being any situation of "distress or urgency." The pilot also asked the judge to take judicial notice that the FAA, by its own regulations pertaining to the requirements for obtaining an instrument rating, (namely 61.65(c)(5) lists as a simulated emergency any instrument malfunction. It was also argued that it was all the more an emergency since the flight test guide for an instrument rating does not even require recovery from unusual attitudes following the loss of an artificial horizon.

The pilot also referred to Webster's definition of emergency as being "a sudden unexpected happening, specifically a perplexing contingency or complication of circumstances or a sudden or unexpected occasion for action, exigency or pressing necessity."

FAA argued that since the pilot never declared an emergency, no emergency in fact existed and that by inference the loss of the attitude indicator was a fabrication used in an attempt to explain away the altitude violation. This put at issue the credibility of the witness, which was a matter solely for the Administrative Law Judge to examine and rule upon.

In furtherance of the pilot's defense, those sections of the ATC Controller's Manual which govern the controller's duties and responsibilities were put in evidence. In particular, Section 9 of the manual requires a controller who may be in doubt as to a particular situation to treat it as an emergency and provide the pilot with every available assistance. Oddly enough, the Administrator chose to try this case without the live testimony of the controller and thus had to rely on the controller's supervisor for evidence as to whether or not the controller performed properly and in accordance with the manual during the course of this undeclared emergency. The ATC Supervisor testified that, when he listened to the tape, he could not detect any indications of distress or urgency and that the mere use of the words "I'm all screwed up" and "I'm in trouble" did not indicate any problems. He further testified that, in his view, the pilot's declaration that "I'm in trouble" meant to the supervisor that the pilot simply was acknowledging that he was in trouble with the FAA for violating the altitude restrictions.

The Administrator also put on an avionics expert who admitted that, although he was unfamiliar with the Malibu and its systems and had not examined any of the parts or components of the vacuum system or the attitude indicator, that he knew of no reason for such a system to fail under the circumstances described by the pilot. On cross examination, however, he readily acknowledged that transient instrument failures are commonplace in aviation. The mere fact that no physical evidence was found which would corroborate a malfunction does not disprove that a malfunction, although temporary or transient in nature, did indeed take place.

The Administrator's witnesses also acknowledged that although there was a technical violation of the altitude clearance, no other aircraft were affected with regard to separation standards, as the controllers of the adjacent sectors were alerted to the situation and rearranged any potential conflicting aircraft accordingly.

After deliberating on the evidence, the Administrative Law Judge found that the pilot's testimony was credible and that indeed an emergency condition existed which justified the pilot's deviation from his altitude clearance. He found this even though the pilot didn't formally declare an emergency by the use of the words "emergency," or "mayday." Therefore, the judge dismissed the Administrator's Order of Suspension.

In addition to the good news of having the Order of Suspension dismissed, the pilot may even be reimbursed for his attorney's fees pursuant to the newly implemented rules under the Equal Access to Justice Act of 1980.

One might think that the ATC system would normally respond to a situation as described above by providing the pilot having any kind of problem with affirmative and immediate assistance. But the lesson to be learned from this particular case is that if there is any doubt in mind of a pilot, resolve that doubt by declaring an emergency to assure that those requirements of the ATC Manual are adhered to by the controller. Without the formal declaration of an emergency, the matter is left to the subjective determination of the controller as to whether or not an emergency exists.

There was a time where you could believe in the statement, "I'm from the FAA and I'm here to help you become a safer pilot." Those days are history. Any discussions with FAA representatives, whether by telephone, in writing or at "informal conferences," are not for the purpose of providing pilots with counsel and guidance to become safer users of the airspace system. They are for the purpose of gathering evidence for use against the pilot if and when an enforcement action is instituted.

Another thing this particular pilot learned is that general aviation aircraft are not required to have failure indicators for flight instruments such as are required in transport category aircraft. An attitude indicator failure can be quite insidious. When it occurs within a few hundred feet of the ground only a few seconds are available to detect and correct the situation.

And what did this pilot do as a result of his experience? Well, at least one Malibu now flying has a newly installed set of copilot flight instruments with a dual vacuum system.

When You Need Help, Ask

In many cases, a pilot doesn't have to deal with the problem all by himself; there's plenty of help available for the asking, but it goes begging if the need is not communicated. One of the most dramatic examples of this occurred in January of 1990, when a South American airliner crashed while approaching JFK Airport.

The NTSB indicated that the pilots of Avianca Flight 052 never used the proper terminology for alerting ATC that they had a critical fuel situation.

The 707 was en route to New York's John F. Kennedy International Airport from Medellin, Colombia. At the time, weather associated with a deep surface low over Lake Huron was causing extensive ground and in-flight air traffic delays along the East Coast. The 707 was put into holding patterns three times for a total of 77 minutes. During the last hold over the CAMRN Intersection, 35 miles south of JFK, the crew told ATC they could hold only five minutes longer and did not have enough fuel to proceed to their alternate, which was Boston. The 707 was one of four aircraft being held over the intersection.

The Avianca crew was promptly cleared for the ILS approach to JFK's Runway 22L. They missed the approach, however, and subsequently told both Kennedy Tower and the New York Tracon that they were "running out of fuel." Nevertheless, the aircraft was vectored 20 miles to the northeast of the airport for sequencing to land behind three other aircraft. The 707 was 15 miles from the outer marker for the ILS 22L approach when the crew reported losing two engines. It was their last transmission. The 707 crashed at Cove Neck on Long Island.

At no time did the Avianca crew state that they had "minimum fuel" nor did they declare an emergency. Although some of their statements were explicit, such as when they reported "running out of fuel," the crew never got the point across to ATC that they had an emergency.

Though the NTSB cautioned that it's too early to determine whether communication or ATC coordination problems caused the Avianca accident, it recommended that pilots know and use standard phraseology and that controllers be alert to statements, especially from foreign pilots, that may indicate an emergency situation and a need for special assistance.

"Monday morning quarterbacks" might suggest that the Avianca captain—knowing he was nearly out of fuel—should have continued to a landing on that first approach, even in the face of below-minimums weather and with no landing clearance. But that's a direct violation of Federal Aviation Regulations, and we all know that the rules must be followed, come hell or high water...or must they?

One of the least used provisions of the Federal Aviation Regulations is that portion of FAR 91.3 that permits the pilot in command to deviate from the operating rules, "in an emergency requiring immediate action...to the extent required to meet that emergency."

This broad authority gives any pilot the subjective right to determine a) whether or not an emergency exists, and b) whether or not immediate deviation is required for safety.

The reasons why this provision is underused are not altogether clear; however, two thoughts come to mind. The first is that the macho image generally associated with being a pilot carries with it some suggestion of infallibility, and a declaration of an emergency is, in that scheme of things, a virtual admission of incompetence. Thus, it might be a fear of being humiliated by one's peers.

The second, and perhaps more likely reason, is that by declaring an emergency an investigation will ensue and a possible certificate action might follow.

Whatever the reasons for not declaring an emergency, there have been many instances where hindsight suggests the crew might have been much better off if they had declared one.

An example involved the crew of a Boeing 737. On departure from Newark, smoke was noted in the forward lavatory. The crew advised Newark Departure Control, New York Center, Boston Center, and Boston Approach Control of the situation, but never declared an emergency nor sought any deviation from previously issued clearances. The smoke continued unabated throughout the flight, much to the consternation of the passengers, yet the crew continued undaunted.

With the lessons learned from the tragic Air Canada lavatory fire several years ago, hindsight suggests that this crew might have been treading on thin ice by not treating the smoking bathroom as an emergency. They were lucky.

Another example of failing to declare an emergency involved a low-time VFR pilot. He was attempting a single-engine eastbound crossing of the Adirondack Mountains into Burlington, Vermont. In "VFR flight not recommended" weather, he climbed up through a sucker hole only to be caught between towering cumulo-nimbus clouds in all quadrants. He continued pressing eastward in IMC at various altitudes and attitudes (including inverted).

He finally raised Burlington Approach Control on the radio and asked for his position. Burlington picked up his transponder and suggested a turn to the south to avoid a solid line of showers. Instead, he turned north toward the line and descended in IMC, breaking out at 1500 feet in heavy rain. He landed on a highway with a 40 to 50 knot tailwind and totaled the aircraft. A reconstruction of the descent profile indicated several near misses with mountain peaks.

In both of these cases, the pilots never declared an emergency. The Boeing pilots did not have to, because they did not deviate or seek to deviate from any regulation.

But the VFR pilot was already busting the regs all over the place, i.e. attempting VFR flight in IFR conditions, flying in instrument conditions without an IFR rating and without an IFR clearance, without recent IFR experience, without declaring an emergency, etc.

Interesting, these pilots actually never had to use the word "emergency" in order to be handled as one. In fact, it is not a requirement that an emergency be "declared" in order to have the option of deviating from any rule or clearance provided by FAR 91.3. For example, an electrical fire or failure which required an immediate shutting down of all electrical systems would preclude any "declaration" of an emergency.

Under the requirements of the FAA controller operating manual, if there is any doubt as to the status of any aircraft, that aircraft is to be handled as an emergency.

A good example is that of a low time private pilot who lost his only attitude indicator shortly after lifting off while in the clouds. ATC had cleared him to climb to and maintain 2,000 feet, but he became so concerned with his attitude indicator he missed the level off and continued to various altitudes between 2500 and 2900 feet before settling down and returning to 2000.

The FAA argued that this was not an emergency as none had been declared, and thus the pilot could not advantage himself of FAR 91.3. The Administrative Law Judge found that the communications from the pilot clearly indicated that the pilot was in distress and in need of assistance, which should have been sufficient to alert the controller to the fact that this was an emergency situation.

On the other side of this coin, the controller manual permitted the smoking Boeing 737 to be given priority handling even though no emergency was declared.

No certificate actions were taken in either of these cases; but it is very important to note that FAR 91.3 does not insulate the pilot who deviates from the operating regulations when the emergency is one of his own making.

With a forecast of late afternoon thunderstorms en route and marginal VFR conditions, with VFR flight not recommended, our intrepid Adirondack aviator with 80 hours total time, and 10 hours in make and model, might be said to have created his own problems by attempting a VFR flight in mountainous terrain with such a pessimistic forecast.

The Boeing 737 drivers—if they required a deviation on approach to Boston—may have also created their own emergency by not landing at the nearest suitable airport upon discovering the inflight smoke, rather than taking a chance that it would escalate from smoke to uncontrolled fire during the 45 minute flight to Boston.

Some readers may recall the tragic Pan Am cargo flight which, in the vicinity of Montreal en route to Europe, had a cargo fire of unknown origin and intensity. The crew, blindly adhering to the company's request to deviate to Boston, almost made it, crashing just short of runway 22L when they were overcome by smoke and toxic fumes. Next to the loss of a primary flight control or structural failure, few would disagree that an inflight fire is high on the top-ten risk list, and usually warrants an immediate landing.

Sound Off

If you are approaching emergency conditions, then say it: *Emergency!* Running out of gas *is* an emergency. Even if the tanks are not yet dry, but you are plodding ahead, you are approaching an emergency condition. Might as well declare it now.

Say it loud and clear—"I am an emergency." Or, at least—"I will be an emergency when I get to Metropolis." Tell them you are running short of fuel, but make sure you tell them just how short. Even if you don't know the best alternate short of Metropolis, those guys on the ground will know. Let them know you have a problem.

They still don't respond? Not likely; but if in doubt, squawk them a 7700 on your transponder. Bet you get a quick reply then. If needed, try transmitting "pan, pan, pan" or even three "mayday" calls. If there's a lot of congestion on the comm frequency and you can't get a word in edgewise, why not switch to your own private channel? Give them a call on 121.5 MHz. That ought to get you a quick reply.

Flight 052, an old Boeing 707, plowed into the hills of Long Island out of fuel. And, apparently, nobody really understood that the crew had a fuel problem—at least not a real "dry-tank" fuel problem.

In such a situation, though, don't be quick to blame the controllers. They are often overly busy and should not be expected to read between the lines when a pilot hints about a low fuel condition. It's up to the pilot to tell them—loud and clear—that there's a problem.

Not Their Job

Don't count on controllers also being pilots and knowing what you're hinting about. There's no requirement in ATC for a pilot's ticket. Controllers expect that you know how to handle your airplane, and how to manage fuel vs. range. They expect that you will arrive with a safe amount of petrol...*unless* you tell them how low you really are.

If you don't have enough fuel to make a go-around, better let them know ahead of time. If you have enough for only one short go-around, let them know that, also. If you can't accept standard handling and traffic procedures, then it's likely you have an emergency.

Don't count on controllers being perfect. They can make mistakes, too. Maybe the one you just talked to doesn't know that previous sector controllers have already given you several en route holds, re-routings, or unfavorable altitude or airspeed changes. Maybe he doesn't comprehend that ATC delays have already eaten up all of your planned reserve, and more.

It looks like Avianca got at least three en route holds, for a total of at least 85 minutes. The pilot would have been held even longer, except he finally got word through that he was running a little low on fuel. One of the crew members told ATC, "I think we need priority," and the 707 was cleared for the approach.

The phrase "minimum fuel" was added a few years ago to the minimum fuel Pilot/Controller Glossary in the Airman's Information Manual after a several airplanes had fuel close-calls. When a pilot says "minimum fuel," the controller is alerted that little or no delay can be tolerated when the aircraft reaches its destination. "This is not an emergency situation," AIM says, "but merely indicates an emergency situation is possible should any undue delay occur."

_In order to provide priority handling, controllers have to hear the pilot
utter the magic word: emergency._

That's a good way of letting ATC know that things might become
sticky. But saying "minimum fuel" is a little dangerous if it really
means you will be running on fumes if you don't get an immediate
straight-in and that you don't really think you have enough for that
possible missed approach. If this is the case, you need "priority"
handling. Better make sure that the controllers understand.

Take Command

Why not just declare an emergency? If you get special handling and
ripple the flow of other traffic, you may have to fill out all of the FAA
paperwork, anyway. Either way, you may get a flight violation. But
that's better than crashing, out of gas, just because the controller
didn't quite understand just how serious your problem really was.

I still recall the senseless death of a friend in a sailplane almost 20
years ago. He reported to the tower on downwind and was cleared to
land. Then, abeam the landing end of the runway, the controller
asked if he could do a 360-degree turn on downwind, because there
was a jet on long final approach. My friend and his glider instructor
consented, and set themselves up for a real emergency. They got too
low during the orbit and spun in trying to tighten the turn.

Don't blame it on the controller. He wasn't a pilot. He didn't know that gliders can't extend landing patterns that much. Blame it on the pilots. They needed priority and didn't ask for it. They didn't insist on landing *right now*.

As pilot-in-command, you don't have to accept dumb requests like this glider pilot did. You don't have to plod ahead toward Metropolis or sit forever in a racetrack hold, like Avianca apparently did. Exercise your PIC authority, if need be. Do what is necessary to assure a safe arrival. If your problem is primarily a lack of understanding by the guy on the ground, make him understand! Bite the bullet. Declare an emergency. Get it on the ground in one piece. Don't leave unsuspecting passengers in bloody shambles just because you were afraid to say the magic word.

I was lucky to have walked away from an incident several years ago: a sudden engine failure in an underpowered two-engine amphibian. Broken crankshaft and an unfeatherable propeller—no climb or level-flight performance—just a gentle descent on the still-operating left engine. No, I didn't declare an emergency. I just told the tower that I had lost one of the two motors, and they automatically gave me priority and rolled the crash/fire truck. But they knew my voice and recognized the airplane. They had only light traffic. It was good VMC.

But, suppose that dead engine had caught fire from oil leaking from the cracked crankcase. Suppose we had had to make a nonstandard pattern to land on an off-duty runway or the midfield grass. Suppose the landing had not been successful, and we had rolled up into a flaming ball. Where was the additional crash, fire and medical support? Had I just said the magic word—"emergency"—the whole county contingent of special vehicles would have been rolling toward the landing area.

"Can't Do it Now."

Some of the Avianca passengers were fortunate. Rescuers reacted quickly, and there was no fire. Many lives were saved that might have been lost. Many volunteers appeared to assist. But, it looks like the controllers didn't even know the 707 was going to run out of gas. If the aircraft had made it to the runway on the first attempt, probably nobody would have ever known just how close it had been. But, the aircraft didn't make it. The pilot never declared an emergency.

Sure, all the facts aren't in yet. As this volume went to press, NTSB was still many months away from issuing its findings, and there's been some talk about the accuracy of the 707's fuel gauges. But you can be sure the investigators will spend a lot of time studying the communications.

Here's a preliminary transcript of the transmissions between Avianca 052 and New York Center after the flight held for 29 minutes at a fix just south of JFK International and just before it was turned over to approach control for an immediate ILS into Kennedy:

Avianca: "I think we need priority."

Center: "Roger. How long can you hold and what is your alternate?"

Avianca: "We'll be able to hold about five minutes, and that's all we can do."

Center: "Roger. What is your alternate?"

Avianca: "It's Boston, but it's full of traffic, I think."

Center: "Say again your alternate."

Avianca: "It was Boston, but we can't do it now. We will run out of fuel now."

Center: "Avianca 052, cleared to the Kennedy airport via heading zero four zero, maintain one one thousand, speed one eight zero."

Avianca 052 tried the ILS but had to execute a missed approach. The reported weather was an indefinite 200-foot ceiling and 1/4-mile visibility in light drizzle and fog. A wind shear alert had been issued.

Preliminary review of the cockpit voice recorder tape shows that a ground proximity warning sounded. Apparently, all four engines quit from fuel starvation during the vectoring for a second approach. And, still, it appears that nobody on the ground understood that Avianca was running on fumes the whole time.

The Book

There are some recommended procedures for handling this sort of misunderstanding between flight and ground personnel. Like the alerting phrase, "minimum fuel," they're in the AIM.

My copy is a commercial soft-back (yep, out of date) that includes a lot of the FARs, NTSB stuff and a Customs guide, in addition to the AIM. (I should review a current copy every year, but I haven't been. Bet'cha most of you haven't reviewed the AIM recently, either— probably not since the last time you were getting ready for an FAA written exam.)

Boy, there's a wealth of good stuff in the AIM, and it's all written in plain English. You don't have to be a lawyer to understand it. It's much better than the language of the FARs.

Let's take a look at some passages from the AIM. From the foreword: "This Manual is designed to provide airmen with basic flight information and ATC procedures for use in the National Airspace System (NAS) of the United States...contains the fundamentals required in order to fly in the U.S. NAS. It also contains items of interest concerning...factors affecting flight safety."

Here's more on minimum fuel: "Advise ATC of your minimum fuel status when your fuel supply has reached a state where, upon reaching destination, you cannot accept any undue delay. Be aware this is not an emergency situation but merely an advisory that indicates an emergency situation is possible should any undue delay occur. Be aware a minimum fuel advisory does not imply a need for traffic priority. If the remaining usable fuel supply suggests the need for traffic priority to ensure a safe landing, you should declare an emergency because of low fuel and report fuel remaining in minutes."

How many of you really knew that a call of "minimum fuel" would not get some priority? I didn't know that until I re-read my AIM. Did you really understand that you should declare an emergency if you need traffic priority because of low fuel?

Let's read some more from AIM, which restates the pilot's golden rule, FAR 91.3: "The pilot in command of an aircraft is directly responsible for and is the final authority in an emergency as to the operation of that aircraft. In an emergency requiring immediate action, the PIC may deviate from any rule...to the extent required to meet that emergency."

Also from the AIM: "An emergency can be either a *distress* or *urgency* condition as defined in the Pilot/Controller Glossary. Some [pilots] are reluctant to report an urgency condition when they encounter situations which may not be immediately perilous but are potentially catastrophic. An aircraft is in at least an urgency condition the moment the pilot becomes doubtful about position, fuel endurance, weather or any other condition that could adversely affect flight safety. This is the time to ask for help, not after the situation has developed into a distress condition."

Your Job

Now, that is pretty specific. It's your job to announce the impending crisis. It's your responsibility to get that plane on the ground safely. Don't lay it on the controller if you haven't made your distress known.

For a different type of emergency, here are some AIM tips on how VFR pilots getting radar service can avoid being vectored into IMC:

"If continued flight in VFR conditions is not possible, the non-instrument-rated pilot should so advise the controller and, indicating the lack of an instrument rating, declare a distress condition."

Now, that means you are hollering "emergency," unless a different direction or altitude would keep you VFR. Those FAA prosecuting attorneys will have a field day with you, but it's better than spatial disorientation in the clouds and a spin into a bean field.

If both you and the airplane are equipped and current for IFR, better immediately request an IFR clearance before you accept vectors into IMC.

The AIM also says: "When a distress or urgency condition is encountered, the pilot...should squawk 7700." That's right, you don't have to have an engine on fire before you twist the transponder knobs to the emergency squawk. The AIM will tell you all about using "pan," "mayday" and 121.5 MHz. No point in copying all those AIM words here; open the book and read it yourself. Whether you are a student pilot or an ATP, you just gotta know this stuff. I've been through stacks of accident reports involving very experienced pilots who crashed without word one or an emergency squawk to anyone...and often after wandering aimlessly for many minutes.

How to Ask

You are paying the bill for those guys on the ground, so get your money's worth. If you need help, ask for it. But know how to ask.

There are three pertinent definitions in the AIM's Pilot/Controller Glossary: *"emergency*—a distress or an urgency condition; *urgency*—a condition of being concerned about safety and of requiring timely but not immediate assistance, a potential distress condition; and *distress*—a condition of being threatened by serious and/or imminent danger and of requiring immediate assistance."

The words "pan, pan" are the internationally recognized signal of an urgency. "Mayday" is the distress signal.

Once all the evidence has been collected and studied, it may turn out that Avianca 052 will be a tragically relevant example of what can happen when a pilot doesn't know or doesn't use the proper procedures and doesn't communicate effectively with controllers. It happens in general aviation all the time. Few pilots ever scream "emergency," let alone "pan" or "mayday" when they should.

So, quit worrying so much about the FAA's enforcement policy. If you find yourself in trouble, if you need some help, if you need priority, *tell somebody*—and use the right words, so there's no misunderstanding. (Maybe the FAA will pull some of their people off the bothersome ramp checks and put them to work digging into the real cause behind some of the emergency situations. Meanwhile, I'm on my way to the airport to buy a current copy of the AIM. It will be money well spent, especially if the latest changes to Part 91 and other FARs are included.)

Proficient Pilots Prefer Proper Procedures

Fuel emergencies generally fall into one of two categories; fuel starvation or fuel exhaustion. In the first, there is simply no fuel available to the engine(s), and the most common cause is misplaced fuel selectors. Fuel exhaustion, on the other hand, is the situation that exists when every drop of fuel on the aircraft has been consumed. The result is usually the same; a forced landing for a single, or an unscheduled engine-out procedure for a multi-engine pilot.

There are a thousand excuses for running out of gas (virtually none of them justifiable), but an engine failure on an airplane with plenty of fuel on board demonstrates a monumental lack of pilot proficiency. Every checklist in the land includes some sort of reminder to switch to the fuller tank before takeoff or landing, and for good reason, as illustrated by this accident.

No one was injured when a Cherokee Six was force-landed after an apparent case of fuel starvation on approach to its home base at Roanoke, Virginia.

The pilot in command was a 27-year-old commercial pilot with 374 total hours and 46.5 in the Cherokee Six. He told investigators he was asked by the FBO to give two people an airplane ride. The passenger in the right seat was taking lessons at the FBO and had brought his friend from out of town to give him a ride, but the plane normally used for flight lessons was being flown by someone else. The pilot of the Cherokee Six agreed to make the sightseeing flight to Smith Mountain Lake and back.

The outbound trip was unremarkable, and on the return, the commercial pilot allowed the student to fly the plane during the approach. Upon being sequenced behind a Lockheed Jetstar, the commercial pilot cautioned the student to stay high on the approach in order to avoid the jet's wake turbulence.

When they reached the proper point in the approach, it was necessary to pull the power back to idle to descend. The

Every emergency checklist includes a reminder to switch fuel tanks when the engine quits or seems rough. Yet every year, a few pilots plow into the ground just short of the airport, with fuel to spare in a non-selected tank.

pilot said because he and the student were wearing headsets, they didn't hear the engine stop. Upon reaching a low altitude, the commercial pilot attempted to add power and found the engine had quit. At the same time he noted the student pilot pulling back on the yoke, in a manner that would result in a stall. He took over the controls and maneuvered away from some towers before landing the plane across a road.

Investigators found the plane's fuel selector positioned to the left main tank, which was dry. There was fuel in the other tanks. The pilot conceded to investigators that he had gotten involved in talking with the passengers and had forgotten to switch tanks.

More Fuel-Starvation Problems

The simulated emergency is perhaps the most frequently used tool when flight instructors are building their students' proficiency as pilots. A CFI is to be praised for developing innovative techniques to make his simulations as realistic as possible—but not to the extent that safety is seriously compromised. Heed this example of an instructor and his student who escaped injury when their Cessna 152 was forced into an actual emergency landing following a simulated power failure.

> The instructor had 757 total hours, including more than 500 in make and model. He had logged 400 hours as an instructor, including 170 in make and model. His student had a total of 29 hours, all but one of them in the Cessna 152. The two were returning from their practice area when the accident occurred. As the CFI later told investigators, he initiated a simulated engine failure by either pulling the mixture control or turning off the fuel selector—"I can't recall which."
> The exercise began at about 2,200 feet AGL and when the engine couldn't be restarted, the instructor made an emergency landing in a soybean field. The plane nosed over inverted upon landing.
> As the student pilot related events to investigators, he established a 60-knot glide speed at the onset of the simulated engine failure, pulled on carburetor heat and insured that the mixture was in the full rich position. After that, he checked the fuel selector and found it in the "straight up and down" or "off" position. He turned it back on, but the propeller had stopped windmilling during the glide, and the pilots were unable to restart the engine with the starter.

Facing a Forced Landing

In earlier years, it often was a miracle when an engine ran without a hiccup for an entire flight. Pilots learned to accept power outages and forced landings as routine events. Today, engine failures for mechanical reasons beyond the pilot's control are fairly rare, but they do happen. Early detection of the impending failure can go a long way toward saving the day, as can remaining calm and working with all available resources.

A good illustration was provided by the forced landing of a Mooney M20K during an air taxi cargo flight in the Northwest. The pilot was unhurt in what almost wasn't a reportable accident. The Mooney was substantially damaged after it hit an irrigation pipe and some wooden fence posts during the rollout in a stubble field.

In an Emergency, Stay Cool and Fly the Airplane

The pilot, age 29, was an experienced flight instructor, with 4,286 total hours. His experience in the Mooney was limited, however—he had accumulated only 7.5 hours in it, including the accident flight. The journey started at 8:21 a.m. when he departed Salem, Oregon, on an IFR flight plan for Pasco, Washington. In contact with Seattle Center, the Mooney was established in cruise at 11,000 feet with nothing out of the ordinary until 8:45, when the pilot noticed "a slight and irregular engine roughness, similar to detonation."

He tried to stop the apparent detonation, but his efforts were futile. In moments, the manifold pressure had fallen off to 25 inches. Shortly after this, he noticed the oil temperature climbing and the oil pressure falling. Engine failure was imminent, and he called the controller for some help.

Pilot: Seattle Center, Mooney four two niner.

Controller: Four two niner, go ahead.

Pilot: Yah, what's our, ah, current distance from Madras?

Controller: Madras is bearing one two zero degrees at 38 miles.

Pilot: Okay. Well, it's about the same, ah, as The Dalles at this point. Ah, I think we're gonna have to make a beeline for The Dalles at this point. We've lost our turbo and are losing oil pressure.

Controller: Four two niner, say again.

Pilot: Four two niner, we've lost our turbo and ah, ah, our oil pressure is gone at this point, so we're expecting engine failure at any time.

Controller: Ah, four two niner, roger, and ah, I'll have to keep you on that heading for a while to keep you clear of the terrain around Mount Hood and ah, distance now to The Dalles Airport is 32 miles.

Pilot: Four two niner, roger, we're steering direct for The Dalles. We have Mount Hood in sight.

The Mooney was VFR on top, and the pilot wanted to stay that way. The controller relayed The Dalles weather, noting that other aircraft had cancelled IFR near there, "so the weather should be pretty good."

Four minutes after the pilot had announced the imminent engine failure, the power started winding down.

Pilot: Seattle, four two niner, we're losing the engine.

Controller: Four two nine, roger, understand and The Dalles Airport is, ah, 21 miles, bearing 310 magnetic and turn five degrees left, direct to The Dalles.

The controller, in an effort to help, began scanning a chart above his radar scope, looking for a closer airport than The Dalles.

Controller: And four two niner, there is another airport, ah, just south of the town of Dufur, southwest of the town of Dufur. It's a private airport, and looks like, ah, elevation 1,440 feet.

Pilot: Okay, can you give us direct directions to it?

Controller: I don't have it marked on my scope, but it looks like, ah, just interpolating from my overhead map, that it would be, ah, fifteen miles south of The Dalles Airport. And Mooney four two niner, do you have the ground in sight?

Pilot: Yah, we can make a VFR descent, that's no problem. The problem's going to be finding a place to put her down.

Altitude and options were running out. The controller was working hard to try to direct the Mooney toward the small strip he had found on the overhead map.

Controller: Mooney four two niner, that airport should be just about your 12 o'clock position and no more than five or seven miles.

Pilot: Four two niner's looking for it.

Controller: And there's a north-south highway, fairly straight until it gets north of that airport, and then it has a shallow turn to the northeast. If you spot that, let me know.

Pilot: Okay, I think I see it, I'm not real sure.

Controller: Er, roger, and I don't know what condition that airport might be, but there may be some flat ground in that area, if you don't think you can make it to The Dalles.

Pilot: Naw, The Dalles is definitely out. We're still showing 23 DME and I don't know if we'll be able to make this one. We're looking for it.

Controller: Roger, understand.

Pilot: Four two niner, we have a town just off our left. Is that Dufur?

Controller: Affirmative, that should be the town of Dufur. The airport should be southeast of that town.

Pilot: Okay, it appears we should be able to make that.

Controller: Roger, understand. Four two niner, The Dalles radio advises that is a dirt strip and it may be soft.

Pilot: That's okay, it's probably better than my other option.

It may have been better than the other option, but the pilot could not find the strip. The controller kept trying to guide the pilot using the pilot's descriptions of what he saw out the window, but the Mooney was getting lower all the time. The pilot was able to find features which made it look like he was in the vicinity, but after four minutes of looking, he decided to try for a nearby farm field.

Pilot: Four two niner, I sure can't see an airport down there anywhere. I think we're just gonna have to shoot for one of the fields.

Controller: Roger, if you've got a nice big field, that's probably going to be your best bet.

Pilot: Yah, they all look pretty, ah, pretty soft really.

Controller: Yah, four two niner, radar contact is lost and, if you can't let me know when you get on the ground you might try for a telephone from one of the farmhouses nearby.

Pilot: Four two niner, will do.

Controller: I should be able to talk to you on the ground, but I'm not sure.

Pilot: Okay, we've got a field scoped out.

Controller: Four two niner, roger. Good luck.

Controller: Four two niner, The Dalles altimeter is two niner six eight.

Pilot: Four two niner.

No more transmissions came from the Mooney. The pilot had selected a stubble field. He set up a good approach to it and got in. But when he stepped on the brakes, the wet ground let the wheels lock and slide.

The Mooney slid down the field, decelerating slowly. At the far end, almost out of energy, it slid through a light wire fence and into an irrigation pipe. The pilot was uninjured, but the left wing, the right wingtip and right aileron had been damaged in the collision with the fence.

The pilot had spent almost 15 minutes flying the Mooney down from altitude. Coincidentally, he had almost made it to The Dalles, having run out of altitude only two miles short, according to the accident report.

The accident investigation centered on the engine. Initial inspection showed the engine compartment covered with oil, as was the belly of the Mooney. The source of the oil leak, "was not obvious at the accident site," said the investigator.

The engine was disassembled and a hole was found in the No. 4 piston; the spark plugs had misfired due to carbon tracking in the right magneto distributor block.

With the hole burned through the piston, the crankcase became pressurized, forcing the engine oil overboard through the crankcase breather tube, eventually exhausting the supply and stopping the engine.

The pilot's calm approach to the emergency certainly helped to keep the power loss from causing a disaster.

The Problem of the Incomplete Procedure

Engine failures should provoke more from a pilot than trimming for best glide. After trying to restart the engine and getting no response, pilots must commit to a forced landing. This means making sure the engine is *really* dead. Just because it won't respond to the restart procedures doesn't mean that all the horses have died; sometimes one must administer the *coup de grace* to make sure the engine doesn't burst back to life.

During flight training, many pilots go through the motions for engine failures and forced landings, but never really go through the procedures very well. Flight instructors may pull the power and watch as the student points to the fuel selector or pantomimes a mag check, but after that, the set-up for a forced landing rarely includes securing the engine.

An example of what can happen with a "semi-dead" engine took place near Corona, California, when a Cessna 150G crashed. The 45-year-old pilot received minor injuries, but his passenger was seriously injured and the aircraft was substantially damaged.

The pilot, with some 1,385 hours in his logbook and commercial, instrument, and instructor ratings on his certificate, was well qualified for the flight. His logbook showed 850 hours in the Cessna 150.

The flight had departed Lompoc, California, at about 10 a.m., bound for Lake Elsinore. Weather was described as clear skies with ten miles of visibility. Before departing Lompoc, the pilot had the Cessna serviced with 10 gallons of 80 octane avgas. According to the factual report, this gave him a total of 16 gallons of fuel on board at takeoff.

The flight progressed for an hour and 50 minutes when, with only 23 miles to go to reach Elsinore, the engine sputtered and died...fuel starvation.

The pilot later recalled in this accident report that his first action was to trim for a 70 mph glide. He then started looking for a place to set it down. An empty mobile home lot that was his first choice turned out to be studded with powerline poles. His second choice—a road—had too many cars on it. His passenger said there was a blacktop road on his side of the plane, and the pilot turned toward it.

He was all set to land on the road; the approach was good, but as he flared to touch down, the engine burst into life and the Cessna started flying again. Despite the pilot's efforts to force it onto the ground, it careened into a concrete abutment before he could get it down and stopped. When the airplane finally came to rest, the pilot dragged his unconscious passenger from the wreckage.

Post-crash examination showed that there were less than two gallons of gas in each tank. The Cessna, total capacity 26 gallons (22.5 usable), had consumed almost all of the 16 gallons of fuel on board. But there was just enough to produce that last surge of power at the wrong time.

One of the often overlooked items on many engine failure checklists is securing the engine when committed to the forced landing. Pulling the mixture to idle/cut-off, turning the mags off, turning the fuel off, and turning the master switch off all seem to get lost in the all-consuming task of the forced landing. Yet, having the engine suddenly surge with power can wreck even a properly executed off-field landing.

Open Sesame—But Not in Flight

We'd have a lot fewer problems with airplanes if they were built like Sherman tanks; of course they wouldn't fly very well, but if you closed and locked the cabin doors, they would probably remain secured. Occasional door openings in flight and subsequent accidents continue to plague general aviation, but the real shame lies in the fact in almost every case, such an event should result in nothing more than an inconvenience.

Virtually all light airplanes fly quite nicely, thank you, with open or loosely latched cabin doors. It may be noisy, but the airplane continues to fly—unless the pilot lets the open door distract him to the point of losing control.

Neither occupant of a Beech Duchess was injured when the plane was landed gear-up at Pensacola, Florida, after the pilot discovered his cabin door had popped open just after takeoff. The pilot told investigators he had just lifted off, and was at about 100 feet AGL when the door on his side opened. He said the airplane began to behave erratically and he elected to pull back the power and land on the remaining runway. He said he did not hear the gear warning horn activate, but during the landing realized he had forgotten to extend the landing gear. The pilot also stated he had had previous problems with the plane's door on the passenger's side, and had been told of other problems with Duchess doors.

The pilot reported a total of 279.4 hours, 161.9 of them in multi-engine aircraft, all of which were in the Duchess.

The NTSB investigator said when the plane was later checked, the pilot's door latch mechanism was found to be operable and within adjustment limits. The landing gear warning horn was also found in working condition.

The investigator consulted FAA records and found no Service Difficulty Reports on file for Duchess cabin doors. He consulted Beech Aircraft, which checked its computer for a five-year period and found only three items, including two reports from people who contacted the company about door-openings and one warranty claim for an adjustment.

The investigator said Beech factory personnel also told him when a Duchess door does come open, it has no adverse effect on the plane's flying qualities.

Pilot, Know Thyself

Surely, one of the most important facets of pilot proficiency is being aware of existing or potential problems in every regard; in other words, being familiar "with all available information concerning the flight"—FAR 91.103. This includes knowledge of personal condition (fatigue, stress, etc.) and ability to handle whatever conditions might show up on the flight, as well as the condition of the airplane, the weather, and airport facilities at destination. Adequate knowledge tends to suppress unpleasant surprises.

But some flights seem to be a chain of problems, with one hazard being cured, or endured, only to have another crop up. This ATP-certificated pilot had struggled her way through just such a flight, only to have her Cessna 303 Crusader run off the end of the runway at North Carolina's Hickory Municipal Airport. The accident left the Crusader with substantial damages, but the pilot and her five passengers were unhurt.

> The 7,614-hour pilot had logged 110 hours in the Crusader, all of it as pilot in command. Her credentials included an instructor certificate for single- and multi-engine aircraft and instrument instruction. She was well experienced and qualified for the flight.
>
> The trip had begun earlier in the day when she had flown the Crusader from Hickory to Fort Lauderdale, Florida. The first inkling of things to come was the left alternator dropping off line. The pilot later reported she had considerable difficulty getting it back on, but she eventually did.
>
> By 6:25 p.m., she and her five passengers—all co-workers at a Hickory FBO—were back in the air heading for home on an IFR flight plan. The pilot had gotten a complete weather briefing by telephone before departing. Cruising at 9,000 feet along the coast of Florida, she encountered some of the forecast weather.
>
> Now she found the Crusader's weather radar was inoperative. She later reported flying through several "storm cells" which she felt might have been avoided if the weather radar had been working.

In about the same area, the outside air temperature was 38 degrees Fahrenheit, and the pilot now discovered that the aircraft's heater wasn't working. She noted in her report that "the girls in back had a blanket over them," trying to keep warm. But the pilot couldn't have a blanket wrapped around herself and still fly, so she stayed cold.

About 50 miles south of Hickory, Atlanta Center cleared the flight down to 4,000 feet. The flight continued without incident until Center cleared the Crusader for the visual approach to Hickory's Runway 6 from about 15 miles out.

Now they began to encounter turbulence, so the pilot told her passengers to snug up their seatbelts. The FSS at Hickory advised that a commuter flight which landed earlier had found considerable turbulence on the approach to Runway 6. They suggested she try landing on Runway 19 instead. But Runway 19 was shorter, and the VASI system on 19 had been decommissioned.

NOT OUT OF THE WOODS YET

Darkness introduced another problem. At the start of the flight, the pilot had found that the cockpit dome light couldn't be turned off, nor could it be dimmed. The girl sitting in the copilot's seat held her hand over the light in an effort to allow the pilot's eyes to adjust to the outside darkness.

The pilot came around the pattern for Runway 19, and found the turbulence getting worse. Coming down final with full flaps and the airspeed at blue line, she felt the turbulence "like air current eddies going every which way, and I had trouble getting the airplane on the ground."

The touchdown was normal, as she and the passengers recalled it. But it was too far down the runway. The girl in the copilot's seat recalled, "We were all excited when we touched down and [we] applauded [the pilot]. I realized we were in trouble when we passed [the FBO] too fast, but I still thought we could get the plane stopped before the runway ended.

"At the end of the runway, when we went into the field, the plane was still rolling fast and she was pumping the brakes fast and hard. We hit a knoll and went down into the fence at the edge of the field. I was not jerked in any manner on impact, so we must have been almost stopped at that point."

The Crusader had run into the airport boundary fence.

None of the passengers was injured, and all described the impact with the fence as almost unnoticeable. But the impact was hard enough to damage the nose, as well as the right gear door, stringer, and skin around the wheel well. Two offending items got theirs—the radar and the cabin heater were also damaged by the impact.

The Cessna sat with its nose against the fence. Inside, the girl who sat in the right seat recalled, "when we stopped, we all just sat there sort of shocked, and then we started laughing. No one screamed or was upset."

One of the FBO's employees had seen the Cessna slide off the end of the runway. He came out and helped the girls open the rear door, and all six climbed out unhurt.

The pilot had some recommendations on how the accident could have been avoided. In her accident report she wrote:

1. Do not fly when under stress or when fatigued.
2. Definitely need a dark cockpit area on landing.
3. Have the heater working when flying in cold conditions.
4. Use oxygen at night if possible.
5. Recommission the VASI on runway 19."

An Inflight Fire and a Proficient Pilot

Indications of a fire in the engine compartment is guaranteed to increase the pulse rate of even the coolest pilots. In this case, good training and even better procedures and technique saved the day, or more specifically, the night.

An emergency landing successfully concluded what might have been a first-class catastrophe following an engine fire in flight. The CFI and his four passengers escaped injury when he put the Turbo Lance down in a harvested corn field.

The pilot, with 2,750 total hours and 320 in the Lance, was en route from Fondulac, Wisconsin, to Waterloo, Iowa, when the 10:20 p.m. emergency occurred. The pilot told investigators he noticed a loss of manifold pressure, a slight burning smell, and a glow coming from the area of the engine. He shut off the fuel, pulled the mixture, began a best-angle glide and notified controllers of his emergency. During the descent, he had one passenger get the plane's fire extinguisher ready to use, and the landing was made with the doors open for a quick exit. There was no fire upon landing, and the passengers exited without incident.

Investigators said the source of the fire apparently was a loose gasket in the area of an exhaust crossover pipe at the rear of the engine.

Don't Rush into an Emergency

Sometimes it seems the combination of a novice's natural apprehension and his recent schooling in the "what ifs" makes a student pilot "too ready" for an emergency. Much of the training regimen orients the student to rapid-fire responses to critical situations, when sometimes, a moment to just sit and think about it may be all he needs.

Take, for example, the case of the 76-hour student pilot who departed Norwood, Massachusetts, in a Piper Warrior and went out to the local practice area for solo airwork. When he got ready to return about 40 minutes later, he noticed that he could not hear the ATIS on his radio, nor could he raise the tower. At this point, he noticed that both fuel gauges were reading empty, the fuel pressure gauge was below the green, and the oil pressure was in the yellow arc.

Feeling that Norwood had "too busy" a traffic pattern to attempt to work his way in there with no radios, he chose nearby Norfolk Airport. He couldn't raise Unicom there (investigators found he had neglected to tune the frequency for it), so he set up an approach to Runway 36 (this put him in a four-knot tailwind situation, he later conceded) and landed. However, there were patches of ice on the runway, and he slid off the side, crunching the landing gear and damaging other parts of the airplane.

Investigators found that not a thing electrical or mechanical was wrong with the airplane—and there was plenty of fuel in it. In all likelihood, investigators said, the student had inadvertently turned off the master switch sometime during the airwork. He had no "real" emergency at all. The situation could have returned to normal at the flick of a switch.

Let's Get Out of Here—If We Can

A pilot's proficiency extends to consideration for his passengers. There's a lot to be said for choosing an altitude that isn't bumpy, for making each takeoff and landing as smooth as possible, and for briefing passengers with regard to emergency procedures...use of safety belts and harnesses, and operation of emergency exits. The shock and confusion that prevails immediately following a crash does not produce an environment conducive to instruction on how to get out of the airplane.

Aviation Safety's comprehensive study of the emergency egress problem in general aviation speaks to not only the mechanical aspects of doors and windows, but also provides guidelines for development of effective procedures for getting out of a crashed airplane.

One Way Out—Is That All You Get?

It isn't enough, as illustrated by the crash of a Piper Cherokee near Lavina, Montana, while the plane was attempting to take off from a dirt road. The pilot's family and friends saw the crash and rushed to the wreckage. They were able to see at least one person alive inside the aircraft; unable to extricate herself, she begged for help. The people on the scene tried unsuccessfully to open the main door to get the girl out. They then attempted to break the windows out to remove her. This was also unsuccessful. A small fire erupted which eventually consumed the entire aircraft, killing the girl trapped inside and the other incapacitated occupants.

The date of this accident, taken from NTSB files, was 1977. But the FAA rules, the methods of aircraft construction, and the airplanes in the current fleet make the same kind of accident possible every time a pilot gets into a typical light aircraft.

One Way Out—Unless You Make Another

The crash of a Gulfstream AA-5A left the aircraft inverted, effectively locking the canopy and sealing the pilot in. Although suffering from a head injury, the pilot managed to force his way out through the baggage door.

In another accident, the pilot was literally blinded when an inflight fire in the engine compartment of his Beech A36TC Bonanza welled up into the cockpit. Following the subsequent forced landing in a field near San Diego, California, the right-seat passenger was trapped in the blaze when the cabin door jammed, and he died. But the two wives in the back seats were able to get out and drag the pilot with them...because the plane had a large, easily accessible rear door.

Emergency egress is an area usually ignored by pilots and aircraft purchasers. If one were to ask the aircraft salesperson about it, the most likely response would be a glossing over of a particular aircraft's lack of egress or perhaps a glib reference to the size of its main door.

Most owner/operator manuals do not even mention evacuation in the event of an emergency. Most light single-engine aircraft have only one way out—the door through which you entered.

The regulations regarding emergency egress are quite explicit. Based on seating and engine arrangement, the FARs tell us that our typical single-engine airplane seating less than six people, or a twin with both engines mounted on the centerline of the fuselage (like the Cessna 337), need have only one door. Lightplanes seating six or more must also must have an emergency exit on the side of the cabin opposite the main door. Twin-engine aircraft which have the engines mounted on the wings must have an emergency exit regardless of number of passengers.

Typical light singles run the range from models with one door which offers little hope of escape from the wreckage, to those which allow everyone to jump out as needed. Single doors are usually on the right side of the aircraft next to the front seats. In some aircraft, such as the Piper singles, this door also has a double latch system which can pose some difficulty for egressing passengers.

This Way for the Tour

Let's take a look at some of the more popular light singles on the market today. The results of this tour might surprise many people, especially those who have not considered the egress problem before. Even a pilot who realizes how bad the situation is regarding his own aircraft may not know how universal the problem really is.

The low point of the tour is the low-wing singles, such as Piper and Mooney aircraft. The typical Piper single, with the exceptions of the Tomahawk, the Saratoga, and some Cherokee Six models, has only one door. It is located on the right side of the aircraft, and has a unique two-latch (top and bottom) door latching system. Used properly, this provides exceptional protection against inadvertent inflight opening of the door and serves quite well to reduce cabin noise levels. It also presents a problem for those who must get out in a hurry.

The NTSB felt that the top latch presented a hazard to occupants in an emergency egress situation. In a safety recommendation issued March 20, 1981, the Board drew attention to the top latch system on Piper singles noting that the top latch could (and did) lock occupants inside the aircraft. It also noted that rescue personnel who are not familiar with this type of latch mechanism might not be able to spot the top latch handle or be able to operate it quickly and properly in an emergency.

Opening the single cabin door of a Piper aircraft could be impossible if the upper latch is damaged or pinned against the ground in an overturn accident.

The NTSB called for the elimination of this mechanism and establishment of a requirement that all aircraft manufactured after a specific date have only a single handle or latching mechanism with a simple and apparent means of operation. The Board also felt that emergency exits should be provided on light single-engine aircraft.

FAA at first responded that "the rules the Board has recommended may be economically feasible, but the data provided with the recommendations are not sufficient either to substantiate or to justify the additional rules." FAA did promise to "investigate the potential safety benefits and economic impact" of the proposal. But in a follow-up response dated June 18, 1982, FAA repeated the assertion that "currently available data do not adequately support this recommendation," and therefore, "FAA dos not intend to take further action."

Flip Side of the Coin

A point not addressed by the Board, but one which must be considered, is the aircraft flipping over after touchdown. In many Piper singles, this can be tantamount to being locked inside the cabin. The upper latch of the door latch system can be pinned against the ground by the airframe, holding it closed.

Unfortunately, this double latch system persists in virtually all Piper singles. From the Cherokee to the Dakota, these aircraft offer only the single door with the double latch system.

The Tomahawk primary trainer aircraft, having two doors, seems to offer a bright spot in the low end of the Piper line, but this aircraft also has the double-latch system. A Tomahawk crash at Punxsutawney, Pennsylvania, in May of 1982 forced a student pilot to kick out the back windows to escape after the aircraft came to rest upside down after a forced landing. (Luckily, there was no fire after impact, as there is in about 10 percent of all lightplane accidents and about one-quarter of fatal ones.) The top latch could not be moved to open the doors because it was pinned between the aircraft and the ground.

For those who find themselves trapped in an inverted Piper single, the only solutions at hand are breaking a window, or going out the baggage door. It's unlikely that a pilot or passenger using hands or feet could break an airplane window. Plexiglass is noted for its strength, and has a tendency to simply bend without breaking. For this reason, the windows of light aircraft are usually impervious to efforts to kick them out or break them, unless the person is lucky or skilled enough to bash it out of its mountings.

Baggage Doors May Be Better

On Pipers, the baggage door is a viable option. Most are constructed with weak latches, and usually all that is needed to open one from inside the aircraft is a good kick or punch. The only problems here are encountered when trying to reach the baggage area. In some aircraft, it is impossible, while in others, it may require considerable gymnastic prowess for passengers to wriggle over seats and out the door.

The best of the Piper singles as far as egress is concerned may be the Saratoga and those Cherokee Six models equipped with the optional cargo door. The forward door on the right side and the large cargo door on the left rear offer excellent means of escape. Both are operable from outside the aircraft, and the cargo door offers an escape route away from the fuel and fire sources.

Flip-overs present much the same problem in the Saratoga and Cherokee Six as in other Piper singles—the top latch on the forward door. In this case, however, the rear cargo door still offers the chance of escape without having to do a martial arts act on a baggage door.

The new Piper Malibu, a pressurized single which seats six, also has only one door. This door, because of the pressurization of the aircraft, is a clamshell-type, opening outward from the fuselage. Because of the number of seats, the Malibu is equipped with an emergency exit. It is a window exit which opens inward (also a concession to pressurization). Located next to the forward passenger seats (just behind the flight crew), this exit promises a fast answer to that burning question after a crash.

Mooney, in the M20 series, also offers only one door on the right side of the cabin. We deem the design slightly better than the Piper system, however, in that it does not have the upper latch to contend with in a flip-over type accident. It still may be difficult, if not impossible, for rear-seat passengers to get out of Mooney aircraft fast enough to avoid incineration in the event of fire. The single door requires the rear-seat passengers to climb over the front seats and out the door over the wing. In a flaming aircraft, or where one or more of the passengers may have suffered incapacitating injuries, this can be impossible.

A typical Mooney does have a baggage door in the rear, which can be used in emergency egress.

Best of the Bunch

The really bright stars in the single-engine emergency egress picture, in our opinion, are the aircraft produced by Beech and Cessna. The Beech Bonanza (which nominally seats six) has some of the best-designed emergency exits of any single-engine aircraft we've seen. These are easily accessible, easy to operate, and would not seem to have any deleterious effects on performance, structure or noise levels. They are in the form of hinged windows placarded with red handles. Their location beside the seats helps to ensure that they will be used when the occasion arises, and windows are usually the first place which rescue personnel will attack when the door won't work. Additionally, these exits are fairly large and will accommodate most adults with a minimum of struggle or gymnastics. They are not, however, marked or operable from outside the aircraft.

Slightly lower in the Beech line, the Sundowner, Sierra and Sport/ Musketeer models are provided with the elusive second main door. Both doors are fairly large and permit easy, fast egress for both front- and rear-seat passengers, minimizing the athletic prowess needed for escape in many aircraft.

When it comes to doors, the Cessna line shines. The Cessna singles all have at least two doors, one on each side of the aircraft. The 172, as a prime example, features those large doors to allow everyone to get out with a minimum of fuss. Additionally, the handles for operating the doors are large and obvious in their use. There is only one, and it, like many automobile door handles, is located on the armrest. It even operates the way a car door handle does—a real plus for non-flying passengers who might not be familiar with aircraft door mechanisms.

A little farther up the Cessna line, the Model 206 has doors galore. With what amounts to a door for each row of seats, on some models, the Stationair 6 provides the most chances for escape during an on-ground emergency. There is a minor fly in the ointment here, though. The rear doors may be pinned closed when the flaps are extended. Even when this occurs, however, it does provide a starting point for rescue personnel to work with, and does not require tools more advanced than a crow-bar to force entry.

While Cessna doors may be among the best in the light-singles, they have a drawback in that the doors are located directly under the wing, raising the possibility of occupants becoming trapped by fire in the wings. As with the Piper singles, though, the baggage door is accessible from inside the aircraft and can be opened with a kick or punch. While not very large, it does provide another way out.

Canopies—A Mixed Blessing

Gulfstream American Tigers, Cheetahs, and Travelers offer an interesting twist on the egress situation. With sliding canopies, these aircraft offer fast, easy egress through the simplicity of opening up and jumping out. The size of the opening which the canopy provides also offers the possibility of leaping away from flames to a clear area, if the passengers are still able to do so, or allowing rescue personnel to reach in and grab the incapacitated to drag them to safety.

But let's turn our Gulfstream upside down. Suddenly, the picture changes dramatically. The asset of the sliding canopy is now a deadly liability. The weaker structure of a canopy, as compared to a standard cabin, presents the possibility of being crushed as the canopy caves in. If the canopy does not cave in, the occupants had better hope that it opens before the aircraft comes to a halt. If not, then they are effectively locked in, leaving only the baggage door for escape.

Five Seats, One Door

Occupants of twin-engine aircraft generally fare better in terms of emergency egress, since compliance with certification standards requires emergency exits in most cases. The most notable exception to this is the Cessna 337 Skymaster. With both engines mounted on the centerline of the fuselage, this twin falls into the light-single category under FAR 23.807 when equipped with five seats.

This has led to the creation of an interesting, and perhaps dangerous, loophole. It is possible to purchase the aircraft with only five seats, and so without a second door or emergency exit. After purchase, however, it is possible to have a sixth seat added. Thus, we can have "non-complying compliance" to 23.807. The aircraft was constructed and sold in compliance with 23.807, but can legally be modified out of compliance. Potential purchasers of used Skymasters ought to be aware of this when shopping for a 337.

An optional advantage can be gained on the Skymaster through an STC'd modification. This STC permits installation of an emergency exit on the top of the fuselage. Such modification is highly desirable for pressurized versions of the 337 which have only the right-side clamshell door for entry and exit.

The venerable Cessna 310 provides the occupants with a main cabin door over the wing for primary entrance and egress. Unfortunately, the emergency exit is also located over the wing, on the left side of the aircraft alongside the pilot's seat. With placement like this, the pilot and copilot are afforded easy escape, while the rear passengers must still make like world-class gymnasts to crawl, climb, and wriggle their way out over and around the front seats.

Other Cessna twins offer multiple doors as options. The added expense and slight increase in empty weight are well worth the added security provided by the extra door. However, the majority of the Cessna twins come with only the single main door and the required emergency exit(s).

The emergency exits on most Cessna twins suffer from some common problems—namely, inoperability from outside the aircraft. This, combined with superb matching of exit to airframe (sometimes including a factory putty and paint job that is nearly seamless), can render these exits worthless to rescue personnel who must act quickly. The slight seam around the exit can be almost invisible to would-be rescuers in an emergency situation.

Notable exceptions to this include the 404 Titan and the 441 Conquest which at least have external release handles for the emergency exits (although the exits are not outlined). For the rest of the Cessna twins, however, the emergency exits are unmarked and can not be opened from outside the aircraft.

Piper opens new doors with some of its twin-engine entrants. The Seneca stands out for its dual doors. These not only are on opposite sides of the aircraft, but are at opposite ends as well. The rear door is large, operable from outside the aircraft, and situated away from the fuel and engines.

Piper still retains the upper latch mechanism for two of its twins, the Seminole and Seneca. The Seminole is handicapped by having only one main door, although it is, by federal law, equipped with emergency exits.

Only when we begin looking at those Piper models equipped with airstair doors do we find the top-latch system has been discontinued. Those chic airstair doors can also function to the disadvantage of escaping passengers as, with the gear collapsed, the door will not deploy fully on most aircraft so equipped. This leaves the unextended steps to contend with on the way out.

Chained In

Airstair doors may also suffer from an additional drawback in that some are equipped with a safety chain which holds the door closed in flight. This chain was the subject of an NTSB safety recommendation in 1979. The Board found that Beech 99 aircraft had such a safety chain and that it could significantly hamper both escaping passengers and rescue personnel attempting entry to the cabin. Lack of familiarity with the chain and its location could lead to passengers attempting to open the door without first removing the chain, in which case the door will only open about 6 inches. The Board discovered, during its investigation of this matter, that as early as November of 1976, FAA had been concerned about the matter of safety chains on airstair doors.

The NTSB recommended in 1979 that FAA issue an Airworthiness Directive requiring compliance with a Beech service letter which had advised the removal of safety chains on Beech 99 aircraft. Additionally, the Board had recommended that other aircraft that have these chains be investigated with an eye toward removing the chains on these aircraft as well (the Board points out the Piper Navajo in particular). Piper's higher-performance twins, which all have airstair doors, suffer from most of the same disadvantages as the Piper singles. All have only one main door (even the Cheyenne series), and although they have emergency exits, these are not operable from outside the aircraft. In some cases the emergency exits have been so well mated with the airframe, they are difficult to locate by eye. Lack of external markings in the form of a colored band outlining the exit compounds the problem.

The Beech line of twins has to be the best as far as egress is concerned. By using the same type of emergency exits on the Baron and Duke as found on the Bonanza, Beech has combined ease of operation with the psychological advantages which window exits afford—namely that the windows are usually the first place which rescue personnel are going to attack after a crash if the doors don't operate.

The exits themselves are clearly marked inside the aircraft. The red handles are easy to locate and obvious in their operation. The windows, while conforming to type IV exit specifications under the FAA rules (a 19-by-20-inch opening, as opposed to much larger openings required on large aircraft), would still seem to offer plenty of space to squeeze even the largest passengers outside to safety.

The emergency exits on the Beech twins also show the same lack of external marking and inoperability from outside as is common to other twins. Some Beech twins, like the Baron, offer more than one emergency exit, however, which is certainly a big plus. Beech's upper-line models feature emergency exit door-type windows. Just like the exits offered by Cessna and Piper, they are nearly invisible from outside the aircraft, and cannot be opened from outside.

Where's the Door?

While twin-engine aircraft with the engines on the wings must have emergency exits under FAA Part 23 rules, the utility of these exits has been diminished in a number of ways. The single largest detractor of emergency exit utility is the almost total lack of markings on the outside of the aircraft. Coupled with the lack of external handles for operating the exit, this leads to the situation of incapacitated passengers being unable to open the exits and ground personnel being unable to save them because there is no way to open, or even identify the exit from outside the aircraft.

Emergency exits which are not only unmarked but also inoperable from outside the aircraft are nearly pandemic to the industry. Cessna doesn't start marking the emergency exits until you buy a Citation. Questioned by *Aviation Safety* as to why this practice persists, Cessna stated that the principal need is for exits to be openable from inside the aircraft. This "avoids complications and the aircraft retains aesthetic value." Cessna went on to assert that the exits on small aircraft are easily found, thereby obviating the need for external markings.

Piper and Beech don't mark the emergency exits on any of their general aviation aircraft (though it should be noted that certain of Beech's models used in Part 121 operations do come from the factory with marked exits as required by FAR Part 25).

The NTSB had recommended to the FAA in May of 1979 that the

certification rules be amended to require that emergency exits be conspicuously marked and operable from outside the aircraft. The FAA responded by publishing the proposal in the form of an Advisory Circular in January of 1984 (AC 23.807-3), but the FAA has stated that it will not consider any further response to this issue.

It should be noted that the Advisory Circular is just that—advisory, not mandatory. Apparently, compliance has been slow in coming, as a recent tour of several general aviation airports found no light aircraft with externally marked emergency exits, and we've heard of no rush to aircraft paint shops to get the job done. The situation of unmarked emergency exits still persists throughout most of the fleet.

In response to a series of questions regarding emergency egress, GAMA wrote to *Aviation Safety* magazine, calling attention to the pilot's operating handbook (POH) standardization it had implemented in the mid-1970s. According to GAMA, information regarding emergency egress can be found in Section 3 of a GAMA format handbook. GAMA went on to say, "This information deals mainly with the location and operation of emergency exits. Additional information...is issued in other POH sections.... This standardization...would be GAMA's contribution to 'guidelines' on publishing emergency egress information."

Cessna, in response to an inquiry regarding AC 23.807-3 which suggested external marking of all emergency exits, sent *Aviation Safety* a copy of its crash/fire rescue (CFR) procedures guide. Much to its credit, Cessna has produced and distributed this booklet for crash/fire rescue personnel illustrating the location of emergency exits and doors. It also specifies whether the emergency exit is operable from outside the aircraft.

Additionally, the Cessna CFR booklet offers illustrations of "cut-out" areas. These are places in the structure of the fuselage where power cutting tools can open the structure to free people trapped inside. While this kind of direction is good, it may be virtually useless, since all across the country, most airport CFR groups do not have such tools at ready disposal and must rely on local municipal fire departments for such equipment.

Potential Solutions

So why don't the manufacturers simply add another door? The answer lies in several areas. The primary reason has to do with structural considerations. Every time another cutout is made for windows and doors, it degrades the load-carrying ability of the fuselage. The alternative would be to beef up the structure to the point where addition of another door cutout would still permit compliance with the regulations. The trade-off here would be a serious reduction in useful load as weight is added in the form of reinforcement to the structure.

Another consideration is aerodynamics. The addition of door handles in the slipstream, perhaps adding a step (either a reinforced area on the wing or an external step), and the inevitable seam around the door all add drag to the airframe. The airflow engineering required to reduce this drag to an acceptable level might add unacceptable engineering hours to the design stages of the aircraft, with consequent manufacturing costs, all passed on to the customer.

The noise levels in the aircraft also increase, not only because there are additional openings in the structure, but also because increased drag-induced noise is created as handles, hinges, seam lines, etc., protrude into the wind. Another consideration must be that sections with doors are very hard to sound-proof compared to intact aircraft structure with no door.

All in all, the prospects for additional doors for the bulk of the light single fleet seem pretty dim. The required changes in design, the trade-off of useful load, and the decrease in occupant comfort would tend to override any benefits derived from the additional door.

What can be done? The NTSB has addressed the issue of emergency egress from general aviation aircraft, recommending to the FAA in 1981 that the rule be changed to require any aircraft manufactured after a certain date which seats more than two people, have at least one emergency exit in addition to the normal entrance door.

More Window Exits

During preparation of these recommendations, the Board looked for solutions to the egress problem. The addition of window-type emergency exits would seem to be the most practical solution. NTSB has discussed this with Piper engineers who indicated that a rear window opposite the cabin door could be readily converted to an emergency exit without airframe structural modifications.

Other aircraft could also be easily converted in this manner. The windows are already there, and the design changes required to hinge them and make them openable would not be unacceptable either in price or performance. Also, since these exits would not be governed by FAA size standards (being extra exits not required under the certification rules), such a change would not require enlargement of the existing window structures while affording the security of another way out.

Another possibility was not mentioned by the Board, but it could address the problem. In the absence of hinged windows, certain windows could be designed to have weaker supports or mounts. This would make them easier to kick out in an emergency. It would also offer ground personnel the chance to get at passengers without having to resort to axes or other potentially dangerous methods.

The NTSB had not recommended any change in the existing fleets, but merely, a change in aircraft constructed after some future date. Nonetheless, since aircraft are still in production with type certificates dating back three decades, the FAA considered the proposal to be "retroactive rulemaking." The FAA eventually responded in June of 1982, saying that "the available evidence does not indicate a need for emergency exits of any type on small general aviation aircraft," and that "retroactive rulemaking is almost always an economic burden. Such rulemaking must be quantifiable as a net benefit to society." To put it bluntly, the FAA has declared that preventing the deaths of a small number of people is not worth the cost to the aircraft manufacturers (and ultimately to the aircraft buyers, it's true) of adding a couple of hinges and a latch to an airplane's back window.

Do it Yourself

What can owners and operators do with current aircraft? Aircraft already in the fleet, as we have seen, are deficient in terms of emergency egress. What can be done to minimize this deficiency? The wise pilot should examine his aircraft with a jaundiced eye. Look for ways out besides the main door. For all practical purposes, one should assume this door would be unusable in the event of a crash. Try climbing over the seats and out the baggage door to see how long it takes. If the aircraft has emergency exits, look at them and try to envision crawling out. It might be worth having a good hatchet mounted securely and within reach for hacking your own way out.

An added measure of safety can be gained by twin-engine operators through the judicious use of red or international orange tape. Applied around the outlines of the emergency exits, it could aid rescue personnel in reaching the occupants quickly.

Perhaps the most important gains in egress-ability are realized when ordering the aircraft. Sign up for as many doors as can be fitted to the aircraft. As predesigned options, the weight and drag penalties are minimal. The bonus of additional ways to get out far exceed any transient benefits that could be derived from a slightly higher useful load. These extra doors can, in certain aircraft, also add to its utility by allowing bulkier loads to be moved in and out with greater ease, as well as allowing passengers to board and deplane with less need for gymnastics.

Brief passengers before engine start on the exits and their use and location. Even exits big as barn doors won't save anyone if they are not used. Studies by the NTSB have found that even in airline operations, a significant portion of the passengers are unaware of the location and operation of emergency exits. Make sure that everyone aboard knows how to get out quickly through the nearest available exit, not just the main door.

Above all, make sure that the aircraft exits work as they are supposed to. Sticking or sealed exits are useless decorations—make sure they are able to do the job required when required. In the interests of aerodynamics or aesthetics, some operators (and even some manufacturers) have applied putty and paint in the seam around the emergency exits. While providing an almost insignificant reduction in drag, this practice may result in the putty drying out, which can effectively glue the exit closed, rendering it useless.

According to FAA guidelines from Washington, an annual inspection is not complete if the emergency exit has not been exercised, so all that paint and putty is legally required to be cracked open at least once a year. It's a good drill for the airplane, and for the pilot.

6 | Other Proficiency Considerations

Most of the articles and mishap reports that were considered for inclusion in the Pilot Proficiency volume of *Command Decisions* fit rather nicely into the subject-matter categories we selected. But when that process was complete, there remained a significant list of material that deserved illumination—information that we felt was important to pilots who are serious about becoming more proficient. So we have created a section that contains just what the title implies—recountings of accidents and incidents, and educational articles covering a wide range of "other" pilot activities. We hope you'll benefit from this potpourri of pilot problems.

Airworthiness: The Pilot's Role

One of the most commonly used words in aviation is "airworthiness," yet nowhere in the Federal Air Regulations is that most important term defined, yet airworthiness is a burden placed squarely on the shoulders of the pilot. Some indication of its legal significance may be found in FAR 91.7(b), which states: *The pilot in command of a civil aircraft is responsible for determining when that aircraft is in condition for safe flight. He shall discontinue the flight when unairworthy mechanical or structural conditions occur.*

The legal question immediately raised by FAR 91.7(b) is how can a pilot who holds no A&P credential determine whether or not a particular aircraft is safe for flight (airworthy), except by reliance on the representation of others who are rated and trained to make such observations and determinations?

The answer is that except for the manufacturer's preflight inspection guidelines, and that portion of basic flight training which deals with determining airworthiness, pilots have no alternative but to take the representations of others in assessing whether or not an aircraft is in condition for safe flight.

No regulation, for example, pretends to require an owner or pilot to monitor an annual inspection to determine that the A&P and IA have performed all of the regulatory inspections, and that the components and/or systems inspected meet the minimum safety standards. There are no enforcement decisions that hold that a pilot may not rely on logbook entries indicating an annual or 100-hour inspection signoff, in determining airworthiness for a particular flight. In airworthiness, you have to take somebody's word for it.

On the other hand, common sense and FAR 91.13 (careless or reckless operation) would probably dictate that if a pilot finds preflight inspection items that raise any reasonable suspicion of airworthiness, that doubt should be resolved by referral to a qualified A&P mechanic.

Can't Even Trust a Painter

Not too many years ago an owner/pilot of a popular light twin performed what he thought was a thorough preflight inspection following a complete repaint job on his airplane. Having found nothing to indicate that the aircraft was in any way unsafe, he taxied to a nearby FBO to have one of their mechanics re-inspect the aircraft. A smart move as it turned out, since it was found that in reinstalling the left aileron, the paint shop failed to line up the aileron hinges with their mating holes on the wing. Consequently, the aileron bolts, which appeared to be in their proper position, were not attached to any part of the aileron. This was rather dramatically demonstrated by the mechanic who with a playful tug pulled the aileron off the wing. After regaining his composure, and having the aileron reattached properly, the owner/pilot flew off into the sunset with a dramatic realization of the importance of selecting competent repair facilities.

A short time thereafter the paint shop lost its license and went out of business.

Other than complying with the manufacturer's recommendations concerning preflight inspections, and checking such basic items as fuel contamination, strut extension, fuel, oil, or hydraulic leaks, how can any pilot possibly comply with FAR 91.7(b)?

The answer is that no pilot can possibly be aware of hidden—or as they say in the law, "latent"—unairworthiness items. No pilot can possibly know, for example that an alternator has 2.2 hours of life remaining when lifting off on a 4-hour flight.

Likewise, no pilot can possibly be aware of low compression on a cylinder when it is not accompanied by other symptoms of distress. Since hidden incipient failures or malfunctions are not capable of being detected by even the most thorough and knowledgeable pilots, reliance on the representations of airworthiness in the maintenance records and by mechanics is unavoidable. Keep in mind, the FARs again put the burden of maintenance and record-keeping requirements on the owner/operator, so that the PIC has every right to rely on the accuracy and the completeness of those records.

Some years ago a Part 135 carrier and several of its pilots were cited for regulatory violations for operating a light twin with missing wing rivets. It seems that this particular aircraft had over 3,000 such rivets and the A&P who regularly maintained the aircraft advised the operator that the missing rivets did not constitute an airworthiness problem. That representation was enough to insulate both the operator and its pilots from further action, particularly since the A&P had the good sense to get his advice confirmed by the manufacturer.

Often FAA inspectors have attempted to take the position that any condition less than factory-new constitutes an unairworthy condition. If that were the case, even delivery flights would not be possible, as every moving part on an aircraft begins to wear as soon as it is first operated. The reasonable test is whether or not the suspect part, component or system is in a condition such that the proposed flight can be completed safely.

Of course, some items are readily within the pilot's ability to observe—for example, when he powers up the panel and half the instruments are out of commission.

The Notorious "Bottom Line"

The pilot in command bears the burden under the regulations to ascertain whether or not an aircraft is safe for flight both before takeoff and during flight. That same pilot, however, has every right to rely on maintenance records, including annual and 100-hour signoffs as well as AD compliance signoffs, in arriving at the subjective judgment as to whether or not the aircraft is safe for initial flight and safe for continued flight.

The Big C

There are a number of critical before-takeoff items a fighter pilot can't see once he's strapped into the cockpit, and so he relies on groundcrew personnel to make a "last chance check" for him. General aviation pilots should be no less concerned about the condition of the machine they're about to take into the air, and the critical items should be checked immediately before taking the runway.

Some pilots use a printed checklist, some use mnemonics such as CIGARTIP, or CIFFTRS, or some other home-made reminder. But in every case, the "C" stands for controls, and guarantees that if the flight controls are checked for freedom and proper movement, there's no way a control lock can be left in place.

> Five persons were killed when a Beech Baron crashed during takeoff from Ithaca, New York. Investigators quickly found the airplane's control column lock still in place, having likely prevented the pilot from using aileron or elevator controls.
>
> The 1968 Baron, a corporate aircraft carrying four passengers and commanded by an 8,500-hour ATP with 397 hours in type, became airborne on takeoff and climbed very steeply to about 100 or 150 feet, then rolled left and descended near-vertically to impact, witnesses told the NTSB.
>
> The crash site was near the approximate midpoint of the 5,800-foot runway, meaning that the Baron could have been stopped in ample time, if the pilot had rejected the takeoff before becoming airborne.

Older Barons and Bonanzas have a three-part control lock assembly, consisting of a rudder pedal lock, a plastic throttle guard, and a control column pin, all linked together with thin cables. With all three in place, it would be impossible to work any primary control, and difficult to use the throttles. However, it is possible to remove the rudder and throttle locks (or not bother to install them) while leaving the column lock in place.

The column lock is a steel pin inserted through a hanger (column guide) from underneath the column. A C-shaped wire bail wraps around the column to hold the pin in place. This is largely out of sight from the pilot's seat. Some versions do not have the wire bail, and owners say the weight of the throttle lock dangling by its cable would pull the pin out even if the pilot forgets it. However, roughness on the

Most control locks, such as the one on this Baron, have a conspicuous flag to warn the pilot that the controls are not functional. Often, however, the flags are removed or obscured.

pin, or pressure on the yoke might keep the pin in place while taxiing.

In the Baron that crashed, the column pin was slightly scuffed and the hanger was broken, probably upon impact. The rudder and throttle locks were not in place. The cable from the throttle lock to the column pin was broken, leading to speculation that the pilot might have pulled down on it in an attempt to remove the column pin.

The old-style column pin design also involves a hole location which locks the pitch control at or slightly aft of neutral.

Newer Barons and Bonanzas have a column lock that inserts from the top, and is crowned by a large, red metal flag which is in plain view of the pilot and interferes with use of the throttles. In addition, the pin hole locks the aileron control 12 degrees to one side, and the pitch control well forward of neutral. Thus an attempted takeoff with the lock in place would not only be evident to the pilot, but it might be impossible for the airplane to get airborne.

In 1973 and 1974, Beech issued Class II (recommended but not mandatory) service bulletins for the Baron and Bonanza series to be modified for the new control lock system. No warranty help was offered, and a relatively high labor time plus parts costs might have influenced owners not to have the work accomplished.

In the B55 Baron manual, removal of the control locks is in the preflight checklist, and "Controls—check full travel and freedom of movement" is in the pre-takeoff checklist.

"I Was Convinced I Had Time..."

Like most airplane makers, for years Cessna has put "controls—free and correct motion" in its pre-takeoff checklists. And it takes a little extra effort to get the key past the control lock flap just to start the engine. However, if a pilot is determined to ignore all the deterrents, it's still possible for him to get the engine running, taxi out and attempt a takeoff with the control lock still pinning his ailerons and elevator rigidly in place.

While we hope most pilots would pull back the throttle instantly when they feel the frozen yoke, Safety Board files contain at least one case where the airman attempted to continue the takeoff.

> The pilot, an aircraft salesman flying an almost-new Cessna Skyhawk, said "Upon completion of run-up and check for traffic, I announced my intentions and started rollout. Reaching rotation point, the control lock for elevator and ailerons was still in lock position.
>
> "With 4,200 feet of runway, I was convinced I had time to pull out the control lock. I was struggling with the lock when the right wing began to lift, causing the aircraft to leave the runway to the left. At that point, I was unable to apply right rudder to return to the runway, still unable to remove the control lock, and reached for power reduction, when the nosegear hit a ditch and the aircraft nosed over."
>
> The plane had extensive damage to the propeller, engine, windshield, wings, landing gear, tail and instrument panel, but the pilot walked away with minor injuries. Investigators said the pilot admitted to having a checklist aboard, but failed to use it. They also noted that the control lock did finally come out—when the yoke broke off across the holes where the locking pin is inserted.

Partial Preflight

Aviation accidents can be broadly categorized in two ways. There are those the pilot could not have prevented, no matter how careful he was, and those that could have been avoided by the use of good judgment and caution. One that definitely falls into the latter category is the case of a pilot whose Cessna 182 crashed in Paxson, Alaska, due to fuel exhaustion.

Fuel exhaustion is only part of the story, however. The pilot also put himself in the position of having to mix autogas with 80/87 octane avgas in order to get home, didn't call for a weather briefing (and got stuck in instrument conditions as a result) and didn't even try to use his radio until he was already in trouble. He was definitely not a proficient pilot.

The pilot and one of his two passengers escaped the night forced landing in mountainous terrain with minor injuries; another passenger emerged with nary a scratch. Their luck continued after the crash as well. Though they did not have the legally required emergency equipment on board, they were able to rig a makeshift shelter using one of the airplane's wing covers. The plane's ELT was instrumental in their rescue.

The pilot had flown the Cessna to Valdez Creek from Anchorage two weeks earlier to work at a mining camp, and it was the first time he had flown to Valdez. During the flight, the engine had not performed to his liking, running rough on one magneto.

While he was in Valdez, he had an uncertified mechanic check the engine. The mechanic found that the magnetos were working properly but noted that two of the spark plugs were fouled with soot. He cleaned and regapped the plugs but did not run the engine. He said the pilot told him all the plugs would be replaced when he returned to Anchorage. The pilot stated that after a preheat and a 15-minute run-up, the engine appeared to operate normally. Witnesses who saw the Cessna take off also said the engine sounded normal.

The pilot said he was careful with his weight and balance calculations, since one of the passengers was heavy and he knew the airplane would be operating near gross weight. Since avgas was not available at Valdez Creek, he was forced to add 10 gallons of auto fuel to the approximately 20 gallons of 80/87 avgas already on board in order to have a sufficient supply to get to Palmer, the first planned stop en route to Anchorage. The 182 had not been STC'd for using autogas.

The pilot did not call for a weather briefing before he took off. According to investigators, he based his decision to depart on his own observation of the weather at Valdez Creek and was planning to get a weather update by radio once he had climbed high enough to contact the nearest FSS. The sky was clear over the airport; but according to two witnesses on the ground, the pilot knew there was a solid ceiling to the south and west (the intended direction of flight) before he took off at 8:15 that evening. The mechanic who had worked on the plane said that the clouds appeared to be between 8,000 and 10,000 feet and noted the pilot told him he intended to climb to 10,000 feet.

The pilot taxied out, did a run-up at the end of the runway, set his directional gyro and took off. He climbed to 9,500 feet and headed south-southeast. He said that after leveling off, he noticed a cloud bank in his path that "seemed to appear on the horizon." As the Cessna continued south, the pilot became more and more concerned about the weather and started to consider changing course. He still wasn't worried enough to turn around and go back, however. The next thing he knew, he was in the clouds. He later said that he was "just flying along and it seemed like it just glommed on to me."

The pilot was quite confident that he would be able to make a 180-degree turn and go back the way he came. He looked at his directional gyro and discovered that the heading was still locked where he had set it just before takeoff. The setting knob had remained engaged.

The pilot initiated a standard-rate turn by setting up a 30-degree bank and watching the clock. He said that his compass was swinging wildly in the turn; investigators later said the pilot did not display an adequate understanding of magnetic compass problems.

After he rolled out on a heading of about 330 degrees, the engine began to lose power, and he was unable to get it running properly again. The pilot said it felt as if he still had partial power, and he tried to keep the airplane in level flight. In this attempt, he went through a "light stall" that he was able to recover from.

"I noticed that I could not regain airspeed past about 60 mph, but I went ahead with the recovery anyway," he said. "Now I tried to fly without losing any altitude." By this time, he was down to 6,500 feet and knew there were some 6,100-foot mountains in the area. He tried the radio but was unable to raise anyone. In his attempt to maintain level flight, he went through another "light stall." He was getting close to the ground and just missed a ridge line before eventually crashing into spruce trees near a lake at an elevation of about 3,000 feet. The crash site was only 32 miles from the airport at Valdez Creek. The airplane had been airborne a total of one hour and twenty minutes.

The FAA inspected the wreckage at the site. The spark plugs were once again fouled with soot despite having been run no more than two hours since they were cleaned. No fuel was found either in the tanks or in the carburetor. The mixture control was set full-rich, the primer was unlocked, there was no oil in the crankcase and the oil breather pipe was blocked. The magnetos and carburetor were tested and found to be in good working order.

The Safety Board concluded that the pilot did not lean the engine properly, which would account for both the fouled plugs and the fuel exhaustion after less than two hours of engine operation.

Investigators noted that, despite the pilot's claim of 609 hours of flight time, he showed a marked lack of knowledge in basic principles of airmanship, including the proper use of the mixture control.

Little Things Mean a Lot

To close out this section on pilot proficiency, here's a discussion of "little things" noticed by a highly experienced pilot evaluator as he recalls checkrides and personal experiences with a variety of pilots. This is constructive criticism, offered for the sole purpose of helping you improve your proficiency by benefiting from the mistakes and poor procedures of fellow pilots.

IT'S NOT IN THE BOOK

A friend of mine—an A&P mechanic—almost lost his leg because a customer had not advised him that a magneto was still hot with the ignition switch off. The mechanic was just doing routine trouble-shooting of fuel injection problems, and had no reason to suspect a loose P-lead or a bad mag switch might cause problems. Okay, so it was not so smart on the part of the mechanic—he should have checked for ignition grounding before easing the prop through a compression

Every preflight should include visual inspection of the magnetos, plus a P-lead check during the run-up.

stroke, and he should have stayed well clear of the prop arc. But when he moved the prop, it kicked off on a power stroke and badly cut his leg. What about the aircraft owner? He had been flying this small machine for a long time with an unsafe ignition—and didn't know it!

For the vast majority of pilots, all shutdowns are accomplished with the mixture control, with nary a real check of ignition grounding with the mag switch in the "off" position. "Ignition grounding check?" What's that? It's probably not in the *Aircraft Flight Manual* (AFM). The manufacturer can only go so far in telling the owner how to operate the aircraft—it is not required to spell out the basics of how to fly and how to check for safe engine operation. The owner/operator/pilot is expected to bring a certain level of expertise with him into the flying arena.

Imagine what might have happened to the owner/pilot of that small machine if he had ever pulled the prop through during preflight, with the mixture a little out of the cut-off position, and with the throttle out of idle. It would have been another runaway airplane on the ramp. It's no joke; hot ignition systems still cause fatalities and unpiloted flights each year. Why not check that ignition system at the end of each flight?

FAMILIARITY BREEDS PROBLEMS

What I'm hitting on in this article is those simple little items that too many pilots miss. I see them often during Flight Reviews, and I see the worst performances with owner/ pilots—the ones who have gotten too familiar with a particular airplane. It's easy to think we know it all. How could any check pilot or examiner know this plane better than I do?— maybe by being cautious; perhaps by checking a few things not covered in the AFM; and, of course, by doing all the checks called for in the AFM!

One thing I like to do before a Flight Review in the owner's airplane is to beg off flying for an hour while I read his AFM. I check the systems description, normal procedures, and emergency procedures. Why go to all this trouble? First, I'm supposed to check this pilot on his procedures and knowledge of the check airplane—not just look at his airwork. And quite often, I find that I have just learned things about the bird that the owner/pilot either never knew or has forgotten.

My second reason for AFM study is protect myself; the NTSB, the FAA and the courts might consider me pilot in command, and thus responsible for any incident or accident during this flight.

Let's start our nit-picking with preflight inspections; in particular, the engine installation. Many airplanes nowadays come with cowlings that can't be removed for preflights. And there are no easy-access doors that allow a good view of all the innards. So, it's easy to just peek into the cooling air inlets, check the oil dipstick, drain the fuel strainer, and proceed to the "left wing checks." What about the alternator belt? What about the baffles and flexible baffle seals? What about bird nests? How about those exhaust pipes?

A flashlight is a big help on engine preflights, even on a sunny day. The light means you will be able to inspect more than just the forward fins on the two front cylinders when you look into the air inlets. You might catch that pile of straw atop the No. 4 cylinder that means sparrows have set up housekeeping. And just behind the bird nest you will be able to check the flexible seals between the rear baffle and the top cowl; if the seals are bent to the rear, a lot of the cooling air is being dumped before it has a chance to cool the cylinders.

GREASE SPOTS ON YOUR FLYING SUIT

It's nice to see what's behind the cylinders also, and to trace the exhaust stacks, and fuel and oil lines. But again, those non-removable two-piece clamshell cowls make this difficult. Well, how about kneeling or lying under the cowl flap area and looking up the backside of the engine? Sure, it's a little dirty down there, but here are a few items found by grungy local pilots during preflights.

Joe didn't own this two-seat trainer, he just rented it occasionally, but he didn't like what he saw in the rear baffle seal area when looking into the air inlets. So, while the dipstick access door was open, he slid his forearm inside and felt around the rear baffle.

Sure enough, the entire seal was blown to the rear, and there was a big gap between the baffle and the top cowl. With the help of a mechanic, he got the top cowling off and discovered that the entire seal was out of place. The last time that cowling had been off, nobody checked the condition of the seal. The rubber was already rotted and cracked, and several of the fasteners were out of place.

Joe missed his flight that day. The mechanic didn't like the looks of one rear cylinder—all of the paint was burned off. That jug had to be replaced. It was badly heat damaged from inadequate cooling.

Or how about Tom, a CFI who did a lot of instruction in an old twin. One morning he noted an augmenter tube in the right nacelle was loose. This six-inch stainless steel tube acts as an ejector pump to pull cooling air though the engine. The exhaust pipe ends at the firewall, right at the front-end inlet of the augmenter, and the pulses of exhaust into the larger tube produce the pumping action for the cooling air. Tom also noted a line of popped rivets in the rear of the nacelle, close to the loose augmenter tube. Again, it was a cancelled flight and a call for the A&P.

What the mechanic found was startling: The augmenter tube was broken completely in two. The right side exhaust pipe was dumping hot exhaust directly into the nacelle and trying to blow the nacelle into a balloon shape. The exhaust heat probably wasn't doing the top wing skin much good, either. And there were openings for fuel and pneumatic lines, engine control cables, and wire bundles in the nacelle area that made carbon monoxide entry into the wing, and thence to the cabin, a distinct possibility. Good preflight, Tom.

Another nit-pick: One of our local pilots owns a big Cessna 400-series twin. He knows this plane so well that he doesn't even bother with a preflight—just a quick splash of fuel from each quick-drain onto the concrete. He doesn't even kick a tire before lighting off. And what a light-off: 2,000 rpm on starting and the plane's already moving as he cranks up the other one. I'll bet he doesn't make it to TBO on either engine.

I'll also bet he doesn't get much service from the local avionics shop. Last week, he made a sharp right turn after starting up, pointed his tail at the open door of the avionics hangar and blew sand, dirt, empty bottles, test equipment, and assorted airplane interior parts to the back hangar wall.

What's the hurry on start-up? Why not use the pre-start checklist? Why not set the parking brakes? Why not let the oil get flowing by running at a low rpm on start-up? This guy is just asking for a spun bearing, spalled tappets, and a self-ground camshaft with those roaring starts.

Time to Do Lots of Things

The pre-taxi set of checks is one nit that I'll still pick at early on a Flight Review. While that oil is starting to flow, why not get the instruments and avionics set and adjusted? Now is a good time to get the DG aligned to the wet compass, and when you get to the runway you will have some idea about the amount of precession in the gyro. Also, if there is a VOR within line of sight, now's a good time to check the No. 1 nav unit against No. 2. The same with the ADF: Set it now, to a local broadcast station if necessary, then watch the needle during taxi turns. It's a lot easier than discovering, at the LOM on an actual ILS approach, that the ADF won't point.

And while waiting to taxi, consider that magneto grounding check. It's usually considered adequate to perform this check only once per flight, just before shutdown. But I have gotten a little touchy about ignition recently. I've had several occasions of getting clear out to the run-up pad, then finding that I had only one mag or maybe a bunch of badly fouled plugs. So, shortly after start, at about 1,000 rpm, I like to do a quick check of the mags. Pull the throttle back to full idle and switch to "OFF" just long enough to hear the engine quit and see the tach start to unwind.

I always find lots of bad procedures when we get out to the run-up pad. Even during taxi I can find things to bitch about. For example with a fuel-injected engine, why not lean the mixture a little before starting to taxi? Most of these injected engines run quite rich at low power settings, and that extra fuel with all that lead isn't doing the valves and plugs any good. So, set the throttle to 1,000 rpm, and lean the mixture until max rpm, then richen it just a hair. Lots of carbureted engines will be helped by this also. But don't forget to return the mixture to full rich for run-up.

Taxiing out is also a good time to check on the operation of the fuel system by selecting each tank to see if it feeds. Again, make sure to go back to the proper tank for the run-up and takeoff.

I see a lot of mistreatment of constant-speed propellers during run-up. That hard pull aft on the prop control, followed by a stiff-arm back to the high-rpm position isn't doing the engine any good, and it really isn't proving much except that the prop lever is still connected to the governor. Many of the engines have dynamic, or "floating," counter-weights on the crankshaft and sudden rpm changes tend to bounce the counterweights against their bearing surfaces. This spoils what must be a smooth bearing if the counter-weights are to do their job. That yank-and-shove routine with the prop control is bad for the engine and maybe dangerous for the prop—it relies on the counterweights to damp some of the vibration modes that otherwise induce fatigue stresses in the prop blades.

How about a nice, slow retardation of the prop rpm—no faster than the way you would change rpm while flying. The idea is to check governing, so why not just slowly reduce engine speed 200 to 300 rpm below the initial rpm, using the prop lever? Let the rpm stabilize. If it holds constant, the governor almost has to be working properly. To double-check the governor and prop, while holding that 200 to 300 rpm low, add one or two inches of manifold pressure. The rpm may surge a little, but it should settle back to what was set before with the prop lever.

If the AFM calls for moving the prop control through the full range during this governor check, then do it before running the governor check previously discussed and move the prop lever slowly. This full-travel check gives the governor an oil change; it pumps the governor full of new oil as the blade angle increases, then flushes the oil out (maybe a lot of sludge, too) when the lever is advanced again.

There's a distinction to be made about multi-engine props—the feathering variety. Too many pilots think, and at least one AFM indicates, that the feathering check and governing check can be done as a single maneuver. The feathering check should be performed at a speed below the minimum governing rpm, which is typically about 1,200 to 1,500 rpm. Set the rpm with the throttle (prop levers full forward), then slowly move the prop levers aft through the normal governing range to the beginning of the feather detent. The rpm had better not decrease during this slow prop lever retardation. If it does, you might experience an inadvertent feathering while setting climb rpm after takeoff!

At the beginning of the feather range, move the prop lever sharply to full-aft, and observe the rpm rapidly decreasing. Then, move the lever rapidly forward before the rpm can drop more than 200 to 300 rpm—unless you want to see the prop actually feather during the test, and maybe overstress the crankshaft. The full-feather movement of the prop lever positively and mechanically lifts the governor pilot valve into a position where all oil pressure in the prop is dumped and the feathering mechanism (prop dome air or nitrogen charge, springs, or counterweights) can move the blades toward the feather angle. But, this check does not prove that the prop will govern!

Governing is checked next, with the prop rpm set by the throttle, well into the governing range. Run this check just the same as for single-engine airplanes as previously discussed. If the two engines seem to respond differently, add that one or two inches of manifold pressure while the prop is set to a lower rpm with the prop lever. If the two props respond very differently, check both powerplants at the same time. If there is a big difference in governing (or in feather action during that previous feather check), cancel the flight!

ON, OFF—BUT DON'T TARRY

Magneto checks are often mishandled by pilots who stay too long in single-mag operation—that is just asking for a fouled plug or two. Only a couple of seconds is needed to note the rpm drop or any roughness when you switch to one mag or the other. And there should be some drop in engine speed; if there's no rpm drop, it can mean a bad mag switch, a broken P-lead, or horribly advanced ignition timing. A big difference between the two magnetos can be a sign of bad timing also—adhere to the AFM limits.

Key-type ignition/starter switches can be misused. Many pilots move the key very rapidly from the BOTH position to one of the single-mag positions, then rapidly back to BOTH. Why move it so fast? If the innards of the switch are working properly, there shouldn't be any dead spots between the positions. If there is a dead spot, you want to find it—the switch might be ready to fail. Also, moving the key too rapidly back to BOTH might let it overshoot and engage the starter, which is bad for the starter ring and other engine parts.

Alternatively, moving the key too fast toward a single-mag position might allow it to overshoot and go into the OFF position and allow the engine to conk out. If this ever happens, leave the mag switch off and pull the throttle back to idle, then switch the mags on again. At high rpm with the ignition off, the exhaust stacks will be full of raw fuel vapor and turning the mags on will make the exhaust stacks act like little rockets.

Everyone has his own idea of how to handle indications of fouled spark plugs after a bad mag check; I'll share one I learned from an old-timer. First, don't lean the engine at high power. Some pilots try to burn off the fouling at mag-check rpm, which is usually in the vicinity of 60 percent power, and it's not a good thing to heat up cylinders unless they have plenty of airflow. Also, the heat produced might bake some of the offending sparkplug deposits into something harder.

Instead of the high-power procedure, throttle back to about 1,000 rpm. Then lean the mixture slowly until the tach indicates a slight rpm increase. Continue leaning until the rpm peaks, then lean some more—very slowly—until the rpm just starts to decrease. Now the combustion chamber is over-leaned—too much oxygen for the fuel provided. Running the engine for about one minute in the over-leaned condition might allow the excess oxygen to combine with the offending plug deposit and burn it off. After about a minute, put the mixture back to full rich and throttle back up to mag-check rpm for another look at rpm drop.

Is there still a 200 to 300 rpm drop on one mag? Okay, so the burn-off didn't work. Let's do the "blow-off" technique. Try full throttle, full rpm, and full-rich mixture for about 30 seconds. Now check the mag again. My success rate is about nine out of ten using these two techniques. What about that tenth time when the mag won't clear? I go back to the barn! Sure, it probably will clear up in flight, but why take the chance? Over the past year, my A&P mechanic has found two bad high-tension leads and one bad magneto after my magneto aborts.

I've done all of this nit-picking before the airplane even reaches the runway. But, during the average Flight Review, I pick more nits on the beginning of a flight and on the subject of "is this plane really ready to fly?" than what I scratch on in-flight operations.

A last thought: Maybe you disagree with me or with your flight reviewer checker. But do you really know your airplane? Can you perform a preflight that really protects you and your passengers from a detectable mechanical failure? Does your engine run-up and takeoff check cover everything that you can possibly cover to be absolutely sure that something doesn't screw up right after liftoff?

The Armstrong Starter

Time was, when hand-cranking was the only way to start a car and hand-propping the only way to start an airplane, and broken thumbs and arms were almost *de rigeur* among motorists and pilots. But there's a big difference between the kick of a Model T's crank and the damage that can be done by a propeller.

There are precious few times when it's absolutely necessary to resort to hand-propping, and very few pilots have the knowledge or training to do it properly or safely. The hazards grow in proportion to the size of the engine—the big ones are much harder to turn over by hand, and when they do start, there's a lot more energy to cause damage to people or property. But even in a pilot population that should know better, propping accidents and incidents continue to take place. Especially in the case of large, powerful airplanes, there's almost always a better way, a safer alternative than hand-propping. Witness these examples of what can happen.

The pilot of a Cessna 210 found he had a dead battery. Told by mechanics that the battery would not hold a charge and that he would need a new one, the pilot took the battery to the airplane, installed it and prepared to hand-prop the engine. He told his passenger to hold his feet on the brakes. The pilot then successfully started the plane.

However, though the passenger pressed with great force on the rudder pedals, he was apparently unaware of how to place his feet to operate the toe brakes. The Centurion taxied smartly into a hangar and its prop ate the wings of a new Stits biplane. There were no injuries—but replacing the biplane probably cost a lot more than a new battery.

In a mishap at Seattle's Seatac Airport, the pilot of a Cessna 210 suffered serious foot and head injuries when the plane dragged him 1,200 feet into a VOR facility—and he wasn't even trying to start the engine.

The pilot was aware that compression in the No. 1 cylinder was higher than the others, which stopped the propeller near top dead center whenever the engine was shut down. This made starting difficult unless the prop was backed up to give the engine a running start past top center in this cylinder.

Very unfortunately, the magneto switch was on when the pilot moved the propeller. The engine started, at about half-throttle. The pilot quickly got around to the plane's door and tried to reach in and shut the engine off, but the Centurion was already in motion. The airplane dragged him a fifth of a mile, across an active runway, over a ditch and into a VOR antenna building. The pilot managed to get to the magneto switch and turn it off just before impact, which was severe enough to drive the engine through the cinder block wall of the building.

In yet another low-battery fiasco, the pilot of a Beech Bonanza was asked by Ground Control to keep his landing light on while taxiing to its parking space at Seattle's Boeing Field; 'twas a very hazy day. The pilot was aware that unlike an alternator, the Bonanza's generator system would not keep charging the battery if taxied at low rpm. This resulted in a drain on the battery and the engine wouldn't start when the pilot got ready to leave.

The pilot set up the airplane first so that he could turn the prop through before starting. When he went back into the cockpit, turned on the mag switch and set the parking brake, he unfortunately did not notice that he left the throttle in the full forward position.

The Bonanza started at full power, and began to creep forward against its brakes. Even so, the pilot was able to get around the wing, into the airplane and pull back on the throttle. But this pilot had spent most of his flying time in a Cessna 172, and by the time he remembered that he needed to release the vernier button on the throttle of the Bonanza to pull it back, the airplane had taxied into a Beech 58P Baron, causing an estimated $60,000 worth of damage.

Though there was some danger—the Bonanza's tires were smoking and fuel was pouring from the damaged airplanes—there were no injuries.

The FAA's Advisory Circular 91-42 has specific cautions that apply whenever the propeller of an airplane is to be hand-rotated. An excellent rule of thumb, however, is to not even *try* to hand-start an airplane whose systems include a battery and starter. Remedy whatever is keeping the engine from starting normally. It's the safest procedure, especially with engines of 200 horsepower and higher.

It also should be noted that some insurance companies may void coverage in hand-propping cases, particularly where a rated pilot or mechanic is not stationed at the controls during the starting attempt.

I Can't See You; Can You See Me?

Flight operations at uncontrolled (non-towered) airports represent the most likely environment for midair collisions, and the statistics confirm it. Here are some thoughts on the subject from a long-time professional with a deep interest in helping pilots live longer.

COOL HARBOR AIRPORT, USA

Collision avoidance has been a hot topic for as long as I've been flying. Until some fool-proof device comes out to keep airplanes apart, we're all stuck with relying on procedures and eyeballs to prevent unplanned mid-air meetings.

Some situations seem to foster more than their share of near mid-air collisions. Places like uncontrolled airports, for example. I sometimes fly out of an uncontrolled field near my home. I'll call this place Cool Harbor Airport.

Cool Harbor Airport isn't real busy—it's got two hard-surface runways, each 4000 feet long, some usable grass areas, Unicom on 122.7, avgas and a little jet-A, and lights on one of the runways.

But Cool Harbor has a lot of diversity; little planes and big ones, new and old varieties, antiques and homebuilts. There's even a Citation jet and several turboprops. But wait, that's not all; Cool Harbor has two sailplane operations going, one of them seven days a week. Several ultralights, including a two-seat model for instruction. Occasional hang gliders get taken aloft under tow. And a seaplane training operation in a lake just off the end of one runway. The Sheriff's Aviation Department is based here also. I live 15 miles away, but have found Cool Harbor a pleasant place to work; flight instructing, and conducting flight tests. During a recent meeting of local pilots at the airport, the new airport manager went over the rules for uncontrolled airports. He covered basic things like "see and be seen," look for the other guy, look at the wind sock and tetrahedron, listen on Unicom and call on 122.7 for field advisory, make your calls on downwind and base, Unicom is only advisory...on and on.

Obviously, lots of us had not read the rules on uncontrolled airports for a long time. Some figured that an airport advisory was mandatory, and that they *had* to land on Runway 04, just because Unicom so advised. Others concluded that the tetrahedron was the final word on the active runway (at Cool Harbor the tetrahedron is not tied down, and swings slowly in light winds).

Several pilots, with that one-sided view that I have learned to expect at such meetings, predicted dire consequences if all of the "sub-normal" flight operations weren't banned from the airport. Others had real experiences with traffic conflict. I've had a few conflicts there also, including one just the day before the meeting.

I had been listening on Unicom, and heard a Navajo get an advisory to use Runway 22. Shortly after, he reported "downwind for 22." About three minutes later, I entered downwind, and reported. There was no sign of the Navajo. He wasn't on the runway. He wasn't on base leg, final, or the downwind. I figured he must have already taxied to the ramp. So, I let my student turn a normal base leg, and reported "turning base."

There came an immediate radio call from the Navajo. He was on base leg, and wanted to know why I was cutting him out. Sure enough, way out there, about five miles away, was a little two-engine speck on the horizon. Needless to say, we continued with "cutting him out," but politely advised the big-plane pilot that we were doing so.

Now, uncontrolled field or not, you have to fly a normal pattern. I have developed an "eagle eye" for catching the straight-ins and right-hand base leg time-savers at Cool Harbor—and there are a lot of them. But I missed the Navajo, until he called to complain.

I'm especially wary when the first call from another plane is "base leg for 04", or "on final for 29". These are usually the pilots sneaking in with that backwards base leg, or improper straight-in. *Don't do that!* What about that old J-3 or Luscombe that has no radio? We have lots of the oldies at Cool Harbor, and those pilots are counting on everyone else flying a standard pattern so that the no-radio aircraft can pick them up visually. We also have several pilots with well-equipped airplanes who routinely taxi out and take off with nary a radio call. It sure would be safer to alert other radio-equipped planes of what you intend to do.

A friend recently taxied out on a dual instruction flight. He got the Unicom field advisory to use Runway 22. As he passed midfield, and went onto the parallel taxiway to get to the active, he noticed a light twin leave the ramp at the other end of the field. The twin made no radio call, taxied for Runway 04, and didn't answer a call on 122.7 from the little trainer trundling toward 22. Only when the twin announced, "departing on 04," followed instantly by the CFI in the C-152 announcing, "and I'm departing on the active runway, 22," did the twin chop power, burn rubber, and come to a screeching halt. Sort of nasty, maybe. But, a lesson was learned.

What if they had both been no-radio airplanes? Boy, they had better both have a good look around! Even if only one of the planes is not radio equipped, everybody needs to keep the eyeballs moving, and the head swinging. Not just that short instant before releasing the brakes for takeoff, but all the time during taxi-out and run-up.

We have one blind spot on the airport. From the departure end of 04, you can't see the departure end of 29—there's a row of T-hangars in the way. The city intends to relocate those hangars, but until they do, that midfield intersection has the potential for being real hairy.

My only complaint at the meeting was that free-swinging tetrahedron. I'd sure like to see it tied down on those light-wind days. There is a good windsock right close to the tetrahedron, so the putt-putts can still get a gander at the winds.

But, even if the tetrahedron does get staked on the light-wind days (and Runway 04 is the specified "light-wind" runway), there are still those guys who will want to depart from the strip closest to their tiedowns or T-hangars. That's bad when there are parking areas at each corner of the airport. But that's one of the reasons this meeting was called—let's all follow the rules.

The professionals flying the Citation are new to the airport, but obviously not new to uncontrolled airports. They usually enter from overhead, above the traffic pattern, and get a good look around before breaking out to enter the pattern on downwind. A good tight pattern every time— never a straight-in approach. They fly a tighter pattern than some of the putt-putts. And, they use the Unicom.

Occasionally someone, usually one of the smaller high-performance singles, will pull a real tight pattern. So tight that it's a continuous 180-degree turn from downwind to final. That's not good; that's not kosher; that's not standard. And, it spoils the chance for a good look around on base leg; in a low-winger, you can't see the other guy on the outside of your base turn. That might be the guy who flew a little wider pattern—or maybe the sneaky one who is trying an unannounced straight-in approach. Of course, in a high-wing type, you are blind to the inside of the turn, and probably won't even see the runway until almost on final. You might not see the plane pulling onto your runway. You won't have the opportunity to watch *all* runways to make sure that someone isn't landing or taking-off on a cross runway.

But keeping an eye open for traffic extends beyond the airport traffic area. There are lots of gliders now—high-performance sailplanes, really—at the airport. If the buzzards and ospreys are circling in the thermals, those sail-planes will be soaring also, way outside of the traffic pattern. Cool Harbor sits real close to a Victor airway—so look around for the transients. Look down for the seaplanes returning to the lake—they always stay low to keep clear of the runway traffic. The ultralights may be below normal traffic also.

Lots of us have picked up a real bad habit of spending too much time with eyes in the cockpit. We are even training a whole new generation of "non-lookers" with the altitude/heading/airspeed limits criteria that a student pilot must achieve to meet the private pilot flight test requirements. I find lots of pilots, even those with loads of flight time, either looking at the panel, or looking for traffic straight ahead through the windshield. It's better to swing your head, and check out to both sides and up and down.

A fair number of the midairs and near midairs over the years have occurred when both of the front seats were occupied. Now, if you're the pilot, and the guy in the right seat is only a passenger, why not put him to work? Assign him a lookout sector—from 30 degrees left of straight-ahead to 45 degrees behind the wing on his side. That extra pair of searching eyeballs could save your fanny, and it's a good way to keep the right-seater occupied, fairly silent, and not distracting you from your flying and looking. Of course, you had better cover his sector yourself, as a back-up.

Instructional flights are inherently plagued with less-than-optimum looking around. The student is busy with his tasks, and usually not putting enough time into looking outside. You CFI's, just watch a new student some time; make a checkmark on your notepad every time he turns his head to look out to the sides. I timed a third-ride student last week, in a C-150. During one period we went for 4.5 minutes without his head ever making the slightest movement to either side. Five times during the flight I saw an airplane on *his* side of the airplane before he saw it.

But along with the student's looking around being almost worthless at this early stage, my own looking was certainly not optimum. Too much time talking to the student, pointing out pitch attitude references over the nose, maybe getting both our attention focused on the airspeed indicator. The CFI has to pay particular attention to maintaining a double-good lookout on instrument training flights.

I scared myself real good last year while trying to talk a hooded student into a holding pattern entry in good VFR weather. Too much of my time was spent pointing at the DG and VOR indicator, and too much time talking. Just as we rolled out on the proper heading for a "parallel" entry, *there was an Aztec at one-o'clock, level!* And *close!* I just had time to shout, "I've got it," make a hard turn and climb, then quietly state, "you've got it again." It was a 90-degree crossing situation, and the Aztec had right-of-way.

Nobody appeared concerned except me—my pulse rate jumped into triple digits. From the depths of his hood, my student mumbled "What's the matter—did I do it wrong again?" Certainly the Aztec pilot was not concerned; I distinctly remember looking into his left ear as I started the panic evasive maneuver—not his eyes, just one ear. Certainly the approach controller wasn't bothered; he never called out the traffic, so I assume that the Aztec was not squawking.

Years (and years) ago, the U.S. Navy ran a special Instrument Training School at Corpus Christi, Texas, using SNB "Bug-smashers" (that's a C-45 or Beech Model 18, a big recip twin). Looking for traffic from the cockpit was horrible. The left-seat student wore blue goggles while the inside of the windshield had a yellow cellophane lining—the student couldn't see a thing outside. The instructor could see through the yellow okay, but the student's head completely blocked vision to the left side. The navy played it smart; a second student rode in a rear seat, on the left side, with the sole duty of looking for traffic, and he was wired into the intercom.

This worked real well for years, until one day two of the Bugsmashers collided directly over the "cone-of-silence" of the Palacios low frequency radio range.

Okay, there are no more LF ranges today. But now it's even more hairy. Anyone, any autopilot, can easily go directly over a VOR. It wasn't so easy with those old ranges. So, if you're approaching a navigation fix, wouldn't it be smart to figure that maybe someone else might also be heading for that same point in space? And, maybe at the same altitude? This is a good time to double your traffic-watching efforts!

And, for you CFIs, if you have a spare seat in back, and if the insurance company or FBO will allow it, would not an instrument training flight be a good time to load aboard another student, or a mechanic, or even the boss's secretary—just to provide a little extra "looking" capability?

Our worst midairs, those most publicized, occurred when each pilot *could* have seen the other airplane. Or at least one of the crew members in each plane *could* have seen the other plane in time to avert the crash. Obviously, a lot of people were not looking. Don't count on the other guy seeing you. *You just gotta see him first!*

Caught in a Vortex

As any general aviation pilot who has experience in a busy terminal environment has learned, some caution is required when mixing in with the heavy iron. The combination of extreme speed differences (both horizontally and vertically) and special operational hazards, like wake turbulence and jet blast, make it wise to give airliners a wide berth.

Terminal controllers do their best to keep small and large airplanes separated as widely as possible, but when things get really congested, even their best efforts may not be enough.

The pilot of a Piper Seneca got a graphic demonstration of the potential inadequacy of "adequate" spacing at Miami International Airport. The Seneca was on a scheduled passenger flight from West Palm Beach, Florida, and was operating on an IFR flight plan, though the weather was clear.

As the aircraft approached Miami, the 18,000-hour ATP was cleared to land on Runway 9R. At the time, there was a nearly direct left crosswind of 12 knots. Two Boeing 737s were waiting for clearance to take off from 9R, one at the end of the 13,002-foot runway and one at a taxiway intersection about a third of the way down. The pilot of the Seneca requested and received permission to land long, so that he would have less distance to taxi to the passenger terminal.

As he was coming down final approach, however, the tower cleared the Pan Am jet at the end of the runway for an immediate takeoff. The controller told the pilot of the Seneca to "do S-turns or whatever necessary" to maintain spacing with the 737 and avoid its wake turbulence.

According to the pilot, he reduced airspeed and attempted to get his aircraft on the ground short of the 737's liftoff point. While still 10 to 20 feet in the air, however, the Seneca encountered the jet's wake and rolled between 60 and 70 degrees to the right and pitched nose-down. The pilot said he recovered enough control to land in the grass to the right of the runway. Neither the pilot nor his two passengers was injured in the mishap.

The pilot's account doesn't quite match the statements of witnesses, though. One pilot, who at the time was a passenger aboard the 737 holding at the intersection, said, "The plane looked to be on the centerline of the runway and flaring to a stall landing, nose up, gear down. Suddenly, the left wing went down on touchdown. It appeared to me that the tail section elevated, and the plane's nose and right main collapsed on the runway, then began sliding down the runway until it went off the right side into the grass strip. As a pilot, it is my opinion that either the plane's left main collapsed or experienced a tire separation on landing."

Another witness was a member of the flight crew aboard the same 737. According to him, the Seneca was still airborne as it passed the 737, more than 3,000 feet down the runway. He looked away for a moment but saw the Piper as it hit the runway and then slid off into the grass.

The investigator's factual report on the accident states that there was at least 6,000 feet between the departing 737 and the Seneca, and it points out that this is the minimum called for in the FAA Air Traffic Control Manual.

The NTSB concluded that there was "adequate" spacing between the two aircraft. Despite this, the safety board determined that the pilot's inability to flare the Seneca due to vortex turbulence from the departing jet was the probable cause of the accident.

Look Out for the Big Ones

Low-level aerobatics are exciting enough for pilots, but doubly so for passengers—especially when they are totally unprepared, and when they're riding in a commuter airplane. Nevertheless, a Cessna 402 rolled at least inverted while conducting an ILS approach to Boston's Logan International Airport one spring evening, the victim of a wake turbulence encounter.

The flight originated in Hyannis, Massachusetts, at 10:40 p.m. and was being positioned for an ILS Runway 4R approach at Boston when the incident occurred.

The commuter pilot, flying at 3,000 feet, was advised that he was directly behind an A-300 Airbus at 4,000 feet; the controller cautioned him about wake turbulence and advised him that he could reduce his airspeed to 150 knots. The pilot slowed to 150 knots and was about 18 miles from the field when cleared for the approach.

At a position 10 miles out, the plane's occupants felt a bump and the aircraft rolled left. The pilot said the roll occurred so rapidly that he could not determine whether the aircraft did a complete roll and continued to stop inverted, or was just becoming inverted, when he got control and stopped the roll. Another bump was felt and the aircraft rolled 40 degrees to the right before the roll stopped. About 200 feet of altitude was lost during the maneuvers.

The flight obtained vectors for another ILS approach and landed without further incident. There was no report of injuries to any occupants or damage to the airplane.

The Golden Rule of Vortices

Anything that produces aerodynamic lift also produces tip vortices. It's a simple matter of understanding that the higher-pressure air underneath a wing is constantly seeking a way to move to the low pressure area above. If wings were of infinite length, there would be no problem, but the wingtip provides a way for equilibrium to be restored; air curls around the wingtip on its way to the top side, and because of the forward motion of the vehicle, the curl turns into a vortex trailing behind the airplane.

Pilots are trained to avoid these vortices, which move downward and outward, leveling off somewhere in the neighborhood of 1000 feet below the generating airplane. Obviously, the airspace behind and immediately below a large airplane is not a good place to be.

A commercial pilot was killed when his Cessna 210 crashed out of control following an encounter with wake turbulence. The pilot had set out on what was to have been a 12-mile flight from John Tunes Airport to Nashville Metropolitan Airport. He departed Tunes at about 7:20, and contacted Nashville Approach Control, advising the controller he was going to Nashville Metropolitan. The controller acknowledged this and radar contact was established at 7:21.

At 7:23, the pilot was told to switch frequencies and

contact Nashville Approach on 133.9. He complied, and the new controller gave him vectors to land on Runway 2R at Nashville. This routing took the Cessna somewhat south of the runway at an altitude of 1,500 feet which was below the altitude of jet traffic heading for Runway 2L.

At 7:26, controllers advised the pilot of possible wake turbulence due to an American Airlines Boeing 727 on final to Runway 2L. By the time the Cessna was three or four miles south of Nashville, the separation between the two aircraft had dwindled to approximately 500 feet vertically and one mile horizontally.

The Cessna was handed off to Nashville Tower and was cleared to land, but minutes later, the pilot reported, "I got a big dose of wake turbulence." The tower then issued a wake turbulence advisory, and the pilot immediately responded, "I done had it." Radar and radio contact were then lost.

At 10:44 p.m., the flight service station at Nashville called the tower to inquire about the Cessna. The tower replied that they still had an inbound strip on it and they thought the Cessna might have landed and could still be on the airport, if it hadn't already departed again.

Between midnight and 2:45 a.m., the pilot's family called the flight service station numerous times, asking if they'd heard anything about the overdue Cessna. The FSS in turn called the tower, which responded that there was still an inbound strip on the Cessna.

By 6 a.m., the FSS again called the tower to request voice recordings and at 7:15, an Alert Notice was issued. Airport personnel conducted a ramp search, but the Cessna was nowhere to be found. The Tennessee Highway Patrol was finally alerted to the possibility that the airplane had crashed at 1:15 that afternoon. Some 45 minutes later, the Cessna was found. It had crashed a mile and a half south of the runway, killing the pilot.

Rotary Wings Create Problems, Too

Wake turbulence literature generally discusses the problem and its solutions in the context of a small airplane landing or taking off behind a big airplane. This covers the most likely situations; but everything that flies leaves a wake, and it may not register in the minds of all pilots that this includes rotorcraft.

The notion did occur to the pilot of a Piper Arrow during his landing approach at Clatsop County Airport, Astoria, Oregon—but he nonetheless got caught in the wake of a Coast Guard HH-3 helicopter (Sikorsky S-61 in civilian dress), and the encounter had disastrous consequences.

The 302-hour pilot (83 hours in make and model) was ending a VFR flight in good weather when he arrived at Clatsop, an uncontrolled field with a Coast Guard air-sea rescue unit in residence. Although the pilot apparently broadcast his pattern announcements on the Portland FSS frequency, which he had been using for advisories, his failure to broadcast on the correct Unicom frequency was not deemed a factor in the ensuing crash.

Just before the Arrow's arrival, the HH-3 had returned from a mission and executed a standard pattern for Runway 21, announcing its position and intentions on Unicom. The wind was from 250 degrees at about 11 knots.

The helicopter flew a final approach that was steep by airplane standards, but normal for helicopters. It executed a roll-on landing, turned left and taxied clear of the runway.

The Arrow pilot saw the helicopter as he entered the pattern, and he extended his downwind because, he told investigators, "I don't know what helicopters leave behind, but I did not want to take a chance." Nonetheless, the Arrow was on short final when it was clearly caught in a ferocious wake. Witnesses saw its left wing drop sharply, then a nose pitch-up, then a snapping roll to the right. The right wingtip struck ground, followed by the nose; the airplane cart-wheeled, broke off its wings and tumbled. Witness and wreckage evidence suggest the pilot went to full power in the few seconds of the wake encounter (the pilot cannot recall this period), but all observers agreed the airplane was simply out of control.

The crash killed the passenger in the right front seat, seriously injured the pilot and another passenger, and left the fourth occupant of the plane with minor injuries.

Helicopters *Do* "Leave Something Behind"

The HH-3 is a 20,000-pound flying machine with a pair of 1500-horsepower engines driving a five-blade main rotor 62 feet in diameter. As helicopters go, it is a big one.

The investigator estimated that the helicopter touched down 1,500 feet beyond the runway threshold, about 30 to 45 seconds before the Arrow began its flare. It is certain that the helicopter was generating a considerable amount of vortex activity as its pilot set up the flare and landing. But how is its vortex related to that of a fixed-wing aircraft, and how can a pilot avoid the danger?

As the Arrow pilot expressed it, "I am certain that helicopters have a vortex of some type and I feel more should be published in regards to helicopters, and maybe waiting longer before landings or using other runways in regards to large helicopters."

In fact, the *Airman's Information Manual* does contain a statement on the subject: "A hovering helicopter generates a downwash from its main rotor(s) similar to the prop blast of a conventional aircraft. However, in forward flight, this energy is transformed into a pair of trailing vortices similar to the wing-tip vortices of fixed-wing aircraft. Pilots of small aircraft should avoid the vortices as well as the downwash."

This said, the same avoidance techniques used for fixed-wing vortex-makers will apply: Land beyond the helicopter's touchdown point; take off before its takeoff point; remember that the vortices drift downward behind it at all times while it's airborne and are influenced by crosswinds. But the main thing is to recognize a large helicopter as a formidable vortex-generator, and give it a wide berth.

We are told that there's a rule of thumb which can be used to guess the relative vortex strength of a helicopter compared to a fixed-wing craft, based on the ratios of weight and relative speed (the lower the airspeed, the more vorticity is generated). For instance, a 20,000-pound helicopter on approach at 40 knots would have about the same vorticity as a 60,000-pound airplane on approach at 120 knots.

The Wrong Stuff

Every pilot has limits—whether imposed by the aircraft or self-imposed, they are very real limits. Pushing the limits (both his own and the airplane's) killed the pilot of a Cessna 172N and his three passengers when their airplane crashed near Del Rio, Texas.

The 30-year-old pilot was an Air Force captain and military instructor pilot based at Laughlin Air Force Base. He had a total of 1,505 hours of flight experience, including 1,420 hours in T-37s, T-38s and B-52s.

As for his civilian flying experience, he had logged a total of 14 hours in the Cessna 172. He also held an FAA commercial pilot certificate, ratings for single- and multi-engine aircraft, an instrument rating, and a second-class medical certificate. Although one of the passengers was also a private pilot, as well as being a lieutenant in the Air Force, he was sitting in one of the rear seats and was not considered as a second pilot by NTSB investigators.

At about 2 p.m. the pilot loaded the rented C-172 with full fuel and his three passengers and departed Del Rio, Texas, for a local pleasure flight. About 20 minutes later, the Cessna appeared over Lake Amistad, near Del Rio. There was a considerable amount of boating traffic on the lake, and the airplane was observed by several witnesses, most of whom were also military personnel based at Laughlin. Some of the witnesses were also Air Force pilots and colleagues of the Cessna pilot.

The pilot made several low-altitude, high-speed passes at some of the boats occupied by the other Air Force pilots. The passes were concluded with sharp pull-ups and hammerhead stalls. According to witnesses, some of the pull-ups were up the canyon walls which border Lake Amistad. The walls are stepped, with an average slope of about 30 degrees.

The various witness accounts begin at different times, but the Cessna apparently continued these maneuvers for 10-12 minutes. One witness said the airplane flew beneath a railroad bridge running across the lake, then pulled up to fly over a 67-foot-high highway bridge running parallel to the first bridge and 500 feet away, nearly stalling while doing so.

Exact details of the witness accounts vary. Some said the airplane came to within 10 feet of the canyon walls during its pull-ups. However, most agreed that the maximum altitude gained during the pull-ups and hammerhead stalls was no more than 300 feet. Several also said that the Cessna pulled out of some of the ensuing dives only 10 feet above the water.

The pilot concluded this series of maneuvers with an aileron roll starting at an altitude of 300 or 400 feet, coming out of the roll only a few feet above the water. The airplane was so low that one witness thought it had actually touched the surface of the lake.

The pilot then left the area, and so did some of the boaters, who were upset by the display. Some went to report the incident, while others chose to get out of the area.

About 25 minutes later, the Cessna reappeared and started buzzing the boats again. After the first pass, the Cessna cleared a ridge and disappeared for a few seconds. After returning, the pilot pushed over into the canyon, made another pass, and pulled up parallel to the canyon wall for what would be the last hammerhead stall.

One witness (who was also an Air Force instructor pilot) was in a boat out of sight of the canyon itself, but he was able to see the airplane as it cleared the canyon rim. He later told investigators, "The nose fell quickly through the horizon, to what I would estimate as a 40- to 60-degree nose-low attitude. The aircraft disappeared below the terrain in this attitude with the lateral axis of the wings forming approximately a 30-degree angle to the horizon. At that time I turned to my wife and exclaimed that there was no way the aircraft could pull out of that attitude with the altitude remaining. Shortly thereafter, she noted a small plume of dust."

Pilot witnesses in the canyon itself said they felt the Cessna pilot let the nose of the airplane get too low and was unable to pull out in time. They saw the airplane impact the canyon wall about 20 feet from the shore line, break in half at the main landing gear attach point, and bounce into the water. The aircraft was demolished by the impact, and the occupants were killed outright.

Post-crash investigation revealed no medical or toxicological problems with the pilot, and no mechanical defect in the airplane itself. A weight and balance analysis showed the airplane to be as much as 323 pounds over its maximum allowable gross weight and more than three inches out of the center of gravity envelope at the time of the accident. The NTSB concluded that weight and balance were not a factor in the crash, attributing the probable cause to aerobatics performed by the pilot in command, with misjudged altitude and a delayed level-off as contributing factors.

There Are No High Wires

Wires have always been a nemesis for airmen. In years gone by, flying into wires has accounted for a substantial portion of all aircraft accidents. But in recent years, the incidence of wire strikes has dropped significantly; from 5.1 percent of all accidents in 1974 to 4.5 percent in 1984. And not only have the numbers of wire-strike accidents gone down, but the pattern of these accidents has changed. What about wire-strike accidents has changed over the years? And what's behind this drop in wire-strike accidents?

Wired Up

During an earlier survey of wire-strike accidents we examined NTSB data for the years 1977 and 1978. During those two years, we found some 462 wire-strike accidents. Of these, 83 were fatal accidents (about 18 percent).

We also examined NTSB records for 1984 to obtain an updated comparison. During that year, there were some 138 instances of aircraft striking wires. Some 40 of these (about 29 percent) were fatal. This is up 11 percent from our previous survey.

On the whole, however, wire-strike accidents have shown a significant decline. While the average number of such accidents was about 230 per year in the late 1970s, by the mid 1980s the number has fallen to around 140 per year. Again, expressed as a percentage of all accidents, wire strikes have fallen from slightly more than five percent to about four-and-a-half percent of all accidents.

Low Flying

About the only way to get airplanes and wires together is to get the airplane to come down near the ground. That was true years ago, and remains true today. During our original survey, low flying accounted for 95 crashes out of the total of 462 (about 20.5 percent). When agricultural low flying was added in, then the low-flying category ballooned to 221 accidents, or more than 47 percent of the total.

Some 55 wire-strike crashes during 1984 fell into the low-flying category (including ag flying), or about 40 percent of the total. If ag flying is excluded, the total falls to 21, or about 15 percent.

Pilot experience doesn't seem to play a large role in wire-strike accidents. During 1984, pilot time averaged more than 2,500 total hours. There were eight pilots with 10,000 hours or more (one high-timer having had 31,000 hours and another had 25,000 hours).

Low flying can be broken down into finer categories. One of these is ag flying; another is plain-vanilla low flying. Pilots cruise along at low altitude and run into wires. This type of accident predominantly happens over water of some sort.

For example, if ag flying is excluded, of the remaining 21 instances of low flying, 11 involved aircraft cruising along at low altitude. But nine of them were cruising along rivers or over lakes. By comparison, in our earlier study, 16 aircraft crashed under similar circumstances.

In most of these crashes, the wire was struck at a very low altitude—100 feet AGL or less. But in two instances, the wire was at a comparatively high altitude—300 feet in one case, 350 in another.

Around the Field

Something else that can bring airplanes and wires together is landing or taking off. All across the country there are airports literally surrounded by nets of telephone wires, high-tension cables, and antennas with guy wires. And all across the country, pilots are finding these wires the hard way.

During our original survey, some 118 accidents occurred in close proximity to the airport (about 26 percent of the total). During 1984, though, the total was 29 crashes (21 percent of all wire-strike crashes). Typically, these accidents involve airplanes that, for one reason or another, are just too low for where they are and for what they're doing.

The crash of a Piper Tri-Pacer near Memphis International Airport is a good example. The 2,253-hour commercial pilot was on a non-precision instrument approach when he descended below the MDA. The Tri-Pacer hit wires and crashed, seriously injuring the pilot.

There were three other accidents like this, with pilots who tried to sneak under the minimum altitude on an instrument approach and found wires strung across their paths. These four pilots were among the 15 who got too low and hit wires while attempting to land.

But the majority of these accidents happen during VFR conditions. In many instances, the wires are well known to local pilots, and may even be mentioned in various airport guides and facility directories. They may be marked with orange balls—but sometimes even these measures aren't enough to prevent an accident.

A 13,000-hour commercial pilot was attempting a landing in his float-equipped aircraft on the intracoastal waterway where his company's home base was located. On base leg, the Cessna hit the top ground wires of a power line array that spanned the waterway.

Although the wires were marked with large orange balls, the investigation revealed there was severe sun glare off the water at the time of the 6:55 p.m. accident. The Cessna was heading into the setting sun, effectively blinding the pilot and making the balls and wires invisible. Typically, however, on a VFR approach, the airplane gets low but the pilot adds power to try and drag it into the field. The wires loom up and the airplane flies into them.

For example, there was the crash of a Cessna 150F near Westfield, Indiana. The 3,000-hour commercial pilot got low on the approach and snagged a wire. He later told investigators he found himself too low on the approach and, "gunned the engine to stay over the corn field but did not see the wires." He also said he "had never known they were there."

Sometimes it seems the wires are placed just a little too close to the runway, making them easy to hit. Although FAR Part 77 obstruction rules are supposed to do something to prevent such situations, it doesn't always happen.

Wasilla, Alaska, was the site of an accident in which a Bellanca hit an unmarked static wire 40 feet above the ground, but only 75 feet from the threshold of the runway while attempting to land. The pilot and his passenger suffered only minor injuries when the Bellanca crashed on top of a parked airplane after hitting the wire.

Accident statistics show 13 instances of pilots hitting wires during takeoff. Again, these accidents are VFR events. It's interesting to note that no airplanes hit wires during instrument departures. Four accidents resulted from late go-arounds, which we count as part of taking off. The rest were all during "normal" takeoffs that had a little twist to them.

Consider the accident involving a Cessna U206G at Dulce, New Mexico. The 4,984-hour ATP was trying to take off from an airport in a valley. The flight encountered turbulence and downdrafts just after takeoff and would not climb, according to the pilot. The Cessna hit a wire, but it kept flying and the pilot managed to land safely. Neither he nor his five passengers were injured.

Buzz Jobs

Some pilots just can't resist the thrill of a few good low passes, generally over, or at, some specific object or person. Nine aircraft met the wires from such buzz-jobs.

Buzzing roads accounted for three of these accidents. In one of them, a police officer who was also a 4,435-hour commercial pilot, had just completed a traffic surveillance flight. He called the cooperating police units on the ground and told them he would buzz them as he left the area. His Cessna snagged a wire some 89 feet above the road and crashed, killing the pilot and his observer/passenger.

But sometimes it isn't the pilot who can't resist the thrill of a good buzz job, it's the passenger instead. For example, just before the crash of a Cessna 172H at Marvell, Arkansas, the passenger asked the 95-

hour private pilot to buzz the passenger's place of business. The airplane snagged a telephone wire during the low pass and crashed. Both occupants walked away and afterwards, the pilot said he didn't know the wires were there when the passenger asked for the buzz job.

Engine Failures

During our previous survey of wire-strike crashes, some 85 aircraft encountered wires while maneuvering to land after an engine failure. This accounted for 18 percent of the total. Eight of these accidents were fatal.

During 1984, however, wire strikes after engine failures accounted for some 30 accidents (about 21 percent). Surprisingly, only one of these was a fatal accident, and that was a helicopter that autorotated into wires while attempting to land.

It's almost inexplicable that wire-strike accidents during engine failures should show such a low percentage of fatal accidents. We can only suggest that pilots attempting emergency landings arrive near the ground trimmed for relatively low speeds, and all else being equal, the lower-speed accident is the more survivable. Also, since the wire strike by definition occurs on short final in a deadstick landing, the wire being struck may be the kind most invisible from higher-up—like telephone wires or low-voltage electric wires—that do less damage than high-voltage powerlines.

An interesting sidelight—during our previous survey, some 47 of the engine-failure accidents resulted from fuel exhaustion (more than half of the total). But in 1984, only five such accidents could be traced to fuel exhaustion.

Scud Running

Another flight regime that brings aircraft down to the level of the wires is scud running. Unfortunately, our previous survey was unable to compile any statistics on this phenomenon. However, during 1984, some 13 wire-strike accidents occurred during attempted scud running. Another two took place during attempted landings after encounters with IFR conditions.

The scud-running accidents followed a predictable pattern; caught by worsening weather, the pilot flies lower and lower until the wires loom out of the fog. As might be expected, most pilots involved in these accidents were not instrument rated. However, most were fairly well experienced, averaging 788 hours.

Five of the 15 accidents were fatal, which is a better percentage than for VFR-into-IFR flying in general (which has been shown to be fatal in about 87 percent of all cases).

Interestingly, six of these aircraft crashed into antenna guy wires. This is even more peculiar when one considers that, for the entire group of 138 accidents, there were only nine instances of aircraft hitting antenna guy wires.

It's worth noting that antennas and their associated guy wires can present hazards even at seemingly safe altitudes. Many television and radio antennas reach up over 1,000 feet above ground, and some exceed 2,000 feet AGL. While most of these are lighted, some are not. And even with lighting, in low visibility conditions, they can be very difficult to spot in time to avoid.

The guy wires associated with these antennas complicate the problem. They are hard to spot even under the best of conditions, and most are not marked. Worse, they can extend up to 1,500 feet horizontally from the base of the antenna. A pilot may spot the antenna in time and turn to avoid it, only to run into the unseen guy wires. According to the *Airman's Information Manual,* a good rule of thumb is to avoid antennas by at least 2,000 feet—in all directions.

See and Avoid

And then there are those wire-related accidents. The aircraft didn't actually hit the wire, but the wire helped to cause the accident.

During 1984, there were ten accidents which fell into this category. In most of these crashes the pattern was the same—the pilot sees the wire and tries to avoid it, only to crash in the process.

> A Cessna 150 crashed at Vine Grove, Kentucky, as its pilot was attempting a go-around after encountering nosewheel shimmy while landing on a sod strip. He managed to get the airplane off the ground, but it was heading for some power-lines off the end of the runway. He started a left turn and pulled back on the yoke, causing the stall-warning horn to sound. The Cessna cleared the powerlines, but mushed back to the ground and nosed over. The pilot and his passenger both walked away.
>
> These events go the other way as well. Consider the crash of a Cessna 152 at McArthur, Ohio. The 62-hour private pilot was attempting to land when, on short final at about 5 feet above the ground, a gust of wind hit the aircraft. It blew the Cessna back up to 20 feet and blew it to the left of the runway.
>
> The pilot was able to climb over a hangar that was in his

way, but coming down the other side he found himself boxed in by wires. He tried to duck under the wires, but crashed when the Cessna hit a fence and flipped over. Again, both pilot and passenger walked away unharmed.

Variations on a Theme

In a number of mishaps the wire strike was only incidental to the accident; the wires just happened to be in the way of an airplane already in the process of crashing. There were five such instances during 1984.

> One of these happened near Davidson, Oklahoma, and involved a 12,000-hour commercial pilot who had gone out to do some aerobatics. Witnesses on the ground saw the Bellanca pull up and enter a spin at about 3,000 feet. It continued spinning until it hit some high tension wires and crashed to the ground below.
>
> Another was the crash of a Corben Baby Ace homebuilt aircraft at Emporium, Pennsylvania. The 37-hour student pilot was attempting to land when the airplane struck several trees on the approach. The pilot lost control after hitting the trees, but before he hit the ground, he managed to hit some phone wires and a phone pole. He received only minor injuries in the accident.

No See-'Ems

By their nature, wires are almost invisible until an aircraft is right on top of them. The visibility of anything depends on its size and its color. And it's generally true that wires tend to be small; a 10,000-volt wire is only about two inches in diameter.

One expert has stated that a person with good eyesight would have to be within 150 feet of a typical wire in order to see it. If the aircraft were traveling at 100 mph, the pilot would then have a mere *1.5 seconds* in which to spot the wire and avoid it.

In mountainous areas, utilities often string wires from ridgetop to ridgetop and the supporting structures blend in with the surrounding terrain, making them virtually invisible. Most of these installations do not qualify as "obstructions to navigation" when evaluated by government criteria. Thus, they are not marked or lighted in any way. In some instances, the towers on each side of the valley may be equipped with strobe lights to let pilots know there are wires strung between them. But this is not a common practice.

The advice of one official of the National Oceanographic Service, offered eight years ago, proves to be just as valid today: "I would advise a simple rule that pilots may not particularly like, but it's this: don't fly below the ridge line in any valley."

Aids to Conspicuity

The most popular way to make wires more visible is installing wire marking balls, the premier supplier of which is the Tana Wire Marker Company of California, Missouri.

Company president Jack Rutledge told *Aviation Safety* that Tana is the leading manufacturer of the plastic wire marking balls not just in the U.S. but throughout the world. At one time the company had some domestic competition from Grumman, which made them out of aluminum, but Grumman got out of the business quickly.

Tana makes balls in various sizes and colors. Sizes range from very small nine-inch diameter models to large 54-inch models. FAA at one time recommended the 20-inch diameter model because it was the first available and it was the cheapest. However, these weren't very effective. FAA now recommends the larger, more visible 36-inch model. "So now we're selling a hell of a lot more 36-inch balls," says Rutledge. But the 20-inch model continues to be the biggest seller.

The nine-inch balls that Tana makes are inexpensive, but in the opinion of Rutledge are almost worthless for pilots. "I don't recommend these for anything, although people sometimes buy those for aviation usage," he said. He pointed out that these balls are recommended by the U.S. Fish and Wildlife Service, but they're not intended for pilots. The F&WS folks have found that while the balls aren't really useful in warning humans away from wires, they have proven to be a great help in preventing birds (primarily swans) from flying into the wires.

Rutledge says that the balls themselves are all relatively cheap—it's the installation that gets expensive. Most power companies use helicopters to install the balls, at a cost of up to $2,300 per hour. Tana has gradually improved the balls to the point where it now requires as little as 31 seconds to hang one on the wire, using an improved quick-setting clamp.

Rising Sales, Falling Accidents

The original markers were designed by Tana in the early 1970s in conjunction with the Arkansas Power and Light Company and the Little Rock, Arkansas, GADO. Eventually, the Arkansas Division of

Aeronautics mandated installation of the markers on all wires in the state that were near the approach zone of an airport.

By 1977, Arkansas state officials were telling California Department of Transportation officials how effective the markers were. Writing to the chief of the California DOT, the director of the Arkansas Division of Aeronautics, Eddie Holland, said "We feel this program [of marking wires] has been most successful, as prior to starting this program there had been six fatalities from aircraft striking wires in the approach zones of airports. Since our wire marking program, we have had no such accidents."

During the 1980s Tana surveyed some 300 power companies about their experiences with the balls. One question asked was, "Have any aircraft accidents occurred in locations after markers have been installed?" All 300 companies said they haven't had any wire-strike accidents where the balls have been installed.

Rutledge said sales of Tana wire markers have been going up steadily since the company was founded more than 20 years ago. Some groups have been especially aggressive in getting wires marked. For example, the state of Texas has bought about 25,000 balls over the years, and continues to buy them. Rutledge once commented to the head of the Texas Aeronautics Commission that they'd soon have the entire state looking like a Christmas tree. The Commissioner responded, "We haven't even started."

Many power companies will install balls upon request from government or local groups. A spokesman for one local utility told us, "We put warning lights on transmission towers or balls on the wires at the request of the FAA or the airport."

Even some unlikely entities are getting into the act. Some railroads, like the Long Island Rail Road, are installing balls along the wires near their tracks. They use helicopters for patrol along the tracks, so the railroad is marking the wires so their pilots can see and avoid them. Other low-flying pilots get to share the benefit.

Improved Markers

Tana continues to work with power companies to develop new technologies for wire markers. For example, one of the problems remaining to be overcome is corona effect. Rutledge says that the magnetic field around some high-tension wires is sufficient to set the marker ball on fire. He's currently working with engineers from power companies across the country to solve this problem.

But the corona effect isn't all bad. The strong electric field can be put to good use. A subsidiary of GTE Corporation has designed a light that can be installed on the wire-marking ball that runs off this electric field. On wires carrying 30,000 volts or more, the "balisor light," as it's known, can make the markers visible in the dark. It hasn't been a real popular seller, according to Rutledge, because of the initial expense (about $1,500 each) and the maintenance costs.

A cheaper solution to the night visibility problem is being worked on by FAA, Tana and the 3M company. Tana has put 3M engineer-grade reflective tape on some models of their markers, and although in total darkness the tape does nothing, "if you've got your landing light on, this thing comes back like a searchlight," according to Rutledge. "This stuff really puts out a hell of a reflection." However, the tape is very expensive, costing up to half as much as the ball itself. "As a result, we don't sell very many of them," says Rutledge.

Charting Changes

Another front in the war on wire strikes is on the charts—the sectional and TCA charts, to be exact. In recent years, the National Oceanic and Atmospheric Administration (NOAA) has instituted some charting changes to help pilots keep an eye out for wires.

Previously, NOAA charts depicted only power lines that were prominent and highly visible. The idea was that these were the ones pilots might be able to use for navigation. Most others were ignored entirely. But in recent years, NOAA has begun depicting more and more wires on the charts. One of the biggest changes has been the charting of catenaries with heights of greater than 200 feet above ground. (A catenary is a large, heavy span of wires, usually across a river or valley.)

Still, NOAA makes no effort to chart every wire. If they did, the maps would become so cluttered as to be unreadable. And the emphasis is still on objects which are plainly visible from the air (most wires are not), or objects which present hazards to air navigation.

Other Efforts

Still other avenues are open in the war on the wires. For those in close proximity to an airport, enough pressure can sometimes be brought to bear to get something truly constructive done about them.

For example, if the wires are close enough to be subject to the obstructions standards under Part 77, the FAA might be enticed to step in. The agency might persuade the owners of the wires to bury them. Or the FAA might just mark the wires and put a note in the facilities directory. Or it may impose operating restrictions on the airport, including such measures as displaced thresholds on the affected runways.

Often, state and local governments can be brought into the fray. Some state governments—like Texas—will install markers upon request. Others, with the weight of their ability to determine utility rates, may simply request that the wires be relocated or buried.

DARKNESS ONLY MAKES A BAD SITUATION WORSE

A 24-year-old private pilot and his passenger suffered severe injuries when their Skyhawk struck powerlines during a low night approach to Runway 35 at Osage City Municipal Airport in Kansas.

The pilot had flown in from Emporia earlier that day to perform electrical tests on another airplane. After that was done, he and the passenger decided to shoot some touch-and-goes at Osage City before leaving for the day. Investigators said they were trying out some communications equipment, either headsets or an intercom system.

The pilot took off at about 7:30 p.m. and performed one touch-and-go. He came around, turned base and then final. Just after getting established on final, the landing light illuminated the wires in front of the airplane. The passenger shouted, "Watch the wires!" and according to the pilot, grabbed the yoke and pulled back (the passenger did not recall pulling on the yoke). The pilot applied full throttle, but it was too late; the Cessna's nose gear hooked a wire, and the airplane was pitched nose-down into the ground, coming to rest inverted. The passenger later told FAA investigators that just before seeing the wires, he noted that the altimeter was reading 100 feet AGL.

According to investigators, in order to hit the wires, the airplane would have had to be below field elevation. The wires are situated in a gully, and the airport is higher than the wire poles.

Call Sign Chaos—Was That for Us?

The entire structure of air traffic control rests on the assumption that it will be possible to know who's out there. Unfortunately, it appears that with distressing frequency, the pilot on downwind might just as well be the Masked Man, because any one of several possible cockpit communications errors involving an airplane's call sign has made

A good headset, such as this Bose noise-cancelling model, goes a long way toward improving the quality of radio communication.

that airplane an unidentified flying object. It's a frequent and potentially lethal human factors error.

In a recent four-year period, NASA's Aviation Safety Reporting System received more than 2,025 tales of communications goof-ups. A thorough study found 462 instances in which call sign chaos was at the root of problems which ranged from an unauthorized climb or descent to simultaneous takeoffs from intersecting runways. Missing a call for breakfast can leave a pilot hungry; missing a call on the radio can leave a pilot dead, seriously injured, or at least scared.

The call sign errors sorted themselves out into five major categories: (1) Faulty radio technique, (2) Frequency congestion, (3) Similar-sounding call signs, (4) Airman acknowledgment/readback errors, and (5) Controller acknowledgment/readback errors.

Faulty radio technique includes such common infractions as talking before fully depressing the mike button. "All too often," wrote one pilot making a report to the NASA system, "the pilot starts talking about the same time that he depresses his transmit button. The call comes out, 'mumble, mumble, on downwind.'"

Controllers also have trigger troubles, as another pilot reported: "The controller said, "mnffm, unh, right one six zero'. I replied, 'What?' Whereupon he said, 'Do a right three sixty and don't argue!'"

Potentially more dangerous is the problem that might be called "Dangling Conversations." In this situation, a pilot decides to add a little something onto his transmission a second or two after pausing.

Usually the addition doesn't add much useful information, but it often manages to walk on part of the controller's transmission—which might or might not be to the aircraft in question, as one airliner jockey found out when he called, "XYZ is maintaining zero nine zero degrees...as assigned." When he finally let loose of the button, he heard "...turn to one eight zero degrees," which he merrily acknowledged and executed. Thirty seconds later, a horrified controller said "XYZ, where are you going? You were given zero nine zero. Turn immediately and climb."

XYZ eventually figured out that what he'd done was walk on the first part of the controller's transmission, which had been the part with the call sign—somebody else's call sign.

I Could Have Sworn He Said...

Frequency congestion makes its own problems, including a heightening of the expectation problem. This is the "you hear what you expect to hear" phenomenon, and it happens with great frequency when pilots are primed by having made a prior request to ATC, or by having been given a temporary hold or vector. The pilot, anxious to resolve the pending business, expects the call to be for him, and anything coming over the airwaves seems fair game.

Smeared, similar or unclear call signs get mentally converted into a call to the waiting pilot, who does what he thinks he was told to do, unless he was just previously told to do something. Then, it seems, pilots turn off the mental primer and can become almost immune to hearing their call sign since they don't think they'll be called shortly after receiving a clearance.

"Many of the ignored call-up messages," says the report, "were associated with the issuance of a prior clearance followed by an amended ATC assigned altitude. Having just been issued a clearance to a higher or lower altitude, immediate change in instructions would not normally be anticipated. Thus, any garbled call sign transmissions would be disregarded by the airmen as "probably not for us."

When the frequency is jammed, getting through to confirm can be difficult, and under such circumstances controllers apparently can get a bit lax about listening for acknowledgments. In 17 percent of the call sign incidents there was a failure to respond to and comply with revised restrictions, yet time and again controllers report not receiving (or demanding) an acknowledgment.

Another frequency congestion problem is non-stop controller instructions to multiple aircraft. A lot of pilots complained about this problem. Said one poor soul, "The controller issued instructions to 12 different aircraft—all in one, non-stop transmission." Others reported instructions going out non-stop to 18, 20 and 22 aircraft, all without opportunity for acknowledgment or reply of any kind.

Great Potential for Confusion

There were 250 reported incidents of call sign confusion, suggesting this is a major source of danger. There are lots of possibilities for call sign confusion. Sometimes it's the same numbers in a different order (54 Tango, 45 Tango); other times it's the same company name, with a different letter. The problem has become worse as more and more small airlines have popped up, often adopting slight variations of names already in use by larger, older airlines. A clipped syllable here, a missed vowel there, and pretty soon somebody is executing somebody else's clearance.

The transposed digit problem is one that's perhaps most familiar to general aviation pilots. "We heard the Center call ABC143 four times. We did not answer these calls. Later, I came to believe that she had been trying to reach us—we were ABC123."

Another pilot reported "When aircraft C suddenly called in on the frequency, the controller trainee became flustered. This resulted in his calling C by another name in several call-ups. C did not acknowledge these calls. A and C were on a collision course until A pilot saw the traffic and took evasive action."

Then there's the "is anyone listening up there?" problem. The symptom, say controllers, is pilots who have to be called repeatedly to get their attention. "GA and most corporate pilots," wrote one controller, "need to be called two or three times before responding to the first call-up."

"Time is very important to a controller," wrote another radar watcher. "I suggest that pilots be required to maintain a better listening watch on the frequency."

"It happens so frequently, it becomes commonplace," reported a third controller.

The other side of this dangerous coin might be called the "is anyone listening *down* there?" problem. Controllers can be remarkably adept at not really listening to acknowledgments and readbacks. In theory, under the best of circumstances, a controller should issue a command, the pilot should read it back, and the controller should listen and confirm the readback as correct. This neat check-and-balance system frequently yields to the realities of busy controllers. "Sometimes," complained one pilot, "you don't even get a mike click to verify an acknowledgment."

"What is the value of readbacks if no one on the other end is listening?" said another pilot who'd been involved in an incident. There were a lot of complaints about this, enough to suggest that the problem is very real and very much alive. In 42 percent of the call sign incidents, the pilots raised the issue of controllers having failed to catch a mistake which was repeated to them.

The safety system report states, "One repetitive phrase characterized both controller and airmen narratives. This typical expression could be generally stated as: 'I figured it out later, how it all must have happened.'" Unfortunately, in some cases, later is too late.

"The inability to comprehend immediately what was happening—or why it was happening—epitomized the hazardous nature of call sign errors in ATC/cockpit communications," said the report. "If not immediately caught and corrected, call sign mismatches often plunged the airman into confusion and the aircraft into hazard. As the *Airman's Information Manual* warns, the communication link between pilot and controller, once broken, may result in disastrous consequences."

Index